DISABLED EDUCATION

Disabled Education

A Critical Analysis of the Individuals with Disabilities Education Act

Ruth Colker

NEW YORK UNIVERSITY PRESS
New York and London

NEW YORK UNIVERSITY PRESS
New York and London
www.nyupress.org

References to Internet websites (URLs) were accurate at the time of writing.
Neither the author nor New York University Press is responsible
for URLs that may have expired or changed since the manuscript was prepared.

LIBRARY OF CONGRESS CATALOGING-IN-PUBLICATION DATA
Colker, Ruth.
Disabled education : a critical analysis of the Individuals with Disabilities Education Act /
Ruth Colker.
pages cm
Includes bibliographical references and index.
ISBN 978-0-8147-0810-1 (cl: alk. paper)
1. Children with disabilities—Education—Law and legislation—United States. 2. United
States. Individuals with Disabilities Education Act. I. Title.
KF4209.3.C645 2013
344.73 07911--dc23

2012045597

New York University Press books are printed on acid-free paper,
and their binding materials are chosen for strength and durability.
We strive to use environmentally responsible suppliers and materials
to the greatest extent possible in publishing our books.

Manufactured in the United States of America
10 9 8 7 6 5 4 3 2 1

to D.P.L.
May you lead an independent life with your own thoughts, feelings, and aspirations.

Contents

Abbreviations

ABA	applied behavior action plan
ADHD	attention deficit hyperactivity disorder
ALJ	administrative law judge
APPE	average per-pupil expenditure
CAPD	central auditory processing disorder
CAS	Cognitive Assessment System
DIBELS	Dynamic Indicators of Basic Early Literacy Skills
EAHCA	Education for All Handicapped Children Act
EHA	Education of the Handicapped Act
ESEA	Elementary and Secondary Education Act
FAPE	free and appropriate public education
FBA	functional behavior assessment
IDEA	Individuals with Disabilities Education Act
IEE	independent educational evaluation
IEP	Individualized Education Program
IFSP	Individualized Family Service Plan
IHO	independent hearing officer
LDA	Learning Disabilities Association of America
LSAC	Law School Admissions Council
MHRH	(Division of) Mental Health, Retardation and Hospitals
NACHC	National Advisory Committee on Handicapped Children
NCLB	No Child Left Behind
NJCLD	National Joint Committee on Learning Disabilities
ODD	Oppositional Defiant Disorder
OHI	Other Health Impairment
PLD	personal listening device
RTI	response to intervention
SLRO	state-level review officer
SST	Student Success Team
STAR	Standardized Testing and Reporting
TBI	traumatic brain injury
TOPPS	Targeting Our People's Priorities with Service

Acknowledgments

Many people have assisted in the writing of this book with their inspiration, thoughtful conversations, devoted research, or careful reading of various drafts. I apologize in advance for those whom I forget to thank.

Deborah Gershenowitz, who was the Senior Editor at New York University Press, had the confidence in my work to agree to publish it on the basis of a bare outline. Her support of my book, and her desire to offer feedback at an early stage, made it a joy from the beginning to write this book.

Through generous research funds made available by the Distinguished University Professor award at The Ohio State University, I was able to hire a team of research assistants for several summers to help me with this project. Andy Gammill, Jonathan Misny, Patrick Noonan, Kevin Snell, and Justin Tillson provided me with enormous assistance during the summer of 2011 with work that influenced nearly every chapter. Kathleen Patterson and Joseph Brown provided assistance during the summer of 2010, and their work is reflected in chapter 13. Melissa Gerber, Grace Miller, and Katie Johnson assisted me during the summer of 2009 with work that is reflected in chapter 8. A well-timed sabbatical allowed me to complete this book during the fall of 2011.

The staff at the Moritz Law Library was also tremendously helpful. Katherine Hall, who was the Assistant Director for Public Services, and Stephanie Ziegler, Reference Librarian, helped me acquire primary source materials from various district court archives as well as from many other sources. They also helped me gather various statistical sources.

This book also benefited from many people who read earlier drafts and offered constructive criticism or editing. Thomas Gallanis, N. William Hines Chair in Law, University of Iowa College of Law, carefully read chapter 2 and helped arrange a wonderful faculty workshop at his institution where I received great feedback at an early stage of this project. Sally Shaywitz, M.D., the Audrey G. Ratner Professor in Learning Development in the Yale University School of Medicine & Co-Director, Yale Center for Dyslexia & Creativity, offered very constructive feedback on my discussion of learning disabilities. Paula Pearlman, Executive Director, Disability Rights Legal Center; Richard Peterson, Director of the Special Education Clinic and Assistant Professor of Law at Pepperdine Law School; and Julie Waterstone, Director of the Children's Rights Clinic and Associate Clinical Professor of Law at Southwestern Law School were kind enough to invite me to present an overview of my argument to the Special Education Law Symposium held at Pepperdine University School of Law. The conference participants gave me fabulous feedback that has enhanced the book. James Rosenfeld, Director, Education Law Programs, and Adjunct Professor at Seattle University School of Law, invited me to discuss my work at the 2012 Administrative Law Judge and Mediator Training Session for California hearing officers. I appreciated the opportunity to receive candid feedback from people who are working in the field. My colleagues at the Moritz College of Law—Professors Amy Cohen and Cinnamon Carlarne—provided helpful feedback on various chapters even though the work was outside their areas of expertise. They helped me craft the argument for a more general audience.

I especially thank my partner, David Paul Levine, Associate Professor of Education at Otterbein University, who undertook the task of reading every chapter of this book and providing tremendously useful feedback. He was also extremely helpful in suggesting sources from literatures outside of law to strengthen my interdisciplinary perspective. And he never seemed to tire of hearing me share my latest idea for how to approach an idea or a chapter. This book is enormously better in light of his assistance. Thank you.

And I thank my son, Samuel Colker-Eybel, who gave me permission to tell his story in this book. I hope that society will benefit from the extra assistance he has been able to receive under the law of special education. And, most important, I hope that all children, someday, have the opportunity to receive a free appropriate public education.

1

Introduction

During the first few years of his life, my son, Sam, missed every develop-mental milestone. He walked awkwardly, had little speech, and was socially withdrawn. Shortly before his third birthday, his pediatrician diagnosed him as disabled. As a white middle-class mother who is also a legal expert in the field of special education, I have been able to devote enormous amounts of time and money to advocate for Sam since that time. Several years ago, I sued my local school district to attain the services Sam needs in order to have access to oral instruction. At age fifteen, he is flourishing. Sam is run-ning cross-country, writing a science fiction novel, and enjoying social func-tions with his friends. There is little question that Sam would be foundering if he had been born into a less privileged household.

That is wrong.

In 1968, Professor Lloyd Dunn, one of the leading researchers and activ-ists in the field of special education, argued that the practice of segregat-ing "slow" students into special education classes was a "sham of dreams" because it simply resulted in poor and minority students receiving inferior educations.[1] In 1974, Dunn testified in opposition to the proposed special education laws because he predicted that "these bills, if enacted, would do more harm than good for the very children they are committed to serve bet-ter."[2] Even though Congress was aware of Dunn's important work when it devised the special education laws, it took few, if any steps, to deal with this possibility.

Thirty years later, one can find books with titles such as *Racial Inequality in Special Education*[3] and *Why Are So Many Minority Students in Special Education?*[4] that pursue the theme: What is so special about special education for poor and minority children? As predicted by Dunn, the authors of these books argue that poor and minority children often receive "inadequate services, low-quality curriculum and instruction and unnecessary isolation from their nondisabled peers."[5] African American children are likely to be overrepresented in certain disability categories and underrepresented in others. The special education classification system is often "the result of social forces that intertwine to construct an identity of 'disability' for children whom the regular-education system finds too difficult to serve."[6] Special education services for poor and minority children often arrive too late to provide significant assistance, are not tailored to remedy the actual deficits these children face, and may result in segregated services in highly inadequate educational environments.

The story for children in middle-class families is less problematic but still troubling. These children are more likely to live in school districts that offer adequate programs for children with special needs. Nonetheless, if their school districts are not offering an appropriate education for children with disabilities, the resources needed to use the special education laws to challenge inappropriate educational practices are out of reach for most of their parents. It often takes expensive and time-consuming advocacy with the assistance of professionals for children to receive an appropriate education.

This book will try to help the reader understand why the special education system is not so "special" for many children. The reasons are complex and no longer due to *de jure* exclusion from public schools that was common until the 1970s. Instead, rules like the expectation that a parent act as an advocate for a child disproportionately harm poor children whose parents do not have the time or skill level to act as effective advocates. The highly subjective disability classification system has led to minority children being disproportionately classified as emotionally disturbed or mentally retarded[7] and exiled into weak educational settings, and white children being disproportionately classified as autistic or developmentally delayed and sometimes placed in strong educational programs. The special education system is also woefully underfunded, especially in school districts that serve poor children. Although Congress has tinkered with the rules over the years, sometimes even in response to concerns about racial equality, these changes have been largely ineffective. And some changes, like the strengthening of school districts' powers to discipline children with disabilities, have disproportionately harmed poor and minority children, particularly African American youth. This book seeks to uncover the history and impact of these and other seemingly neutral rules on the educational experiences of poor and minority children.

The following two stories drawn from my experience and that of another family in Ohio illustrate the difficulties for any child to receive appropriate special education assistance and how those difficulties are compounded for children in poor families.

Sam was born on January 9, 1997, in a suburban community.[8] Soon after he was diagnosed as disabled, the school district enrolled him in an excellent special education program for preschoolers where he made enormous progress.

Even with some extra help, Sam continued to face difficulties during grade school. In particular, he was having a lot of difficulty following classroom instruction. After I co-taught a special education class with an audiologist, Dr. Gail Whitelaw, and shared with her my struggles with Sam, she suggested I bring him to her clinic to be tested. That testing was covered under my health care plan. Whitelaw concluded that Sam had central auditory processing disorder (CAPD).[9] She explained that the consequences in the classroom for a child with CAPD are comparable to those of a deaf child because the child misses so much oral instruction. She recommended that the school district acquire a personal listening device (PLD) for Sam to use in the classroom, along with other accommodations. A PLD brings the sound directly to the child's ear through an FM receiver and costs about $1,000.

The school district agreed that Sam was disabled but refused to provide him with a PLD. After a year of being stonewalled, I filed a due process complaint against the school district under the Individuals with Disabilities Education Act (IDEA). Under the IDEA, parents who file due process complaints are encouraged to seek a resolution through mediation. If mediation is unsuccessful, parents can then bring their case before a hearing officer, who is an administrative law judge hired by the state to conduct such hearings.

I retained two expert witnesses and a lawyer to assist me with mediation. After mediation was unsuccessful, these individuals also helped me conduct a three-day hearing. On the Friday before school was to start, and two years after Whitelaw recommended Sam have a PLD, the hearing officer sent her decision to the parties and their lawyers. She ruled in Sam's favor, concluding that the evidence conclusively demonstrated that he needed a PLD to access oral communication. She gave the school district thirty days to acquire a device and implement a revised Individualized Education Program (IEP). The school district ultimately complied, and Sam's performance in school began to improve dramatically.

Although Sam's story is a success under the IDEA, it is hard to understate the difficulty and stress of filing a due process complaint, even for someone with my level of expertise. As it happened, I filed for the due process hearing at a time of enormous strain in my life. I had broken my femur several weeks before the hearing and was extremely uncomfortable during the lengthy hearing. The lawyer I hired to assist me was diagnosed with stage-four cancer shortly after the hearing ended and could not help me implement the order. My mother, who lived in another city, was dying of cancer that summer, and I was trying to spend as much time with her as possible. And my daughter was getting ready to go to college. But even if those personal circumstances had not been in place, hiring experts, preparing the lawyer for the hearing, and sitting through a week of hearings were very difficult. The wait for the decision seemed interminable. The process was also quite expensive. Although I was reimbursed for most of my attorney fees, I had to pay for the two experts. Advocating for my son was one of the most stressful experiences of my life.

* * *

At about the same time as I was pursuing my case through the state administrative system, another mother, Marilyn, was pursuing a case involving her son Kevin in a different school district.[10] (Both names are pseudonyms.) She was unmarried, pregnant, and unable to afford an attorney. The school district had identified her son as being emotionally disturbed and having attention deficit hyperactivity disorder (ADHD). Kevin had been taking medication to help moderate his behavior and reduce his symptoms but had stopped taking it for a period of time when his mother could not afford any medical treatment for him. He also had a behavioral intervention plan to help him maintain appropriate behavior in the classroom. When the school district threatened to suspend Kevin for violating school policies, his mother filed a due process complaint in order to get the school to recognize that his misbehavior was a result of his disability. She wanted a more effective IEP that would address his educational needs and keep him in school.

Marilyn initially requested an expedited hearing to avoid having her son suspended from school. The hearing, however, had to be put on a regular schedule because illness and childcare responsibilities precluded her from maintaining the pace of an expedited hearing. Marilyn's brother attended the due process hearing with her, trying to offer assistance even though he was not an attorney.

The hearing officer ruled for the school district, finding that it was offering Kevin an adequate IEP and handling his behavioral problems appropriately. In ruling for the school district, the hearing officer noted that the mother "seemed exceptionally frustrated and intimidated by the due process hearing procedures." The parent had no idea how to write a brief and began leaving long voicemail messages on the hearing officer's telephone with the arguments she wanted to make. Then, after the deadline had passed for submitting a brief, she left further messages with statements such as "Just going to let you make decision. . . . Too stressful on me and my children and my unborn baby." The hearing officer—who never received any kind of brief from the parent—ruled, as noted, in favor of the school district. Kevin's reasons for causing trouble in school and what kind of IEP might provide him with an effective education were barely explored.

The difference in treatment that Sam and Kevin received is typical of the stories that this book will explore. Both Sam and Kevin had trouble paying attention in school. Sam saw a private audiologist who diagnosed him with CAPD and helped him get a PLD. Even though the school district fought me over the PLD issue, they did give Sam lots of support to improve his performance and were patient when his behavior was sometimes socially awkward. Kevin, by contrast, was labeled as having ADHD and being emotionally disturbed. He did not get the academic support he needed and was suspended when he violated school rules. I was able to hire a lawyer and two expert witnesses. Kevin's mother could neither participate in an expedited hearing schedule nor file a brief. No system was in place to provide Kevin or his mother with a free advocate. While Sam soon flourished in school, Kevin was suspended.

How did we attain a process that is so heavily biased against low-income parents like Marilyn whose children need assistance in comparison with a mother like me who has expertise in the subject and can afford to spend the time and money to assist her son? Why do we have a statute that requires families to make advocacy a full-time job in order to prevail? That is the story I will tell in this book.

* * *

When Congress adopted the Education for All Handicapped Children Act (EAHCA) in 1975, which was subsequently renamed the Individuals with Disabilities Education Act, it sought to improve educational equity by helping children with disabilities. Since the enactment of the EAHCA in 1975, 90 percent fewer children with developmental disabilities are living in institutions.[11] In 1975, more than 1 million children with disabilities were excluded from public school; today, virtually no child with a disability is excluded from public school.

Nonetheless, the enactment of the EAHCA may have also *increased* educational inequity. Congress has never fulfilled its promise to provide 40 percent of the dollars needed to educate children with disabilities; instead, federal underfunding of special education has exacerbated an inequitable allocation of education resources. Certain racial minorities are disproportionately identified as belonging to particular disability categories; those categories are often also the most stigmatizing. And, irrespective of their disability classification, racial minorities, who are disproportionately poor, are likely to receive inappropriate or inadequate special education and related services when they are so identified.

These disparities have always plagued the special education system. Table 1 reflects the current status of racial disparities in disability classification, using data available for 2010.[12]

As has been true since the early court cases in the 1970s, which chapter 2 will discuss, African Americans are overrepresented in the categories of mental retardation and emotional disturbance and underrepresented in the categories of autism and other health impairments (typically ADHD). In 2010, when African Americans constituted about 14 percent of the school-age population[13] and 21 percent of those classified as disabled, they represented 32 percent of the students identified as mentally retarded but only about 14 percent of the students identified as autistic.

Latinos reflect a somewhat different pattern of disproportional representation. In 2010, they constituted around 22 percent of the school-age population[14] and were underrepresented in the category of "developmental delay," which is used to get children extra assistance at ages three to five before they enter kindergarten. Latinos were 9.6 percent of students identified as developmentally delayed but 23.8 percent of students who were later identified as learning disabled. Whites, who represented 55 percent of the school-age population,[15] were overrepresented in the categories of autism and other health impairments but underrepresented in the category of mental retardation. They constituted 69.7 percent of students identified as autistic, 68.4 percent of students identified as other health impaired, and 51.4 percent of students identified as mentally retarded. From these numbers, one might surmise that an African American boy who "acts up" in class because he has trouble sitting still might be classified as emotionally disturbed whereas a white boy

Table 1
Disability Classification Data from the U.S. Department of Education

	African American	Hispanic	White
Mental Retardation	32.5%	12.8%	51.4%
Speech or Language Impairments	16.5%	18.1%	61.6%
Visual Impairments	16.3%	26.7%	52.3%
Emotional Disturbance	28.5%	11.9%	56.7%
Orthopedic Impairments	14.2%	20.6%	61.4%
Other Health Impairments	18.9%	9.8%	68.4%
Specific Learning Disability	21.2%	23.8%	52.1%
Multiple Disabilities	18.8%	12.6%	64.8%
Hearing Impairment	16.2%	24.9%	52.9%
Autism	14.0%	11.3%	69.7%
Developmental Delay	23.7%	9.6%	59.4%

with similar characteristics would be classified as having ADHD. Similarly, a very withdrawn African American boy might be classified as being emotionally disturbed whereas an equally shy white boy might be classified as being autistic. An African American preschooler who is having trouble keeping up with age-level expectations might be classified as mentally retarded; her white counterpart is more likely to be classified as being developmentally delayed. And a Latino boy who has missed developmental milestones is unlikely to receive early intervention services as developmentally delayed because of Latinos' underrepresentation in that category.

This point about overrepresentation by race in certain categories is different from a point about overrepresentation by race in the general category of disability. Even if poverty is linked to higher rates of disability, that higher rate of disability should not be found in some but not all disability categories. Why are mental retardation and emotional disturbance "black" categories and why is autism a "white" category? As Tom Parrish asks, "Can Connecticut, Mississippi, North Carolina, Nebraska, and South Carolina be in compliance with special education and civil rights law when black students are over four times more likely than white students to be designated as mentally retarded?"[16]

To answer this question, one must also understand the services connected to these disability categories. After all, the point of the special education system is not to classify children merely for the sake of classification. The point is to classify children so that an appropriate discussion can take place about the kinds of services that should be provided for that child. The IDEA is about *services*, not classifications.

Parrish connects classification to services and argues that the overidentification of African Americans as mentally retarded is also connected to limited funding for those children. He finds that in the twenty-five states with the highest overidentification of minority students in the mental retardation category one also finds the lowest funding for special education services.[17] He also found that in states with the highest minority overrepresentation in special education within the category of mental retardation the states otherwise did not overidentify minority students as disabled.[18] In other words, minority students tended to be channeled into one category—mental retardation—rather than channeled more heavily into special education itself. By segregating minority students disproportionately into one category—mental retardation—the state is able to offer inadequate services to children in the racially identifiable category of mental retardation while offering stronger programs to white children in other disability classifications.

The most important conclusion from Parrish's work is that minorities often receive far less effective special education services than whites. Examining data from California, he found that whites are more likely to be mainstreamed than blacks but, when blacks do require more intensive services, they are less likely to receive speech, occupational therapy, and physical therapy than white students. And those who do attend costly, highly segregated services through special education residential placements are most likely to be white.[19] In other words, blacks are more likely than whites to be placed in special education self-contained classrooms but less likely to be placed in the most costly, special education residential schools.[20]

Parrish's work shows how difficult it is to accurately describe the racial problems within our special education system. Special education has led to higher rates of segregation for blacks than for whites. That is problematic, especially when one notes that blacks in those segregated programs are not necessarily even getting the services they need. But the situation is complicated by the fact that whites disproportionately gain access to the most segregated but also often the most desirable programs—costly, highly segregated placements. The comparatively higher rate of autism classification for white children is a reflection of this placement pattern because many of the children in these highly expensive and segregated programs are autistic.

Beth Harry and Janette Klingner add another dimension to our understanding of the differential placement patterns for white and minority students.[21] They emphasize that the purpose of special education is to add support to a child's education, not to classify merely for the sake of classification. Their research demonstrates that minority children face a very low exit rate from special education programs and are likely to be placed in programs with unduly large class sizes in which individualized instruction is not possible. They conclude, "[F]or the [mentally retarded and emotionally disturbed] categories, special education placement was tantamount to exile from the mainstream of the educational system. These are the categories in which Black children are overrepresented nationwide and in this school district. Such outcomes strongly support our view that patterns of overrepresentation in these categories are, in the final analysis, inequitable."[22] Like Professors Maynard Clinton Reynolds and Bruce Balow, who testified in 1974 when Congress was considering enactment of special education laws,[23] Harry and Klingner argue that services should not be tied to a discrete disability label. "A child should be able to obtain specialized services by virtue of his/her level of performance in the academic tasks of schooling, not on the basis of a decontextualized testing process designed to determine an underlying 'deficit.' We do not believe it is necessary to conduct such testing in order to determine a child's educational needs."[24]

Thus, it is true that special education classification and the mental retardation label, in particular, have historically been used as vehicles to segregate blacks from the regular classroom. But it is also the case that the most desirable forms of segregation within special education are disproportionately not available to blacks. The bottom line is that special education did a poor job of serving the needs of poor and minority children when Lloyd Dunn criticized the system in 1968 and continues to do a poor job today, even with the advent of federal legislation. How did we come to have this skewed classification system as well as a system of services that seem to serve African Americans and other racial minorities so poorly? This book will explore those themes to seek to explain how the special education system does not work particularly well for any children but works particularly badly for poor and minority children.

* * *

Chapter 2 will explore the historical and legislative background to the adoption of the Education for All Handicapped Children Act in 1975. From the outset, the story of disability discrimination in education has been intertwined with racial segregation. The lawsuits that preceded the enactment of the EAHCA disproportionately involved African American boys who were being excluded from school for disability-related reasons. Disability had become the new *de jure* model of segregation and exclusion for those boys in the era following the Supreme Court's landmark racial desegregation decision in *Brown v. Board of Education*. The EAHCA sought to end this history of exclusion, but unfortunately Congress did not heed the advice of those who argued that this new statute could actually serve to further stigmatize and segregate many poor and minority children.

Chapters 3 and 4 will take this discussion to a more personal level, to tell the stories of how this statute has affected the lives of particular children. These chapters will discuss two leading United States Supreme Court cases, involving Amy Rowley and Michael Panico, that were based on the 1975 Act, before Congress later amended it. The purpose of these chapters is not merely to dissect these cases from a legal perspective; instead, these chapters seek to show how the 1975 Act affected children who were the subject of extensive litigation. Although the special education laws have often harmed poor and minority children, the statute has not been particularly beneficial to many white children who have faced recalcitrant school districts. The resources needed to achieve success under the special education laws are out of reach of most middle-class parents.

Chapter 3 will tell the story of how the U.S. Supreme Court overturned a lower court decision that had required the school district to provide Amy Rowley, who was deaf, with a sign language interpreter. After winning the case in the Supreme Court, the school district withdrew Amy's sign language interpreter from the classroom and put a lien on the Rowleys' house to recover some of its costs. Amy's family had to move to another city in order for Amy to receive interpreter services. Amy's parents were able to bring this litigation only because an attorney who was deaf made their cause his life's passion, squeezing in their representation on a pro bono basis on top of his full-time job.

Chapter 4 will tell the story of how Michael Panico's parents had to fight for years with the assistance of pro bono legal counsel in order for Michael to win the right to attend a private school that could give him an adequate education. His father was a security guard at the local courthouse and could not have handled the case on his own. It is hard to imagine the stress on the Panico and Rowley families as they faced a series of wins and losses during a five- or six-year fight to get their children adequate educations. Children can never be the "winners" if it takes years to implement an appropriate educational plan.

Chapter 5 returns to the legislative history by discussing Congress's attempts to amend the statute over the years. Because the IDEA is a funding statute, it comes up for periodic renewal and Congress cannot resist the chance to amend various provisions as it reallocates funds. This amendment process has given more power to parents to be involved in the special education process without giving parents the tools to take advantage of that opportunity. Congress has amended the discipline rules over the years to give school districts more flexibility to suspend and expel students with disabilities who violate school rules. These changes have had a disparate impact on African American students.

Chapters 6 and 7 will return to the stories of the plaintiffs involved in some of the leading Supreme Court cases. These chapters will examine the lives of children whose parents brought cases on their behalf after the statute was broadly amended, as discussed in chapter 5. Many children who appear to have "won" faced a very problematic educational experience and an enormous toll on their families.

Chapter 6 will discuss how Brian Schaffer's parents waded through eight years of litigation in which they argued that neither of the educational plans proposed by the school district would be effective because of the large class sizes and lack of individualized instruction. There was a brief window during this litigation when the school district thought it would ultimately lose and agreed to place Brian in the kind of small special education classes his parents had sought all along. Nonetheless, during the course of this litigation the Supreme Court ruled that the burden of proof should fall on parents who challenge the adequacy of an Individualized Education Program (IEP). This burden is so high that few parents—including Brian's parents—can win under it.

Chapter 7 tells the story of Joseph Murphy. His parents pursued ten years of litigation before they were able to secure, through the assistance of a pro bono educational advocate, an acceptable placement for Joseph in a private school. During this extensive litigation, the Supreme Court ruled that parents could not recover the costs of their expert witnesses—which are essential to winning an IDEA case—even if they are the prevailing party. These cases show how the courts have interpreted the IDEA to make it nearly impossible for any but the richest parents to persuade school districts to pay for a private education for their children with disabilities. Judicial decisions have buttressed class privilege—those with the most resources receive the most benefit.

To enhance a ground-level view of the IDEA, chapters 8 through 12 examine the results of hearing officer decisions at the state administrative level. They will examine hearing officer decisions in Ohio, Florida, New Jersey, California, and the District of Columbia. These jurisdictions were chosen because of the availability of their hearing officer decisions in a publicly available database. Because of the enormous variation in the number of hearing officer decisions in each jurisdiction on a yearly basis, as well as large variations in whether hearing officer decisions are made readily available to the public, it was not possible to conduct a comprehensive, national examination of these decisions.[25]

These hearing officer decisions confirm the conclusion of Eloise Pasachoff and others that an enormous enforcement disparity exists between the use of the IDEA's enforcement mechanism for wealthy and poor families: "[C]hildren from wealthier families enforce their rights under the statute at higher rates than do children in poverty and . . . this enforcement disparity has a negative effect on the amount and quality of services children in poverty actually receive."[26] Ironically, parents in high-income districts are more likely to bring due process complaints against their school districts than parents in low-income districts even though "the evidence suggests that wealthier districts both spend more on and provide better special education services than less wealthy districts do."[27] In other words, the IDEA's private enforcement mechanism has become an aspect of the statute's class bias in favor of children from wealthier families because it is a tool that allows them to garner even more resources for these families' children. By examining hearing officer decisions, these chapters provide concrete evidence of Pasachoff's thesis—that the administrative enforcement process presents a nearly insurmountable hurdle for most poor families. While there is evidence that middle-class parents fare better than parents from poorer families, these chapters also document the high toll on any family that pursues an IDEA complaint.

Chapter 8 discusses the hearing officer decisions in Ohio. It begins by recounting the experience of Jacob Winkelman, whose parents filed at least five due process complaints with their school district before attaining effective relief. This chapter will also survey about a hundred cases decided under Ohio's cumbersome two-step hearing officer process under which parents and their children rarely prevail, especially if they are poor and cannot afford to hire a lawyer.

Chapter 9 will summarize hearing officer decisions in Florida. It will begin with the stories of Johnny (a pseudonym) as well as Derek Hughes and then proceed to the summaries. Like Kevin's mother (from Ohio), Johnny's mother could not even navigate the administrative process to present her complaint about a lack of behavioral intervention services for her elementary school child. Derek's parents had to move to a new school district to obtain a safe educational environment for their son, who was prone to life-threatening seizures. Because Florida has a relatively low rate of litigation, this chapter surveys only thirty-three cases. Those cases are very instructive, though, because they show that parents rarely win these cases and, when they do prevail, attain only very modest relief. In virtually no cases in Florida did a parent succeed in arguing that an IEP was inadequate.

Chapter 10 surveys the results from New Jersey, beginning with the story of E.R. E.R.'s grandmother could not get the school district to provide transportation from her grandson's childcare center (rather than from her home) so that he could receive special education services at the local preschool. New Jersey is a very important state to examine because, as a matter of state law, it is one of the few states to impose the burden of proof on the school district when a parent brings a due process complaint to challenge an IEP. As chapter 6 explains, parents typically face the burden of proof when they challenge an IEP. Nonetheless, parents were no more likely to prevail in New Jersey than in other states. Hearing officers deferred so heavily to the school districts' experts that the imposition of the burden of proof on the school district had little or no impact on the outcome of these cases.

Chapter 11 discusses hearing officer decisions in California, a state in which many of the parents or guardians require interpreter services in order to testify. California has one of the most sophisticated hearing officer systems—the decisions are readily available on a word-searchable database and the hearing officer decisions are long and cite considerable case law. Although school districts bear the burden of proof in many of these cases, because they object to a parent's request for an Independent Educational Evaluation or refuse to sign the IEP, the win rate for children is quite low.

Chapter 12 discusses hearing officer decisions in the District of Columbia, where litigation in the 1960s helped lead to the passage of the federal special education laws. Because of its large minority population, hearing officer decisions from D.C. provide rich data on how the statute works for poor and minority families. D.C. is a very unusual jurisdiction in that it has a high level of litigation and much of that litigation is successful even though the children represented in these cases are likely to come from low-income families. This chapter, for example, tells the story of Amanda (a pseudonymn), whose mother was able to use the administrative process to secure a private placement for her daughter; the school district did not even try to meaningfully defend its position at the hearing even though it refused to settle the case privately. Although many low-income parents win cases in D.C. on behalf of their children, the hearing officer decisions catalogue a system that has entirely failed children with disabilities. About half of these cases involve children who are already in high school. Relief provided so late in the educational experience means that many of these students do not receive an adequate education. Chapter 12 provides an example of low-income families' using the private enforcement system with a relatively high rate of success. D.C. can therefore provide some insight into the kinds of resources necessary for poor and minority families to prevail under the IDEA.

Chapter 13 focuses on the largest diagnostic category—learning disabilities. This category has received the most attention, as some have argued that middle-class children are advantaged by overclassification as learning disabled.[28] Congress amended the IDEA in 2004 in response to some of these allegations of class bias. Congress's efforts, however, have been counterproductive as the new definition has caused significant delays in disability classification for all students, enormous variation in disability identification on a state-by-state basis, and little or no improvement in classification or services for poor and minority children. The learning disability mess endures.

Chapter 14 concludes this book by suggesting how the special education system needs to be reformed in order to attain better results for all children and more equity along race and class lines. Many of these reforms require financial solutions—health care to all children from a young age, transportation to special education programs from childcare centers, independent educational consultants to assist parents in navigating the special education system, full federal funding for special education, and equitable funding for all children irrespective of their school district. Special education resources need to be disproportionately allocated to poor families for these changes to be effected.

The political will to make this possible, however, seems unlikely. The learning disability community has been the chief lobbying force for this statute's continued funding, and that community has never focused on the special funding needs of poor families. Eloise Pasachoff documents the peculiar historical fact that although the rest of federal education spending "is often treated as suspect by Republican members of Congress, federal spending on special education has a decades-long history of widespread cross-party support."[29] Special education receives bipartisan support because it is *not* seen as special funding for poor children. Thus it is hard to imagine the funding of special education continuing to receive bipartisan support if it were selectively targeted to reach low-income children. Nonetheless, to paraphrase Ella Baker,[30] we cannot rest until the fate of every black child who is disabled is considered as important as the fate of every white child who is disabled.

* * *

Sam's story is one of disability and privilege. As a child born with an auditory processing disorder, he will always need a personal listening device to access communication in a large classroom or other group setting. And his acquisition of that device did not come easily. Nonetheless, his prognosis is excellent because I have been able to use connections and financial resources, as well as my expertise in special education, to challenge a recalcitrant school district and provide Sam with the support he needs to realize his potential. There are many Sams in poor school districts who sit in a classroom all day unable to hear instruction and who eventually start misbehaving out of sheer boredom. Those children—disproportionately poor African American boys—may eventually access special educational resources but, like Kevin, with the label "emotionally disturbed" or even "mentally retarded" applied because no one ever took the time to determine what is causing their difficulties in the classroom. They are also likely to receive assistance much later in school, when it is quite difficult to remediate the issues they face in the classroom. How we attained this system in which effective special education services are out of reach for most children is the story of this book. The challenge for us as a society is to figure out how to rewrite the ending.

2

The Education for All Handicapped Children Act:
Historical Evolution

Historical Background: The Bad Old Days

The history of disability exclusion is as old as the history of education. And, until the mid-1970s, attempts by parents to challenge these exclusions were largely unsuccessful. One of the earliest reported cases is from the state of Massachusetts. A young boy was excluded from school in Cambridge in 1885 because he was "too weak-minded to derive profit from instruction" and was deemed "troublesome" to other children because he made "unusual noises," pinched others, and was "unable to take ordinary, decent, physical care of himself."[1] A court upheld the school committee's conduct, in excluding this child from instruction, as coming within their "good faith."[2]

The first states to adopt laws requiring the education of children with disabilities were New Jersey in 1911, New York in 1917, and Massachusetts in 1920, but enforcement of those (and other similar) laws was generally ineffective. Merritt Beattie's case was typical of children from that era if they were even able to bring a legal challenge. The school district excluded him from regular public school in Antigo, Wisconsin, in 1919, although he had normal cognitive functioning, because "his physical condition and ailment produces a depressing and nauseating effect upon the teachers and school children."[3] As a result of some paralysis that affected his vocal cords, he had a "slow and hesitating in speech," "a peculiarly high, rasping, and disturbing tone of voice," and "an uncontrollable flow of saliva, which drools from his mouth onto his clothing and books, causing him to present an unclean appearance."[4] The court upheld the right of the public school to insist that Merritt attend a day school that had been established for the "instruction of deaf persons or persons with defective speech"[5] out of consideration for the sensibility of others who might feel "depressed" or "nauseated" by his presence in a regular classroom.[6]

Even though Wisconsin had a constitutional provision requiring a free public education to "to all children between the ages of four and twenty years," the court ruled, "Unquestionably the right of the individual child under such constitutional provision is subject to the equal rights of all other children to the same, and when the attendance of any one child in the public school is a material infringement upon the rights of other children to also enjoy the benefits of free schooling, his right must yield."[7] Merritt Beattie's exclusion from the public schools and placement in a separate facility was typical of the way children with disabilities were segregated and excluded from public education in the early twentieth century. His paralysis was equated with deafness to exclude him from public education and provide him a substandard education in another facility. His educational placement had nothing to do with his actual needs or abilities.

Exclusion and segregation were, in part, a story of good intentions gone awry. Thomas Hopkins Gallaudet and Samuel Gridley Howe were early disability rights activists who sought special public day schools for children with various disabilities, specifically children who were deaf, blind, or intellectually impaired at a time when there was enormous public skepticism about whether such children deserved any education at all.[8] They resisted the notion that these institutions would become "asylums" for incurables and, instead, insisted that "their essential purpose was educational, bolstered by an optimistic ideology that viewed the feebleminded as 'improvable.'"[9] Despite the purported humanitarian rationale for these schools, they were often substandard "with the disabled facing as much ostracism, contempt, and misunderstanding as ever."[10] Hence, Merritt Beattie's parents preferred that he attend the regular public school rather than one of these segregated institutions.

The schools created by Gallaudet, Howe, and others were not for all categories of children with disabilities. These schools did not seek to educate children who used wheelchairs, were not toilet-trained, or were considered uneducable.[11] Nor did they seek to educate children with mental health impairments, who often were placed in residential facilities that were later described as deplorable and offering no education whatsoever.[12]

Meanwhile, antipathy toward students with disabilities was ideologically linked to antipathy toward immigrants and a developing interest in intelligence testing. As a progressive gesture to increase the availability of public education, states began to enact compulsory education laws in the late nineteenth century.[13] When large influxes of immigrants began to move to urban areas in the early twentieth century, some schools began to have class sizes of eighty or ninety students. Some of these students were not literate and, with the advent of intelligence testing, were soon classified as "morons" and placed in special classes for children with intellectual impairments or what was then called mental retardation. The students classified as mentally retarded were typically male immigrants of all races.[14] Special schools or classes for the so-called mentally retarded were largely an urban phenomenon; rural school districts typically sought to exclude or expel children who presented problems as a way to get around the compulsory education laws.[15]

The idea that urban schools should engage in intelligence testing and distinguish students on the basis of race, class, and disability was well accepted in the early 1900s. For example, a writer for the *New York Tribune* explained that courses of study should be "shaded and varied to the peculiar needs and limitations of white people, yellow, black, brown, and mixed within the walls of New York's schools, as those needs and limitations are seen by the individual teachers and principals dealing with swollen classes wherein the vari-colored and vari-national pupils are indiscriminately channeled."[16] Although the author did not refer to the segregation or exclusion of students with disabilities, one can see the seeds of that movement with overt racial and class overtones in describing the "needs and limitations" of children on the basis of race.

Carl Brigham, one of the original creators of Army intelligence tests, was more explicit in connecting race and cognitive ability in a statement that he later disavowed when it became clear that the results he detected were based on regional rather than racial variation. Nonetheless, he claimed in 1923 that there was conclusive proof that "representatives of the Alpine and Mediterranean races are intellectually inferior to the representatives of the Nordic race . . . [and] we must face a possibility of racial admixture that is infinitely worse . . . for we are incorporating the negro into our racial stock."[17]

Those views were widely held as schools began to engage in educational tracking within the school system. Ironically, this system of tracking was considered to be a progressive move that allowed schools to "best serve each child's needs and talents" rather than a racially based move to limit the educational and career opportunities for those considered best suited for the lowest track.[18] Unfortunately, tracking became a mechanism to deprive both students with disabilities and other undesirables (such as immigrants and racial minorities) from obtaining an adequate education.

In a provocative examination of the history of special education in the United States, John G. Richardson and Tara L. Parker argue that "enactment of compulsory school laws had less to do with compelling attendance than with specifying the conditions of nonattendance."[19] While it is likely true that the initial impetus for compulsory education was progressive, it is also true that compulsory education was never truly about equal education for all. Richardson and Parker conclude that public schools accommodated the "laggard" students by adapting the classification scheme (and quality of education) "long practiced by juvenile reformatories,"[20] especially for boys. Thus, some students were excluded from school altogether whereas other students were segregated based on a classification scheme that was heavily influenced by the "mental testing movement."[21] This classification system predates the school desegregation movement although it has its roots in the racialized eugenics movement under which blacks along with various immigrant groups would have been considered to be of innately low intelligence, as described by Brigham in 1923.

Judicial Response: The 1960s and early 1970s

The story of racial segregation in education is well known, but its relationship to special education is less well known. As schools were forced to racially integrate, tracking and special education became a vehicle to maintain racial segregation. Judge Skelly Wright observed the relationship between special education segregation and race in an important 1967 opinion, *Hobson v. Hansen.*[22] He found that the District of Columbia school system unconstitutionally used tracking as a way to relegate African American students to inferior schools and classrooms. The "special academic" track was for students who had "emotionally disturbed behavior, an IQ of 75 or below, and substandard performance on achievement tests."[23] Tracking attained segregation on the basis of race because the students in the "special academic track" were disproportionately African American.[24]

Students placed in the special academic track received a segregated and inferior education. According to Judge Wright, "When a student is placed in a lower track, in a very real sense his future is being decided for him; the kind of education he gets there shapes his future progress not only in school but in society in general." Although the purpose of these programs may be to educate "the student up to his true potential, . . . the miniscule [*sic*] number of students upgraded, and the relatively few students cross-tracking make inescapable the conclusion that existing programs do not fulfill that promise."[25] Judge Wright's hundred-page opinion was a ringing indictment of the relationship between ability tracking (and the special academic track) and racial segregation.

The educational psychologist Lloyd M. Dunn strongly praised Judge Wright's legal conclusions.[26] In a seminal article published in 1968, Dunn documented what he saw as a crisis in special education. The number of segregated "special day classes" for the "retarded" was increasing by "leaps and bounds" with about 60 to 80 percent of those pupils coming from "low status backgrounds—including Afro-Americans, American Indians, Mexicans, and Puerto Rican Americans; those from nonstandard English speaking, broken, disorganized, and inadequate homes; and children from other nonmiddle class environments."[27] Dunn argued that we must "stop labeling these deprived children as mentally retarded" and "must stop segregating them by placing them into our allegedly special programs."[28] In other words, Dunn saw the rapid development of segregated classrooms for the so-called mentally retarded in the 1960s as a response to increased racial integration in public schools.[29] He applauded Judge Wright's decision and urged the Supreme Court to rule that "all self contained special classes across the nation which serve primarily ethnically and/or economically disadvantaged children [be] forced to close down."[30]

In 1972, a federal district court similarly criticized the way school districts used standardized intelligence tests to place children in classes for the mentally retarded in California.[31] The court concluded that racial bias was the only rational explanation for the tracking program because it was used to take African Americans out of the regular classroom and place them in "dead-end" classes that did *not* try to teach them the regular curriculum or prepare them to reenter mainstream classes.[32]

Meanwhile, the problem of exclusion from school also continued as a result of the exceptions in the compulsory education laws. In 1972, Judge Cornelius Waddy ruled in the *Mills* case that the District of Columbia violated the Constitution by excluding various children with disabilities from the educational system.[33] Once again the plaintiffs were African American, but the court's ruling was not dependent on that fact. Instead, the court concluded that denying an education to children with disabilities while offering it to children who were developing typically was a denial of equal protection. The District of Columbia case coupled with the *PARC* case from Pennsylvania[34] helped draw national attention to the million children who were denied an education altogether because of their disability status.

In both the *PARC* and *Mills* cases, the court entered consent decrees that would serve as the foundation for the Education for All Handicapped Children Act. These consent decrees required all school-age children to

receive a free public education (although the *PARC* decree was technically limited to children who were "mentally retarded"). The *PARC* decree
stipulated that each "retarded child [be] placed in a program of education
and training appropriate to his learning capacities." The *Mills* decree used
similar language and also specified that any child who was suspended for
more than two days was entitled to a hearing (and education during the
suspension). The *Mills* decree created an extensive hearing officer system
and provided that parents would be supplied information concerning free
diagnostic services as well as legal counsel. Both decrees created a presumption that a child classified as disabled should be placed in a regular
public school class rather than in a segregated public school class or a special public or private school. This language was based on the integration
mandate from *Brown v. Board of Education*. Congress was quite aware of
both consent decrees (and other court decisions) when it considered and
enacted into law the Education for All Handicapped Children Act in 1975.
These consent decrees were responsive to Dunn's work in presuming that
children should be placed in integrated rather than segregated environments, but they nonetheless did further the practice of classifying children
as "mentally retarded" (or some other label) as a condition of receiving
special assistance.

Congressional Response

By the early 1970s, Congress was aware of the cases in which courts concluded that the constitutional rights of children with disabilities were
being violated by their exclusion from school or by their receiving inferior education in segregated classrooms. Even before passage of the landmark Education for All Handicapped Children Act in 1975, Congress
began to increase federal funding for special education. The next section will trace the congressional developments that led to passage of the
1975 Act. Congress was informed of the particular plight of poor and
minority children with respect to special education, but it never developed a systemic response to that aspect of the problem. Members of Congress also thought that federal funding, along with procedural remedies,
could create an appropriate education for children with disabilities. Testimony from some leading special education advocates that their approach
could exacerbate educational inequities for poor and minority children
was ignored. Instead, Congress simply put the *Mills* and *PARC* consent
decrees into law.

Early Funding: 1954–64

In the 1950s, Congress used its appropriation authority to develop programs for subgroups of individuals with disabilities. On July 26, 1954, Public Law 83-531 authorized Congress to provide $1 million in grants to support educational research for students with mental retardation. In 1957, Congress finally appropriated $675,000 of those funds.[35] For the next several years, other laws supported students who were deaf or mentally retarded.[36]

With the election of President John F. Kennedy in 1960, more attention was brought to the need to educate children with disabilities. He helped establish the Division of Handicapped Children and Youth, which brought "new significance and strength" to the education of children with disabilities under Public Law 88-164.[37] This division dealt with a broad range of children with disabilities, not just a subset of the population. It set the foundation for the approach that would be taken a few years later to make grants directly available to the states to fund special education services.

1965: Direct Support for Special Education

In 1965, Congress enacted the Elementary and Secondary Education Act (ESEA).[38] The primary purpose of this Act was to assist disadvantaged children. In 1966, an ad hoc subcommittee of the House Education and Labor Committee held hearings on the need to support the education of children with disabilities. It learned that "only about one-third of the approximately 5.5 million handicapped children were being provided an appropriate special education. The remaining two-thirds were either totally excluded from schools or sitting idly in regular classrooms awaiting the time when they were old enough to 'drop out.'"[39] The subcommittee also learned that "Federal programs directed at handicapped children were minimal, fractionated, uncoordinated, and frequently given a low priority in the education community."[40]

In response to those hearings, Congress added Title VI to the Elementary and Secondary Education Act, to provide grants to the states for the education of handicapped children.[41] The grants did not go to school districts but rather to "schools for handicapped children operated or supported by [the state's educational agency]."[42] Rather than the modern "full inclusion" model, this funding supported only segregated programs for children with disabilities. The funding then, and now, was only a portion of what states might spend on special education through what the Supreme Court has characterized as a model of cooperative federalism.[43] Congress did not actually appropriate the funds until 1966.[44]

Throughout the 1960s, Congress struggled with the question of how to support children with disabilities. Representative Hugh L. Carey of Brooklyn, New York, chaired a Special Ad Hoc Subcommittee on the Handicapped of the House Committee on Education and Labor.[45] His committee heard nine months of testimony and recommended the freestanding Handicapped Child Benefit and Education Act.[46] Representative Carey was unsuccessful in getting this bill passed, but each of its major features became law within fifteen months through amendments to the ESEA.[47] In the next several years, the ESEA was amended to provide additional funds to programs for children with disabilities, but no freestanding statute was on the horizon.[48]

While Congress considered the needs of poor children to receive Title I money for education, parents of children with disabilities were also banding together to lobby for additional funding for their children with learning disabilities. In 1963, a group of parents convened a conference in Chicago called Exploration into the Problems of the Perceptually Handicapped Child and started an organization called the Association for Children with Learning Disabilities (now called the Learning Disabilities Association of America). This organization worked hard to achieve recognition of the problems of children with learning disabilities and achieved early success with the passage of the Children with Specific Learning Disabilities Act of 1969.[49] By 1970, it helped persuade Congress to enact the Education of the Handicapped Act and allocate $63 million to studying learning disabilities.

The importance of the creation of the Learning Disabilities Association cannot be understated. Its support has helped push for the creation of special education laws and financial resources for the category of learning disabilities. This trend can be traced back to the 1960s.

1970 Amendment

The ESEA amendment process continued in 1970 when Congress amended the Act with Public Law 91-230[50] to include 200 million dollars in funding to the states conditioned on their willingness to "initiate, expand, or improve programs and projects, including [special education] preschool programs and projects."[51] This allocation, 15 percent of the total amount earmarked for "innovative and exemplary local programs,"[52] represented a significant commitment. Public Law 91-230 repealed Title VI of the ESEA as of July 1, 1971, and created a separate Act called the Education of the Handicapped Act (EHA). This was the first freestanding special education statute.

Rather than target a small subset of children with disabilities, the 1970 amendment reached children who were "mentally retarded, hard of hearing, deaf, speech impaired, visually handicapped, seriously emotionally disturbed, crippled, or other health impaired."[53] It also created support for special programs for children with "specific learning disabilities."[54] Reflecting recognition that mislabeling of children can take place, Congress provided that the category of "specific learning disabilities" should not be used to "include children who have learning problems which are primarily the result of visual, hearing, or motor handicaps, of mental retardation, of emotional disturbance, or of environmental disadvantage."[55] This classification category will be discussed further in chapter 13, but for now we can understand that Congress thought that term applied to children with high cognitive aptitude who had trouble in discrete areas such as reading.

The 1970 language about "specific learning disabilities" has always been a part of the special education laws and is one of its more controversial features, although coverage of learning disabilities was added to the general definition of disability in 1975. Today, the statute says that "specific learning disabilities" does not "include a learning problem that is primarily the result of visual, hearing, or motor disabilities, of mental retardation, of emotional disturbance, or of environmental, cultural, or *economic* disadvantage."[56] In other words, Congress has always tried to make sure that special education funds went to children with "learning disabilities," in contrast to children who might be struggling in school as a result of "environmental disadvantage" and, in recent years, has made clear that it wants to exclude from extra assistance children merely because they suffer from "economic disadvantage."

The 1970 statute was pathbreaking in that it provided money to broadly educate children with disabilities, but it did not create extensive substantive rights. No right of action was specified in the statute so that parents could enforce these statutory requirements. It also did not mandate the education of all children with disabilities, so the children who were disabled but not considered "educable" were still denied an education. Its statutory terms were also fairly ambiguous, with terms such as "reasonable promise" and "substantial progress" to describe programs that could be funded.

Although the 1970 statute seems modest by today's standards, it was a very important beginning because it mandated that children with disabilities should be educated and that they should receive the "special education and related services" they needed to make progress. The term "special education and related needs" is still part of the statutory framework.

Nonetheless, by 1971–72, "seven states were still educating fewer than 20% of their *known* children with disabilities, and 19 states, fewer than a third.

Only 17 states had even reached the halfway figure."[57] Thus we had a long way to go before we could claim to have achieved universal education for all children with disabilities. As discussed above, courts were finding that it was unconstitutional to exclude so many children from the public educational system.

1974 Amendments

Congress adopted Public Law 93-380 in 1974, extending the EHA for another three years. It was aware that a broader response was necessary and enacted an emergency one-year authorization provision for greatly increased aid to the states for fiscal year 1975. It also created the first procedural safeguards for parents, modeled after the consent decrees in several of the successful court cases, particularly the *PARC* litigation. These safeguards required school districts to give "prior notice to parents or guardians of the child when the [school district] proposes to change the educational placement of the child" and to give parents a chance to "examine all relevant records with respect to the classification of educational placement of the child" and have an opportunity to seek "an impartial due process hearing that is binding on all parties subject to judicial or administrative review."[58]

The second set of procedural safeguards created the "least restrictive rule." This rule created the presumption that children with disabilities should ideally be educated with children who are not disabled "and that special classes, separate schooling, or other removal of handicapped children from the regular educational environment occurs only when the nature or severity of the handicap is such that education in regular classes with the use of supplementary aids and services cannot be achieved satisfactorily."[59] This rule—which was borrowed directly from *Brown v. Board of Education*—has been a part of special education law since 1974. In many ways, the integration presumption is the strongest substantive right contained in the special education laws even though it was derived from the racial civil rights movement rather than from concrete studies about the needs of children with disabilities.

The amendments also created what today is called the Child Find provision. States were required to have in place a program to identify, locate, and evaluate which children need special education and related services. A part of this new requirement was the explicit statement that there should be a goal of "full educational opportunities to all handicapped children."[60] The era of educating only a subset of children with disabilities was coming to an end.

Education for All Handicapped Children Act: Legislative History

In 1975, there was enough political momentum for Congress to mandate that states receiving federal special education funds educate *all* handicapped children. It enacted the Education for All Handicapped Children Act on November 29, 1975, by an overwhelming majority. The EAHCA received extensive consideration by Congress before being enacted into law. This consideration reflected its landmark importance as signaling a change in U.S. education policy—that all children should receive an adequate education irrespective of their disability status.

Senator Harrison A. Williams of New Jersey introduced the bill in the Senate. Throughout the hearing process, he often interrogated the witnesses and displayed much sensitivity to the race and class issues that were discussed. The Senate Subcommittee on the Handicapped (of the Committee on Labor and Public Welfare) held thirteen days of hearings over a two-year period[61] and produced an eighty-two-page Committee Report on June 2, 1975.

Representative John Brademas of Indiana introduced the EAHCA in the House. The House Select Subcommittee on Education (of the Committee on Education and Labor) held ten days of hearings over a two-year period[62] and produced a sixty-seven-page Committee Report on June 26, 1975. The Senate debated the bill for seven days; the House debated it for four days.[63] Congress produced a Conference Report on November 14, 1975, that reflected the compromises reached between the Senate and House versions. The House agreed to the Conference Report on November 18, 1975, by a vote of 404–7. The Senate adopted the Conference Report the next day by a vote of 87–7.

President Gerald R. Ford considered the proposed funding level to be "excessive," but he signed the bill into law on December 2, 1975, when he realized that veto-proof majorities had adopted it.[64] He promised to have the Act revised before it became fully operative.[65] The procedural and substantive rules he criticized are still part of the law today.[66] The specified funding levels never went into effect. The substantive provisions became effective nearly two years later on October 1, 1977.[67]

THE HEARINGS

Senate

The two years of hearings that preceded adoption of the Act reflected strong concern for the needs of poor and minority children. Witnesses repeatedly brought to the committee's attention the fact that numerous courts had concluded that excluding and segregating children with disabilities violated the U.S. Constitution.

Many witnesses described the unavailability of an appropriate education for poor children with disabilities. For example, Dr. Gerald M. Senf testified, "The ways we now deliver services are truly discriminatory against children who do not have parents who are able and have the time and the personal resources to speak up for them. What happens now is that children who do not have wealthy parents are not able to put pressure on the schools to bring the services we have to these children."[68] He then also said, "The shy, quiet, poverty line child has almost no chance at all of receiving the rather meager services we have available. . . . It is a simple fact that the people who are most attuned with our sociocultural system—that is, the ones who have made it, the wealthier, well-to-do-people—know how to use the system and they are the ones that get resources for their children."[69] He suggested that an "objective" screening process could solve that problem because screening could take place without the involvement of parents.[70] Another witness described the high cost of educating children with autism, highlighting that no South Carolina residents could afford the $550-per-month price tag.[71]

Other witnesses described these kinds of problems in racial terms. For example, a witness from New York complained that "the evaluation and screening process discriminates against black, Puerto Rican, minority and poor children."[72] She criticized the existing system under which parents received tuition grants to send their children to private school. She said that the program "is arbitrary and discriminatory when it comes to the constituency of poor people"[73] because the grants are not available to everyone and are not sufficient for the entire cost of education. Thus, poor people can still not afford an appropriate education for their children. She emphasized the importance of special education's being truly *free*. Another witness from New York tied disparities in services to poverty, stating that school districts with "such mundane problems as trying to get the windows fixed, trying to get the desks to work, and reasonably intact chalkboards . . . can hardly afford these [special education] expenses."[74] Witnesses described examples of students' being misidentified as disabled, and one witness introduced a report which stated that blacks and other minority students, as well as the poor from the inner city, were being placed "into special education programs that are not designed to improve their learning abilities."[75] The report also indicated that blacks and other minorities were being placed in special education programs "because they deviate from established norms."[76] Other witnesses discussed the overrepresentation of minority students in classes for the mentally retarded.[77]

The most articulate Senate witness who chronicled the way special education disserves minority youth was Professor Oliver Hurley, a special education faculty member at the University of Georgia. He said, "Special education has become the tool of society's efforts to maintain a surplus population. Its labels are glib; they are neat; they are made to order for the purpose of institutionalizing racial, class and economic prejudices. . . . The labeling/placement process used in special education, I submit, is an institutionalized extension of society's discriminatory responses to an outgroup, the Black and Brown minorities and the poor."[78] He argued that labeling and placement of children have become a "smokescreen behind which our prejudices and biases could remain unchallenged, even unrecognized."[79]

Hurley recommended that students have an "advocate" to avoid mislabeling. He thought the requirement that there be a written program and due process would improve the quality of professional work in the educational process. He also thought that frequent reevaluation would be helpful because "it is still not uncommon to find children who have not been reevaluated in 5 to 10 years. To us in the black community this seems especially true when the child is black, poor or both."[80]

Dr. Charles Barnett, Commissioner, South Carolina Department of Mental Retardation, agreed with Hurley's statements about overrepresentation of poor and minority children in certain categories, but he seemed less confident that the proposed bill would solve those problems. He said, "There are some real problems here that don't seem to be too close to resolution."[81] Others agreed with Barnett. One report suggested that children really needed an advocate because "too often the notice to the parents is written in educational or psychological jargonese or is so obfuscatory that the parents (most of whom are poor and undereducated) do not understand it."[82] California State Senator Clair Burgener suggested that school districts should be required to offer an explanation if minority representation in special classes exceeds 15 percent of what one would expect from the ethnic balance in the district.[83] That suggestion was never adopted.

Witnesses also pressed the Senate to define what is a "free appropriate public education." For example, one of the plaintiffs from the PARC litigation in Pennsylvania complained that that term was being used in Pennsylvania as an excuse to have a school meet only "minimum State standards" rather than "[establish] quality programs for each individual."[84] Another witness testified that the educational program should be one that "best meets" the needs of the child "whether public or not."[85] A state director of special education testified that "appropriate public education" must be better defined "or we will make a mockery of the intent of this act."[86]

Some witnesses testified in favor of the bill's due process procedures, which were modeled after the PARC consent decree. Those procedures opened "many lines of communication and aid[ed] in find[ing] appropriate solutions of education for many children without the necessity of formal hearings."[87] When hearing officers were used, they were described as "openly questioning the rightness of a program for a child."[88]

Although the committee members often cited the bill's procedural protections as a way to solve the problems identified by witnesses, some witnesses offered testimony that suggested those procedural protections would insufficiently protect poor children. A lawyer who represented poor parents in New Jersey testified that inappropriate placements were occurring "despite the safeguards that have been taken."[89]

A major topic during these hearings was whether it was reasonable to expect all children with disabilities to benefit from an education in a regular public school classroom (with support). The 1974 Act had already created the "least restrictive alternative" rule, and most witnesses strongly supported that rule. Some witnesses, however, expressed concern that Congress was not sufficiently considering the strengths of some of the support at many of the schools for children with disabilities. For example, Dr. Philip Bellefleur, Headmaster of the Pennsylvania School for the Deaf, said,

> Many, my very dear colleagues, afraid of incurring the wrath of militant parents, have developed instant philosophies to cover the situation. Suddenly anecdotal journal articles are showing that education in public day schools and county programs is superior to residential placement. Public School Special Education Administrators speak of residential schools as though they were gigantic wastebaskets providing a care and custody function.[90]

It is not surprising that, as the director of a residential school for deaf children, Bellefleur would favor the continuation of such institutions. At the next day of hearings, however, a mother of a deaf child testified that "integration of hearing impaired children in regular classrooms varies greatly in effectiveness and meaning."[91] Another witness testified, "[T]here can be times when it is advantageous for the handicapped child to be given highly specialized services on the basis that he needs them now so he can be integrated back into the mainstream."[92]

An additional key subject under discussion during the legislative process was the appropriate level of funding for EAHCA. The executive branch made it clear that it opposed large federal outlays to support special education. Stephen Kurzman, the Assistant Secretary for Legislation, Department of Health, Education and Welfare, testified that the Ford administration recommends against increasing the present authorization levels which are already larger than any realistic projection of actual funding possibilities. This, as we have said in a number of other contexts, simply contributes to the phenomenon of unfulfilled expectations. We should promise no more than can be reasonably produced with available resources, and have therefore recommended authorization levels equal to the fiscal year 1974 budget request.[93]

Thus, from the outset, the executive branch resisted providing the financial resources necessary to make special education a reality for all children. The administration was correct to foresee that Congress would never appropriate the funds to support special education at the 40 percent funding level.

Not only did the Senate fashion the procedural remedies on the consent decree in *PARC*, it held hearings in Pennsylvania to become familiar with the state's experience under the *PARC* consent decree.[94] John Pittenger, Pennsylvania's Secretary of Education, testified that the hearing process worked well. Dennis Haggerty, the lawyer who was overseeing the consent decree, however, painted a less favorable picture. He said that parents often did not understand the due process proceedings.[95] He also described special education as a way to segregate and punish: "as a way of getting [special education students] in the front door and putting them out the back door."[96] Don Carroll, who was the commissioner of a state task force responsible for implementing the consent decree, described the importance of having a strong oversight role. He suggested that Congress strengthen oversight of EAHCA.[97]

Peter Polloni, Executive Director of the Pennsylvania Arc, an advocacy organization that represents individuals with developmental and intellectual disabilities and which initiated the *PARC* litigation, testified that many parents had trouble effectively participating in the due process hearings. "[I]t has in many instances put the parent in a very unfair position. They have been fearful of entering into the due process hearing situation. They have felt many times that they have been unprepared and unsupported in going into the due process hearing situation."[98] He also said, "One of the things we have seen in the hearing process is the need for additional training for the hearing officers, and the need for the support for the parents."[99]

Maynard Reynolds, Professor of Special Education, University of Minnesota, spoke against the EAHCA. He opposed the approach found in the proposed Act because it required children to be labeled as "disabled" to get extra help. He said that the "[b]ill provides incentives for the negative labeling of children, a practice which large numbers of educators consider unnecessary and degrading to children."[100] Further, he argued that the "[b]ill would create or solidify artificial boundaries in the schools between regular and special education which would have the effect of limiting options for many children at a time when we ought to be working to open boundaries and increase educational options."[101] Reynolds was not opposed to providing the assistance students with disabilities needed to be successful, but he thought that the EAHCA would simply provide incentives for school districts to seek to classify weak students as disabled to get additional funds to provide the students with assistance, and he predicted that might particularly happen to poor or minority students "from economically deprived homes with previous poor schooling."[102] His testimony did foresee the racial disparity in disability classification mentioned in chapter 1. As we will see, Reynolds also testified extensively during the House hearings.

House of Representatives

As in the Senate hearings, witnesses at the House hearings explained that the existing system of special education had enormous regional, class, and race bias. A RAND Corporation report[103] documented that the funding "variation across states for all handicapped children is extreme: from $213 in the lowest state to $1705 in the highest (excluding Alaska). The reported variation across states within a single handicap is even more striking."[104] This variation was directly tied to affluence (or poverty). "[N]ot only do high income states pay more for special education, but they also give it more emphasis relative to regular education."[105]

Stanley Pottinger, Assistant Attorney General, Civil Rights Division, brought to the committee's attention that courts had found instances of racial discrimination in the classification of children as mentally retarded.[106] He also indicated that his department was concerned about racial/ethnic discrimination as part of special education and that his office was reviewing special education placement practices in the state of New York. Specifically, he was investigating "whether the effect of assigning children to ability groups or tracks, special schools or special educational programs is to create and maintain isolated environments within the schools so as to place children at a disadvantage because of their race, national origin (including language), sex or handicap."[107]

Patricia Wald, an attorney in the *Mills* litigation, testified about how the committee could strengthen the proposed bill. She was concerned that parents would have difficulty navigating the due process system because they "do not know how to follow through with a large bureaucracy. I would like to see it written into a State's policy that there is an independent ombudsman beyond the school system where parents who really feel they are getting the run around, really does not know what is happening, can go to obtain the information."[108]

Wald then underscored the challenges faced by poor and minority parents. She reported that "their phone calls are not always answered; their inquiries are sometimes dealt with cavalierly; often they themselves have difficulty communicating their fears, desires and perceptions of their children." An ombudsman could "obviate tragic confusion and frustration of already beleaguered parents."[109] This emphatic recommendation never became law.

Other witnesses supported Wald's suggestion. Samuel Teitelman, the parent of a severely mentally retarded child, said, "I would personally heartily endorse that because it is almost an impossible task for an uninformed and passive parent to get through a bureaucracy, if you will, which is not specifically interested in the specific problem."[110]

As in the Senate, the House heard strong testimony from Professor Maynard Reynolds, who argued that the proposed bill could do great harm to children by unnecessarily categorizing them as disabled to get extra assistance. Professor Bruce Balow, a special education professor at the University of Minnesota, accompanied him to the hearing.[111] Reynolds objected to the fact that under the proposed statute children had to be placed in a discrete disability category in order to get extra assistance:

> This has to do with the catergorizing [sic] of children and a system of money flow on the basis of individual children in categories. Much of the thinking about categories of handicapped children in education is left over from the last century when children were sent off to very specialized, set-aside institutions. They moved into the public schools very slowly in the first half of this century, mostly in the form of labeled, categorized children in special classes and schools. Recently, we have learned how to be more inclusive of exceptionality, that is, how to deal in more inclusive ways with children. We have negotiated for increasingly integrated situations for the handicapped and made a big start in getting away from crude categories. . . . The parents of poor and minority group children are expressing to us many feelings of resentment and resistance about the categorizing and labeling of their children.[112]

Reynolds and Balow proposed a broad definition of disability that would avoid the need to place a child in a discrete category and would avoid the need to figure out precisely why the child is struggling in school. Their proposed definition was: "Handicapped children includes the mentally and physically handicapped and those who, *for any other reason*, are severely handicapped in their ability to proceed with their school [*sic*] under ordinary arrangements."[113] Their suggestion was the polar opposite of the proposed definition of "specific learning disability." Rather than exclude children from federal funding because their educational challenges are due to income, environment, or cultural factors, they would include children who for *any* reason were having difficulty in school. In other words, a child's difficulties with school would become his or her "handicap."

Reynolds had a heated exchange with the bill's chief sponsor, Representative Brademas, concerning these suggestions. Reynolds cited an example in which a group of Korean orphans could best receive the education they needed from the special education teacher and suggested they should be able to get that help without being labeled disabled. He then asked, "Who is to deny the children access to that program which seems most promising to them? Why should we adopt a system which tends to insert boundaries in programs which work to the disadvantage of children?"[114] Brademas took offense at Reynolds's use of the term "denies access."[115] Reynolds, however, stood his ground and argued, "Your bill would withhold services with Federal support unless the children are categorized. . . . As I understand it, under [the bill] money would go to special education programs only in those communities where children are individually categorized in the terms defined in the bill. It would withhold funds from all other special education programs."[116] He made no headway with Brademas, who said that Reynolds was "misreading" what the bill was saying.[117]

Balow then continued the exchange with Brademas. He stated, "We are suggesting the label is deleterious, is negative and harmful, and I think there is good evidence for it."[118] Brademas replied by suggesting that Balow wanted them to get "apples off an orange tree" by suggesting this bill be used to benefit children who are not disabled. Balow responded that the analogy was wrong: "Plus. It is not apples and oranges. If I may say, but I believe what you are saying is you don't have to call an apple a rotten apple in order to treat it as an apple. . . . [I]t is the stigma that goes with being labeled."[119] Reynolds and Balow repeatedly supported the idea that the federal funding should support *personnel*, who might benefit a broad range of students, rather than children who have to be classified in a discrete disability category in order to get services. Their approach, however, was rejected.

Another witness who supported the positions taken by Reynolds and Balow was Lloyd Dunn, the author of some of the most important work concerning the importance of mainstreaming children with disabilities (discussed above). Dunn testified that "these bills, if enacted, would do more harm than good for the very children that we are committed to serve better."[120] He predicted:

The effects of this legislation will be to *discriminate* frequently *against* children who belong to *minority groups*, are *disadvantaged* and/or are *males*. It could be used to support many programs that run counter to a number of recent court decisions. Much of special education for the mildly handicapped had been to provide relief for the regular classroom teacher and jobs for the special educator at the expense of the disenfranchised child who is non-white, poor, or male—the ones who cause the most trouble in traditional classrooms.[121]

Dunn's testimony was surprising, given his strong support for the *Mills* decision—which was a basis for the legislation he now opposed. But he understood that the *Mills* decision was fundamentally about race, as well as disability, and he was dissatisfied with how Congress had addressed (or failed to address) that issue.

Thus, the House heard even stronger testimony than the Senate about potential problems with the legislation because of the potential for race and class bias. That testimony is not reflected in the reports that followed. And the final bill does not follow any of the recommendations discussed above.

THE REPORTS

Senate Committee Report (June 2, 1975)

The Senate Committee's Report in support of Public Law 94-142 confirms that the racial civil rights movement and the string of disability-related court cases in which parents won the right to send their children to public school influenced the Senate. The report quotes from *Brown v. Board of Education* to confirm that educational opportunity "is a right which must be made available to all on equal terms."[122] Similarly, it references the *PARC* and *Mills* cases as establishing the "right to free publicly-supported education for handicapped children."[123] The Senate committee described the purpose of 94-142 as providing "maximum benefits to handicapped children and their families."[124] The "maximum benefits" concept, however, has never been part of the statute's substantive requirements.

The Senate Report expresses concerns with both race and class disparities in disability identification. For example, the report notes that there are some problems with the disability classification system, including "discriminatory treatment as the result of the identification of a handicapping condition" and the "misuse of identification procedures or methods which results in erroneous classification of a child as having a handicapping condition."[125] It then specifically acknowledges the "erroneous classification of poor, minority and bilingual children."[126] It specifies three steps to respond to this problem: (1) precluding states from identifying more than 10 percent of its population as disabled, (2) providing a priority of educating children currently excluded from education and children with the most severe handicaps, and (3) requiring state certification of the number of handicapped children actually receiving an education.[127] The report expresses confidence that a state's oversight process would seek to eliminate "any discriminatory testing and evaluation procedures."[128]

The Senate Report concluded that children should be able to obtain appropriate educations without recourse to litigation. "It should not . . . be necessary for parents throughout the country to continue utilizing the courts to assure themselves a remedy."[129] The report also considered how best to achieve compliance with the Act's requirements. It concluded that a "State compliance mechanism"[130] was the best way. It chose this mechanism over a strong private right of action or a federal government compliance mechanism.[131] Under this state compliance mechanism, the most significant penalty for noncompliance would be "withholding of payments under this Act."[132] Nonetheless, the report suggested that a private right of action could still exist, although it did not specify how that private right of action would intersect with the state compliance mechanism.[133] The final bill required parents to exhaust all state procedures and not go directly to federal or state court, as suggested in the report. The report reflects a belief in a cooperative relationship between state and federal government, with little need for parents to seek litigation as a way to motivate school officials.

Under prior law, children with learning disabilities were not part of the general definition of children with disabilities. The Senate Report recommended including those children in the definition of disability. It was concerned that too many children might be inappropriate classified as disabled under this vague term, so it recommended that the term not include those "whose learning problems are caused by environmental, cultural or economic disadvantage."[134] (This concern will be discussed at length in chapter 13.) That language became part of the final bill (and is still with us today).

The Senate Report also recommended that an "individualized planning conference" be held at least three times a year. This planning conference should be conducted "with the joint participation of the parents or guardian, the child (when appropriate), the child's teacher and a representative of the local educational agency."[135] Congress assumed that parents would be able to attend such meetings, not considering the challenges such a rule would pose for poor or single parents.

At these planning meetings, the educational plan should be modified, as necessary, but "only with the agreement of the parents or guardians in order to ensure that services to the child are not arbitrarily curtailed or modified."[136]

This suggestion (which did not appear in the final bill) emphasized procedure over substance. The report stressed the importance of these meetings but then recommending deleting language that would have required the use of "objective criteria and evaluation procedures"[137] to ensure that the short-term instructional goals were met. Nonetheless, the report recommended that the federal Commissioner of Education "conduct a comprehensive study of objective criteria and evaluation procedures which may be utilized at a later date in conjunction with individualized data available through the individualized planning conference to determine the effectiveness of special education and related services being provided."[138] No such "objective criteria" have ever been developed, and the special education laws continue to promote process over substance.

The Senate Report extensively considered the priorities that states should use in meeting the educational needs of children with disabilities. It said that the highest priority should be "given to handicapped children not receiving an education."[139] The second priority should be "handicapped children with the most severe handicaps who are receiving an inadequate education."[140] Nowhere in its formula was consideration of the financial resources of the local school district to meet the needs of children with disabilities. In fact, it deflected the argument that Congress should fully fund special education by noting that it is the "State's primary responsibility" to assure "equal protection of the law" by providing special education services to children with disabilities.[141] In other words, states should be *thankful* that Congress was willing to fund *any* of the costs associated with special education because those are local school district expenses, not federal expenses.

The Senate Report reflected no concern about the pervasive inequalities in funding that exist throughout the United States as a result of reliance on property taxes for educational funding, even though it was aware of those problems. For example, the report quoted a passage from the *Mills* decision in which the court acknowledged that the "inadequacies" in the District of Columbia school system, which resulted in many children with disabilities being excluded from school or receiving an inadequate education, could have been the result of "insufficient funding or administrative inefficiency."[142] The proposed bill did not seek to address these funding inequities.

In sum, the Senate heard extensive testimony about the inadequacies of special education, especially for poor and minority children. In its report, it reflected concern for many of these issues. Nonetheless, it chose no mechanisms to directly address these issues. Moreover, it expressed much confidence in various procedural devices that would best suit the resources of middle-class rather than poor families.

House Committee Report (June 26, 1975)

Like the Senate Report, the House Report described the litigation that had resulted in courts' deciding that children with disabilities were entitled to a free and appropriate public education.[143]

The House Report also reflected sensitivity to the problem with determining who should fit the category "learning disability." The committee adopted an amendment to provide a limitation on the number of children who could be served under the Act as learning disabled. "The problem . . . as was underscored in the Subcommittee's hearings, is the absence of any clear or acceptable criteria for judging whether a child is significantly handicapped because of a learning disability. Testimony received from the Office of Education indicated that the entire lower quartile of any normal class could be classified as having some learning disability."[144] The House Report stated that the purpose of placing a cap on the number of children who had learning disabilities receiving federal assistance was to direct assistance to those "children who are the most severely handicapped."[145] The House Committee was correct to foresee that most special education resources would ultimately go to children in the learning disabled category. Nonetheless, it did not foresee how that this category would initially be available to white middle-class children.

Six House members (Albert H. Quie, Peter A. Peyser, John Buchanan, James M. Jeffords, Larry Pressler, and Bill Goodling) criticized in a dissenting report the limitation on the number of children who could receive coverage as learning disabled.[146] They focused on the irony that the Act establishes "a requirement that every handicapped child must be served and then single[s] out one group and limit[s] their participation in these programs."[147] They urged the full House to remove this amendment when the bill came to a vote. Although they did not persuade the full House to remove this rule, Representative Quie did persuade the full House to amend the bill to state that this rule would be in effect only until the Commissioner of Education prescribed regulations establishing specific criteria for determining whether a learning disability or condition may be considered a specific learning disability.

The only other controversy in the report was the level of funding. Two dissenting reports criticized the high levels of funding as unrealistic in difficult economic times. They were correct to foresee that the special education laws have never been fully funded.

The House Report offered no discussion of special issues relating to class or race. Unlike the Senate Report, it does not discuss misclassification as a potential race problem despite extremely strong testimony on that issue.

Conference Committee Report

The Conference Committee Report resolved the differences between the House and Senate versions of the EAHCA. Many of the differences between the House and Senate versions were relatively minor. Some, however, are worthy of discussion.

The Senate bill did not contain the House's language concerning limitations on those covered as having a specific learning disability. The Senate accepted that language with some minor modifications.[148] It retained the Quie amendment, which limited the effect of this rule as soon as the Commissioner of Education adopted regulations defining specific learning disabilities.

The Senate bill required at least three conferences each year with the IEP team. The House bill required only one annual meeting. The conferees accepted one annual meeting.

The House bill, but not the Senate version, required that school districts permit the parent to "be accompanied and advised by counsel and by individuals with special knowledge or training and skills with respect to handicapped children"[149] at a due process hearing. The conferees accepted that language and explained that that language was consistent with rules already established by the Commissioner of Education.[150] This language is important because it makes it possible for parents to be accompanied by nonlawyer advocates at due process hearings.

One of the biggest areas of compromise regarded financing. President Ford had hinted at vetoing the bill if he deemed funding levels to be too high. The Senate version had proposed higher funding levels than the House version, but the Senate version made the bill temporary rather than permanent. The conferees made the legislation permanent but selected authorizations that were lower than those in the Senate version.

STATUTORY LANGUAGE

The statute that emerged from these deliberations represented an attempt to provide a high-quality education to all children with disabilities. The addition of the word "All" to the name of the Act reflected this intention.[151] The definition of disability was changed a bit. The term "crippled," which was included in prior law, was replaced with "orthopedically impaired." And, instead of "specific learning disabilities" having separate statutory coverage, it became part of the definition of disability. In other words, "specific learning disabilities" made the list as a covered disability.

The ambitious funding scheme also sought to make it possible to educate all children. Congress authorized appropriations equal to 5 percent of the average per-pupil expenditure (APPE) in public elementary and second-ary schools for the 1977–78 fiscal year, 10 percent for 1978–79, 20 percent for 1979–80, 30 percent for 1980–81, and 40 percent for 1981–82 for each child identified as handicapped under the statute.[152] That level of funding, however, never survived the appropriations process. It tended to range from 8 to 12 percent of APPE.[153] Congress sought to encourage identification of children as disabled by linking funding to the number of identified children rather than to the number of children overall in the school district.[154] (This was contrary to the suggestion of Reynolds and Balow, who proposed that money be targeted to *personnel* rather than to *students* so that schools could use flexibility in deploying those personnel without labeling children within specific disability categories.)

The 1975 statute created important concepts that are still basic to federal disability education law: the concept of a free and appropriate public education (FAPE) and the concept of an individualized education program (IEP). The two concepts were also connected. A FAPE was defined as "special education and related services which (A) have been provided at public expense, under public supervision and direction, and without charge . . . and (D) are provided in conformity with the individualized education program."[155] An IEP was a written statement developed by a school district representative, the teacher, the parents or guardian of the child, and the child, when appropriate, to help the child attain a FAPE. This written statement must include five elements: (1) present levels of performance, (2) annual goals, (3) specific services and whether the child will participate in regular programs, (4) projected date of services, and (5) criteria for assessing whether objectives have been met.[156] Contrary to the recommendations of some witnesses, the statute did not define what was an "appropriate" education. It also adopted the House's recommendation that meetings take place on an annual basis rather than three times per year.

The 1975 statute repeated the least restrictive educational environment rule contained in the 1974 amendments. Children with disabilities should be educated with nondisabled children "to the maximum extent feasible." Supplementary aids and services should be provided, if necessary, to keep children in the regular classroom.[157]

The 1975 Act also expanded the procedural safeguards established in the 1974 Act. Congress expanded the list of when parents should be provided written explanations (in what is described as "prior written notice"). Under the new language, parents should get written notice when a school district "(i) proposes to initiate or change, or (ii) refuses to initiate or change, the identification, evaluation, or educational placement of the child or the provision of a free appropriate public education to the child."[158] That notice was labeled "written prior notice," as it had been under the 1974 amendments, although it no longer always encompassed situations in which a school district needed to provide notice before taking action.

The 1975 procedural safeguards were an important beginning in requiring that parents be involved in the education process, but the 1975 safeguards lacked a lot of precision. The statute created no timetable for any stage of the process. It also created a multi-tier process that would inevitably be time consuming to navigate. A parent who disagreed with the actions of the school district could file a due process complaint and receive a due process hearing.[159] An impartial review of that hearing was then available to the state educational agency. If a party was still dissatisfied with the result, then an appeal could be made to a state or federal court. In other words, traditional judicial review was not available until the third step in this process.

The purpose of this multi-step process was presumably to make it easy for parents to bring due process complaints. The parent was provided the right to examine the child's educational records and receive a written or electronic verbatim record of the hearing.[160] Hearing transcripts can be expensive, so this provision would benefit parents who bring such actions. But there was no provision to help parents pay for the costs of lawyers or experts whom they might need to use to bring a successful action. They simply were given the right to be "accompanied" by such people at the hearing.[161] The statute did not even include an attorney fees provision for the parent to be reimbursed if he or she were successful in a legal action. Although witnesses had testified in favor of some kind of ombudsman or other person who might assist parents in navigating the process, those suggestions were not found in the statute.

A strength of the 1975 statute has also led to one of its biggest weaknesses. Congress decided that a team—which includes the parent—should devise the child's IEP. Congress tried to involve parents in this process so that it could be a collaborative enterprise. A key problem with this approach, though, is that there is no guarantee that appropriate *qualified* people will make these determinations. The composition of the IEP team merely includes a school district representative "who shall be qualified to provide, or supervise the provision of, specially designed instruction to meet the unique needs of handicapped children, the teacher, the parents or guardian of such child, and, whenever appropriate, such child."[162]

This approach assumes that it is relatively easy to determine what is an appropriate educational program for a child with a disability. The only person required to be present who is arguably an expert in special education matters is the school district representative. Parents are entitled to bring their own expert, but they would have to pay the associated costs, which are rarely even covered by a parent's health insurance policy.

Although Congress has tinkered with the rules about who should attend IEP meetings, the basic structure has remained relatively unchanged since 1975. Congress still believes that a group of lay people can make decisions about highly specialized topics without guidance from an appropriate expert.

Another innovation in 1975 was the "stay put" rule. Under the stay put rule, the current educational placement stays in place during the pendency of any proceedings under the Act.[163] That rule would be helpful in a situation in which the school district wants to change a child's placement and the parent disagrees. The original placement would stay in place during the pendency of the due process hearing and the various appeals (assuming a parent is sufficiently well informed to take advantage of the rule). But this rule has no bearing on a situation in which the school district has offered *no* IEP or an IEP that the parent considers wholly inadequate. Although the IDEA is supposed to provide children with quick and effective relief, the school district has the ability to delay the implementation of that relief considerably by using the appeal process.

Finally, the 1975 Act tackled the coverage of children with learning disabilities. Congress was concerned that children with learning disabilities would be overrepresented within the population of children served by the IDEA. The 1975 Act provided that only one-sixth of children counted as handicapped by the states could be children with learning disabilities.[164] To resolve the controversy about excessive coverage for children with learning disabilities, Representative Albert H. Quie of Minnesota proposed an amendment, which was adopted, that required the federal Commissioner of Education to promulgate regulations that defined a learning disability. Once that regulation was adopted, then the one-sixth rule would be eliminated.[165] As chapter 13 will demonstrate, this attempt to limit broad coverage of "learning disabilities" has been unsuccessful. Today, nearly half of the children covered under the special education laws are categorized as learning disabled.

In sum, the enactment of the EAHCA was a "landmark achievement on behalf of the thousands of children for whom there had been no available schooling prior to 1975."[166] At the same time, however, Congress constructed a framework that some witnesses predicted would harm poor and minority children. As the evidence of such harm accumulated over the next several decades, Congress took few, if any, steps to correct those problems.

Poor and minority children, however, are not the only ones who have faced challenges under the special education laws. In the next two chapters, we will read the stories of two middle-class children whose parents brought legal challenges under the 1975 Act and had tremendous problems obtaining an adequate education for their children despite the assistance of free legal counsel. Chapter 5 will return to the legislative history to see how, if at all, Congress responded to the problems with implementation of the special education laws. Unfortunately, many of the changes made to the statute simply weakened the effectiveness of the special education laws even as the evidence mounted that the statute was not effective for many children.

3

Amy Rowley

Amy Rowley's story is well known in special education circles. Amy began kindergarten in a suburban school district near Westchester County, New York, in 1977. Despite the fact that she was deaf, and spoke fluent sign language, her school district refused to offer her a sign language interpreter.[1] Although both the district court and the court of appeals concluded she was entitled to an interpreter, the U.S. Supreme Court reversed their decisions, concluding that her education was "adequate" because she was performing "better than the average child" and "advancing easily from grade to grade" without an interpreter.[2] As a result of the Supreme Court's decision, Amy found herself in a fifth-grade classroom with no interpreter and a teacher whose beard and moustache made him nearly impossible for her to lip-read. Her parents could help her attain an adequate education only by moving to a new school district where she received the services of a sign language interpreter.

Through detailed review of hearing officer transcripts and other primary sources, this chapter describes the story of Amy and her family. Three themes emerge from this recounting. First, Amy's story reveals the enormous toll on the family as her parents persevered for years to help her obtain an interpreter in the classroom. The school district placed a lien on their house and Amy's brother faced harassment at school, while Amy struggled in classrooms where she could not benefit from oral instruction. Second, her story demonstrates that victories can often be shallow because of the ability of a school district to resist a court order. Even when the school district was ordered to provide an interpreter, it often hired inadequate professionals and instructed them not to assist Amy fully for her entire school day. Third, her story exemplifies that justice delayed is justice denied, because a child can never truly recover lost education. In reading this story, though, keep in mind that Amy's family was fortunate to have a pro bono lawyer who made the representation of Amy a second full-time job. Consider the fate of the thousands of children who cannot attain such assistance.

* * *

Amy Rowley was born to two parents who were deaf, several years before Congress enacted the Education for All Handicapped Children Act.[3] Her father became deaf as an infant as a result of meningitis; her mother began to go deaf at age four as a result of German measles (i.e., Rubella). Because her parents were not born deaf and her older brother had normal hearing, her parents did not expect Amy to be deaf. They spoke orally to her until it became clear when she was fifteen months old that she was deaf. At that point, they began to use sign language in communicating with her as part of the "total communication" method of communication. The total communication method is defined as "the simultaneous use of sign language, finger spelling and audible speech"[4] so that the child is prepared to communicate with or without an interpreter later in life. Amy already knew some sign language because she had seen her parents use it when communicating with each other, so she quickly caught on to this method of communication.

By the time Amy was ready to start kindergarten, she was fluent in American Sign Language, which both her parents spoke. Many children who are born deaf must learn sign language after they begin school. By contrast, Amy began school with strong communication skills.

Amy's parents were aware of two educational options for Amy—attending the local state school for the deaf (Fanwood) or attending the local public school where her older brother was already enrolled. Because Amy's father was a graduate of Fanwood and her mother had taught there, they were quite familiar with the education provided by the school. They believed Amy would get a stronger education at the local grade school than at Fanwood because most deaf students who entered Fanwood had a weak language foundation as a result of the fact that their parents did not speak sign language. The option to send Amy to the local public school in a mainstream setting had become available only a year or so earlier when Congress passed the Education for All Handicapped Children Act in 1975.

Although the EAHCA was relatively new when Amy began kindergarten, the state of New York had already implemented regulations to enforce the statute. These regulations provided that the school district prepare through a "planning conference" an educational plan "at the time" the child enters the school system. The phrase "at the time," however, also gave the school district thirty days in which to hold the planning conference after the child entered the special program.[5] Finally, the plan was supposed to be reviewed and revised on an annual basis.[6] Hence, Amy should have had an educational plan within thirty days of enrolling in kindergarten, and the school district should have revised the plan on an annual basis.

Amy's mother first contacted the principal of the local elementary school, Furnace Woods Elementary School, in May 1976, almost a year and a half before Amy was to enter kindergarten in September 1977.[7] She requested that Amy attend Furnace Woods and receive certain accommodations in kindergarten as well as a sign language interpreter. There is no record of a written plan's being put in effect before Amy began kindergarten at Furnace Woods. The principal of Furnace Woods wrote a memo to the superintendent of schools in June 1977 in which he outlined the options available for Amy: a special education classroom for hearing-impaired children at another elementary school, the state school for the deaf, and a regular classroom at Furnace Woods.[8] He recommended placement at Furnace Woods because of Amy's need to be in an academically challenging environment and her strong verbal skills. He suggested trying various auxiliary services for Amy and noted that Amy's "reliance on an interpreter is still very much a question among members of the committee." He noted that Amy's mother thought Amy needed an interpreter in the classroom and suggested that they were open to that option, although nearly a year would elapse before the school district tried a two-week trial with an interpreter.

The principal's June 1977 memo is interesting, because, at that time, it seems to reflect that he agreed with Amy's parents that Amy should attend Furnace Woods rather than the school for the deaf. Based on remarks allegedly made by the principal, Amy's parents took the position during the course of the litigation that the principal was hostile to Amy's attending Furnace Woods and really wanted her to attend Fanwood, the state school for the deaf. There is no way to ascertain his true position from the available material. His initial memo suggests that he was in favor of Amy's attending Furnace Woods, although it is also clear that he never grasped the necessity of Amy's attending school with the assistance of an interpreter.

Because the EAHCA was a relatively new law, it is likely that Amy's situation presented him with his first opportunity to try to mainstream a deaf child in the classroom. He communicated actively with the state's Department of Education and seemed to follow its guidance without taking into account the specifics of Amy's situation—that her parents were deaf and that she spoke sign language fluently. He also seemed initially interested in being supportive to the family. He had a Teletype machine installed in the school's office so that school staff could communicate by telephone with Amy's parents. Nonetheless, given the subsequent developments, it is also easy to understand why Amy's parents would have experienced the principal as hostile to providing Amy with genuine assistance at Furnace Woods even if those were not his initial genuine feelings. His position that she did not need an interpreter seemed to harden over time, even as school became more challenging.

Amy's parents filed a complaint with the Civil Rights Office of the federal Department of Health, Education and Welfare (HEW) in early September 1977, shortly after Amy started kindergarten, alleging that the school district was in violation of section 504 of the Rehabilitation Act because it was not meeting her educational needs.[9] (They did not use the state administrative process at that time to pursue their EAHCA remedies.) On September 23, 1977, they received a three-page letter from the principal stating that the school district would be conducting various trials in Amy's class over the next month or so in order to determine what services she needed.[10] The trials included the use of an FM wireless system to amplify sound as well as an "interpreter-tutor." Although the promise of an interpreter for a trial period was made in September, the trial did not, in fact, take place for about six months, in February 1978.

There is no way to know if the school district conducted the trial in February of 1978 only because of pressure from HEW. HEW wrote a letter to the superintendent of schools on September 30, 1977, in which it described Amy's parents' request for an investigation as being of an "emergency nature" and said that the investigative period would last no more than 120 days. The trial with an interpreter, however, did not take place within that 120-day period. HEW did not issue its findings until May 1978, about 240 days later and after the trial was conducted. HEW ultimately concluded that the school district was acting lawfully under section 504. HEW's investigation may have caused the school to eventually conduct the two-week trial with an interpreter, but HEW's conclusion that Amy was not legally entitled to an interpreter under section 504 may have also led the school district to feel more confident that it did not need to provide Amy with one.

After a one-week trial with a wireless FM system (i.e., amplification device), the principal sent a letter to Amy's parents in October 1977 saying he was cautiously optimistic about the effectiveness of the device even though he and an HEW investigator had observed that the device did not assist Amy when the class was read a story in the library.[11] They attributed this problem to the fact that her hearing aids were not on the proper setting. The letter indicated that a trial with an FM system would take place for another two weeks. The letter suggested, however, that the school district had prejudged the effectiveness of the wireless FM device. Throughout this entire episode, the school district's perspective was that the solution to Amy's problems was to help her hear better rather than to accept that her primary method of communication was sign language.

The school district met with the Rowleys on January 18, 1978, to develop an IEP even though they had not yet conducted a trial with a sign language interpreter. At that meeting, the school district presented an IEP that stated, "We are committed to a classroom trial utilizing the services of a sign-language interpreter for a period of two to three weeks. We shall implement this phase of our assessment as soon as we are able to find an interpreter."[12] The Rowleys signed this document, stating they "accept and are satisfied with the IEP developed for Amy governing this school year." It is hard to imagine that the Rowleys were satisfied with the IEP, especially because the sign language trial had not even taken place. They probably hoped the trial would now take place, because this was the second school district document promising to try out an interpreter. Their signature on this document reflects the challenges that parents face when confronting school districts—they sometimes may feel they need to appear to agree with the school district in order to keep the process moving forward.

On February 27, 1978, the school district finally implemented a two-week trial with a sign language interpreter. Amy's description of the trial period is that she felt quite uncomfortable having a tall man, dressed in black, following her around all day in kindergarten, and resisted his attempts to interpret for her. Also, because of the data collection that was taking place, he was not the only stranger in her classroom. As an adult, looking back on this experience, she recounted that she could "not wait until the entourage and the oddly dressed tall man left my kindergarten class in its normal state."[13]

In an undated report, the interpreter wrote an "evaluation" of his experience of providing interpreter services to Amy for two weeks.[14] He noted that she "resisted" his attempts to interpret for her except during the storytelling period for twenty minutes a day. He reported that Amy's teacher used sign language sometimes and also used visual cues to indicate the "primary happenings" in the classroom (such as a request that the students lower their voices). Although he observed that Amy does "not get everything," he also found that she would ask people to repeat information she had missed. He described her teacher as "one in a million." He concluded, "I would say that as far as interpretive services are concerned, they are not needed at this time. However, this does not rule out the fact that an interpreter will not be needed at a future date when the classroom work becomes more involved and large group discussion becomes the rule." As the case proceeded in the courts, this two-week trial became critical in determining whether Amy needed an interpreter to obtain an adequate education throughout grade school even though the interpreter had confined his observations to kindergarten in a classroom in which the teacher was able to use some sign language and visual cues on her own.

Because Amy refused to interact with the interpreter, the school district insisted that his services were not needed.[15] No school district employee thought to ask why Amy was resisting the interpreter and whether her "need" for an interpreter in kindergarten was relevant to her "need" for an interpreter in later grades.

Two months after the conclusion of this trial period, and before an IEP for Amy had been completed for first grade, HEW's Office for Civil Rights wrote a letter to the superintendent of schools in Amy's school district and Amy's parents informing them that it had concluded that the school district was in compliance with federal law with respect to the education of Amy Rowley under section 504.[16] The letter to Amy's parents indicated that the school district's report on the sign language trial and its proposed IEP demonstrated that it was "making a sincere effort to educate Amy." This letter likely emboldened the school district to believe it had no legal obligation to provide Amy with an interpreter under the EAHCA even though its conclusions were limited to a different statute—section 504 of the Rehabilitation Act of 1973.

The HEW letter, written in May 1978, references a draft IEP for first grade, but there is no evidence of such a document in the records. At the end of kindergarten, Amy's parents signed a document indicating that they consented to her placement in a regular first-grade class, but no IEP is attached to this document.[17] Thus, even though Amy's parents notified the school well in advance of her enrollment in kindergarten and filed a complaint with HEW at the beginning of kindergarten, the school district had not followed basic procedural rules to have in place an IEP that included parental input within thirty days of the child's beginning instruction in either kindergarten or first grade.

Shortly after first grade began, the school district's Committee on the Handicapped met twice to consider the identification, evaluation, and placement of Amy. At a September 12, 1978, meeting, it concluded that Amy was a "handicapped child" under the EAHCA, and, at the October 3, 1978, meeting, it considered both where Amy should be placed for education and what support she should receive. The chair of the committee sent a letter to the Rowleys on October 10, 1978, summarizing the minutes of the October 3 meeting.[18] The committee recommended that Amy stay at Furnace Woods and then went on to consider what services she should receive. The committee noted that the "state does not mandate an interpreter, but does require teaching of the hearing impaired one hour a day, 5 days weekly."[19] The committee recommended that Amy receive the services "mandated by the state" and that they then "see how she continues to perform." In other words, the committee recommended that the school district institute a plan that conformed to the state minimum requirements for a deaf child without considering Amy's specific situation as a child who was fluent in sign language and who spoke that language at home.

The minutes of the October 3 meeting reflect that Amy's mother objected to the committee's proposal. She said, "We know what is best for Amy. I am not only deaf, but I am a certified teacher of the deaf. If I had to live my life over again, I would want an interpreter while attending a public school. I know how much I have missed."[20] Committee members responded to Amy's mother by saying that there are "differences of opinion as to the value of an interpreter even among teachers of the deaf." Although an IEP is supposed to be, by definition, individualized, the committee referred to no individualized data about Amy's educational needs as a child who was fluent in sign language. Instead, it kept referring to the state's minimum required guidelines for all students with hearing impairments. In reading the minutes, it is also interesting to see that Amy's placement seemed to require discussion even though she had already had a successful year at the local public school in kindergarten. In understanding this case, one must recognize that the Rowleys had to fight merely to have Amy attend the local public school. Were Amy's parents worried that the school district would insist that she attend the school for the deaf if they pushed too hard for an interpreter?

Unsatisfied with the committee's recommendation, Amy's parents requested a due process hearing on October 25, 1978. By that time, they had retained legal counsel. They were entitled to a decision from an impartial hearing officer within forty-five days. The state appointed a hearing officer who had a professional association with the superintendent of schools. On November 29, 1978, the hearing officer recused himself for reasons of personal bias.

Meanwhile, the school district decided to revise the IEP. Amy's first-grade teacher, Regina Globerman, initially developed the educational plan for Amy without parental input. On December 6, 1978, three months into Amy's first-grade year, the school held a meeting to which the Rowleys were invited. They were given a few facts about Amy's educational progress, such as the fact that her IQ had been measured as 122. They were read the proposed educational plan and were not given an opportunity to provide meaningful input. The "parent comments" section was blank, consistent with the parents' position that they were offered no opportunity to provide input at the December meeting. The initial educational plan and the one finally implemented after the December meeting did not include the provision of a sign language interpreter for Amy.[21] Amy's parents did not agree with the proposed plan, and Amy's father signed a document expressing his disagreement. The committee met again on December 11, 1978, to reconsider the plan in light of an affidavit from Dr. Robert R. Davila of Gallaudet College that emphasized the importance of Amy's receiving a sign language interpreter if she were to advance educationally. The plan was unchanged except for an additional proviso that a yearly written evaluation be conducted to determine what services were appropriate.

A due process hearing was finally scheduled for December 20, 1978, nearly sixty days since Amy's parents filed for one. At the hearing, the school district emphasized Amy's educational success during kindergarten and first grade even though Amy was not happy with the structure of the classroom. She was constantly being pulled out of class for speech therapy or testing. She "preferred to be with the other students all the time and not being constantly removed from class to meet with my deaf education teacher or going to speech class and leaving for testing."[22] Amy's experts argued that Amy understood only about 60 percent of oral communication[23] but that she would pretend to have understood classroom communication in the hope that everyone would just leave her alone and let the classroom "return to normal."[24]

The hearing officer rendered his decision in favor of the school district on January 12, 1979. He noted that the Rowleys were not able to participate in the IEP planning process until December 1978 but concluded there was no sanction for an IEP's being prepared on an untimely basis when the child has been offered an adequate education during the period of delay.[25] He found that the school district had to offer Amy only an "adequate" educational program, not one that would "match or surpass a program offered by a private or special school." Because Amy was achieving both academically and socially, he concluded that the educational program should continue through the remainder of the school year.[26]

Amy's parents appealed the decision of the hearing officer to the state Commissioner of Education. Amy's mother provided an affidavit for that proceeding in which she described how difficult it would be for Amy to follow class discussion without an interpreter during the spring of first grade.[27] She described one of the male teachers as having a beard and moustache that hid his lip movement, one female teacher talking with her head down, and the regular classroom teacher explaining new ideas with her back to all the students. She estimated that Amy would be able to understand only about 30 percent of oral communication without an interpreter. She also noted that Amy was now asking for an interpreter even though she had resisted one in kindergarten. Amy's parents also introduced extensive reports and affidavits from others to support the argument that a deaf child cannot receive an adequate education without an interpreter. Some of these reports were based on classroom observations of Amy. Amy's parents made an exhaustive effort to document their daughter's lack of access to classroom instruction without an interpreter. The experts who provided this documentation were expensive. In the district court records, Amy's attorney submitted a document indicating that the Rowleys spent $5,400 on expert witness fees as well as $1,199 in transportation costs.

One of the most important documents submitted by Amy's family for the appeal to the State Commissioner of Education was an affidavit by Amy's interpreter from kindergarten. He emphasized that his original report strongly suggested that Amy would likely need an interpreter "at a future date when the classroom work becomes more involved and large group discussion becomes the rule." He also reported a conversation he had with the principal in which he was told that the school district would not retain an interpreter irrespective of his findings because of the excessive cost and "that it would be in the best interests of all parties for Mr. and Mrs. Rowley to take Amy out of the Furnace Woods School and enroll her in the [Fanwood] New York School for the Deaf in White Plains."[28] His affidavit (which was supported by testimony by others) reflects how difficult it was in the 1970s to get a child with a hearing impairment even into the public schools and was the basis for the Rowleys' conclusion that the principal was hostile to the idea that Amy would attend the regular public schools.

Three months later, on April 10, 1979, the commissioner affirmed the reasoning of the hearing officer and dismissed the appeal. Relying on the interpreter's kindergarten report (and ignoring his updated affidavit) as well as on the school district witnesses who had observed Amy "on a daily basis," the commissioner ruled that "the petitioners have failed to show that the present placement offered by respondent is inappropriate, inadequate or unsuitable [so that] there is no legal basis to grant the relief requested."[29]

Amy entered second grade under the cloud of her parents' having lost two rounds of hearing at the state administrative level. Nonetheless, her parents refused to give up and appealed the administrative decision to a federal district court. The technical issue in the case was whether Amy should have been provided an interpreter in first grade, but she was already in second grade. Her parents continued to refuse to sign educational plans on a yearly basis that did not include interpreter services for Amy. The cumbersome appeal process made it difficult to challenge those refusals on a yearly basis.

Amy's case raised what are called "mootness" problems. Despite a fairly expedited process under which two administrative decisions were rendered while Amy was still in first grade (concerning an IEP that was not put in place until December of first grade), the appeal did not reach the district court until January of Amy's second-grade year. As the district court judge noted, if Amy's parents challenged the second-grade IEP, an appeal "would not reach court until mid school year at the earliest."[30] Because the situation was one "capable of repetition, yet evading review," the district court judge ruled that the case could be heard and his rulings could extend to future school years.[31] Otherwise, a court could not provide relief. Reaching the merits, the district court judge issued an order on December 28, 1979, while Amy was in second grade, that the school district provide a sign language interpreter for Amy.[32] He followed up that order with a written opinion on January 15, 1980.[33]

In reaching his decision, the district court judge relied heavily on testing data concerning Amy's ability to understand communication while using hearing aids and lip-reading, as contrasted with the inclusion of a sign language interpreter. These test results were open to interpretation because Amy's scores improved as she repeatedly took these tests, with scores ranging from 59 percent to 84 percent on a test of word identification.[34] The district court judge concluded that the lower score was more reflective of Amy's ability to understand language without use of a sign language interpreter because the higher score reflected results after she had retaken the test on many occasions. With an interpreter, Amy received a score of 100 percent on comprehension.[35] The judge also considered testing results from first grade and was impressed with her IQ score of 122.[36] That score suggested that Amy should be able to do quite well in school.

The challenging issue for the district court judge was to determine what was an "appropriate education" for Amy Rowley. The principal of Amy's school testified that "only her academic failure would convince the school district that she needed the services of an interpreter."[37] In the post-trial brief, the defendants realized that might be an inappropriately low standard, especially for a child with an IQ of 122. They revised their argument to suggest that Amy's performance was consistent with her IQ score.[38] Amy's parents emphasized that she understood only about 60 percent of classroom communication and that "anything missed in the classroom early in the learning process will have far reaching consequences."[39]

The judge created what he considered to be a middle ground, common-sense standard which "would require that each handicapped child be given an opportunity to achieve his full potential commensurate with the opportunity provided to other children."[40] Like the hearing officer, he rejected the notion that a school district is required to enable a child to "achieve his or her full potential,"[41] because many nondisabled children do not achieve their full potential. But he also thought it was important to make the standard higher than mere advancement from grade to grade. If the standard were the latter, he acknowledged that the school district would prevail because the evidence "firmly establishes that Amy . . . performs better than the average child in her class and is advancing easily from grade to grade."[42]

Applying this middle ground standard that determined educational adequacy in light of the child's potential, the judge concluded that the school district was not meeting that standard for Amy. He concluded that the "deficiency in Amy's understanding supports the conclusion that her educational shortfall is greater than that of her peers . . . Amy's lack of understanding . . . is inherent in her handicap and is precisely the kind of deficiency which the Act addresses in requiring that every handicapped child be given an appropriate education."[43]

The district court judge also gave less weight than the hearing officer to the results from the two-week kindergarten trial. He said, "That recommendation, however, which purported to be applicable only to her kindergarten year, is already over a year and a half old." Further, the judge noted that Amy's refusal to follow the interpreter may have been a reflection of the fact that Amy was not "adequately coached to respond to this change in her classroom setting, or that she was [not] given enough time to adjust to it."[44] Finally, he stated, "It is hard for me to believe that a child who has been raised with the use of total communication cannot be taught to follow an interpreter."[45]

Because an order was issued on December 18, 1979, Amy could have received a sign language interpreter beginning in the spring of second grade. But the appellate court issued a stay of implementation of the trial court's decision on February 27, 1980, pending the appeal. The stay was not lifted until August 14, 1980, after the court of appeals affirmed the district court decision and shortly before Amy entered third grade. Thus, despite a district court victory, Amy attended second grade for the entire year without an interpreter.

As an adult, Amy recounts her recollection of her experience in second grade as being very stressful. She had a wireless FM system but had no way of understanding the various noises emanating from the system. "[T]he FM system certainly amplified everything I heard but I still understood nothing. I think it is difficult for hearing people to rationalize that hearing aids and FM systems are not the same as eyeglasses. I imagine the noises I heard everyday sounded like loud power tools to hearing people."[46] Plus, there continued to be a stream of visitors, including the principal, who came to her class nearly every day. She also very much disliked her speech therapy classes once her other classmates no longer attended them. With all the attention, she "felt like I always had a thousand eyes looking at me the whole time."[47]

At the completion of second grade, the court of appeals affirmed the district court's decision. It upheld the statement from the district court that services of an interpreter were needed "to bring [Amy's] educational opportunity up to the level of the educational opportunity being offered to her non-handicapped peers."[48] The dissent disagreed with this approach, arguing that Congress only intended individuals with disabilities to become "independent, productive citizens rather that their potentials be compared with those of the non-handicapped."[49] The standard cited by the district court, the dissent argued, was appropriate for a different statute (section 504 of the Rehabilitation Act) rather than the EAHCA for the purpose of promoting "gainful employment for handicapped persons by developing rehabilitative services on an equal, non-discriminatory basis."[50]

This court of appeals decision resolved the issue for two years while the Supreme Court considered the case. In third grade, Amy was provided with the services of an interpreter, Fran Miller. For Amy, it was a great year. The interpreter helped her in both the classroom and on the playground. "The added bonus of having an interpreter in the classroom meant that when I got home from school I only had to do my homework and not relearn everything I was supposed to have learned in class that day. So I really had a lot more time to play and 'just be a kid.'"[51] Unfortunately, Amy's older brother, John, who also attended the local public school, did not fare as well. As a result of the hostility against the family, he transferred to a private school.[52]

The experience of Amy's brother, John, highlights the enormous expense involved in these kinds of cases. Amy's parents needed to hire various experts as well as a lawyer to litigate their case through two levels of state hearing officers, a district court judge, a court of appeals and, eventually, the

U.S. Supreme Court, while also transferring their son to a private school to help him escape some of the hostility generated by the litigation. Fortunately for them, their lawyer (who was also deaf) never charged them any legal fees for taking the case.[53]

Even though Amy describes her third-grade experience in positive terms, that experience required continued advocacy on the part of her lawyer. The order from the district court judge stated that Amy was to receive the services of a qualified sign language interpreter during any school period in which academic subjects were taught. Amy's lawyer repeatedly tried to get the court to hold the school district in contempt for not fulfilling its obligations.[54] A hearing was held on September 22, 1980, because the school district's efforts to hire an interpreter were unsuccessful. An interpreter who was initially retained decided not to accept the job, purportedly because he was told he would be paid only during those periods when Amy was in an academic class and because he was concerned that he did not have the required national certification to interpret.[55] Although the judge refused to hold the school district in contempt, he did end the hearing with the request that he be notified as soon as the school district retained a qualified sign language interpreter.

Although the school district hired an interpreter, subsequent events demonstrated its enduring reluctance to provide Amy with an adequate education. The school district interpreted the rule that required Amy to have an interpreter during all academic subjects to mean that an interpreter need not be present during any school assemblies or field trips.[56] Prior to an assembly, the interpreter was told by the school principal not to interpret because the assembly was "entertainment and not for educational purposes."[57] Amy was distraught because she had to attend school assemblies and could not follow what was going on.

The school district also treated the interpreter poorly. She quit after the school district refused to honor its initial salary agreement.[58] The school district insisted on not paying her for any breaks she had during the day while Amy attended non-academic classes.[59] The school district also refused to hire a substitute when the interpreter was not available, and the principal purportedly stated repeatedly that Amy should attend the school for the deaf.[60] This theme—that Amy should attend the school for the deaf and not cause so much trouble for the school district—pervaded this controversy.

With her brother still in a private school, Amy entered fourth grade at the public school. Rather than allow her to continue to use her third-grade interpreter, the school district decided to provide Amy with the services of a teacher of the deaf as an interpreter. This person was less skilled in interpreting and did not facilitate Amy's interactions with anyone other than the teacher. Amy no longer had an interpreter on the playground. There is a difference between someone who is a trained interpreter and someone who can communicate in sign language. The fourth-grade "interpreter" was not trained in the skills of interpreting. Amy found the situation much less acceptable than the one she'd had in third grade, but at least she could receive instruction from someone who knew sign language. Her mother no longer had to re-teach her all the material after school.

The school district continued to have its annual meeting to devise Amy's educational plan. Louise McQuade, who was an advocate for children with disabilities, attended the meetings in the fall of the third-grade year and wrote an affidavit describing the experience. Despite the years the Rowleys had spent contesting the treatment of Amy in the public schools, McQuade felt that they did not understand the procedures very well. She tried to offer explanations to the Rowleys during the first meeting but said that her extended explanations made the principal "more and more agitated." She said that he "created a tenseness and extreme frustration for all of us present at the meeting."[61] She also attended a second school meeting with the Rowleys and their attorney. McQuade, the Rowleys, and their attorney were kept waiting for an hour as school personnel conferred. McQuade described the school as having established a plan before the parents even entered the room. Their lawyer was allowed to speak only after the committee had voted to reject his requests. At the conclusion of the meeting, the school district physician told the Rowleys that they should send Amy to the school for the deaf if they were still unhappy with the school district's program. No member of the school district staff sought to correct that comment. Thus, McQuade was able to independently verify the principal's hostility and the undercurrent that Amy should really attend the school for the deaf. In the face of so much hostility, it is remarkable that the Rowleys kept Amy in the public schools.

Amy's experience—even during the two and a half years when she seemed to have won her case—highlights the difficulty of truly "winning" a special education case. At the end of the day, the entity that needs to implement the judgment is the entity that has fought its implementation.

During the spring that Amy was a fourth-grader, the U.S. Supreme Court heard oral argument on the school district's appeal of her case. Amy's lawyer, Michael Chatoff, who lost his hearing while attending law school, became the first deaf lawyer to argue before the Supreme Court. He was able to communicate orally and used a computer setup that transcribed the justices' questions and other lawyers' arguments into written words on a television-like video display screen.[62] This type of communication is called "real time captioning."[63] Chatoff received assistance from Gallaudet University to make this transcription system possible during his Supreme Court argument.[64]

On June 28, 1982, after the school year had ended, the Supreme Court reversed the court of appeals in a 6–3 opinion.[65] The Court rejected the notion that children with disabilities are entitled to an education "equal" to that of nondisabled children.[66] Instead, it said the appropriate standard is whether the child's individualized educational program is "reasonably calculated to enable [her] to receive "educational benefits."[67]

The issue raised by the "educational benefit" standard was: How much benefit is enough? While not ruling how much educational benefit is appropriate for every child, the Court held that Amy's ability to advance from grade to grade coupled with the special services and professional help provided to her by the school was sufficient evidence that the school district had met the applicable standard.[68] It said that the state satisfies its "free and appropriate public education" requirement by:

> providing personalized instruction with sufficient support services to permit the child to benefit educationally from that instruction. Such instruction and services must be provided at public expense, must meet the State's educational standards, must approximate the grade levels used in the State's regular education, and must comport with the child's IEP. In addition, the IEP, and therefore the personalized instruction, should be formulated in accordance with the requirements of the Act and, if the child is being educated in the regular classrooms of the public education system, should be reasonably calculated to enable the child to achieve passing marks and advance from grade to grade.[69]

In this passage, and elsewhere in the opinion, the Court emphasizes the importance of the "personalized instruction and sufficient support services." It mentions the "personalized instruction" twice within that paragraph. As we will see in chapters 8 through 12, hearing officers often emphasize the "passing marks" passage rather than the "personalized instruction" passage. The record of Amy's having received eight hours a week of individualized instruction and an FM system was very important to the Court in concluding that she was receiving an adequate IEP. Had she not been receiving those additional services, it is unlikely that the Court would have found her record of advancing from grade to grade sufficient to conclude that the IEP was adequate.

The *Rowley* decision is careful *not* to define one educational standard that constitutes the "floor" for all children. It says, "We do not attempt today to establish any one test for determining the adequacy of educational benefits conferred upon all children covered by the Act."[70] Instead, it went on to apply the legal standard to the facts in *Rowley*. And the case was fairly easy under the applicable standard. Not only was Amy receiving what the Court characterized as "substantial specialized instruction,"[71] but there was not even any strong evidence in the record that her performance in kindergarten or first grade would have been stronger had she had access to a sign language interpreter. Further, the Court noted in an often-ignored footnote that

> We do not hold today that every handicapped child who is advancing from grade to grade in a regular public school is automatically receiving a "free appropriate public education." In this case, however, we find Amy's academic progress, *when considered with the special services and professional consideration accorded by the Furnace Woods school administrators*, to be dispositive.[72]

By emphasizing grade-to-grade advancement, rather than the scope of the services being offered, contemporary hearing officers are misreading *Rowley*.

The Supreme Court therefore resolved the substantive issue—whether Amy was receiving an adequate education—rather than remand that issue back to the district court under the applicable standard. The only issue it remanded was whether procedural errors had occurred in the handling of Amy's case.[73] When lower courts use the wrong standard, it is more typical for the Court to remand the case in light of the correct standard. In this case, though, the hearing officer had found that Amy was receiving an "adequate" education because she performed better than the average child and advanced easily from grade to grade.[74] It was therefore obvious how the hearing officer would resolve the relevant issue under the correct legal standard, so no remand was necessary.

By the time the Supreme Court decided this case, which stemmed from a school district decision when Amy was in first grade, she was ready to begin fifth grade. The Committee on the Handicapped met on August 31, 1982, to conduct its annual review regarding Amy. The Court's decision was not technically binding on the services Amy needed in fifth grade, so her parents again requested an interpreter and, again, the committee turned down their request. On September 6, 1982, they appealed that decision to an impartial hearing officer, arguing that Amy's current placement and services should be maintained pending further appeals. The hearing officer denied their request on November 30, 1982.[75]

Starting in fifth grade, Amy was therefore stuck in a school system that had the imprimatur of the U.S. Supreme Court in its insistence not to provide her with a sign language interpreter. Even as school became more academically rigorous for Amy, the school district maintained its position. The result was that, after having an interpreter for two years, Amy entered fifth grade without an interpreter and confused by a teacher with an Australian accent and "big teeth that didn't make lipreading easy."[76] Fifth grade was a disaster as Amy could not follow discussions and often did the wrong homework as a result of miscommunications.

Meanwhile, Amy's lawyer, Michael Chatoff, was having serious health problems. In the spring of Amy's fifth grade, he filed an affidavit seeking a thirty-day extension because he had had three recent operations—two for the removal of a brain tumor and one to relieve pressure on the brain.[77] Co-counsel Barry Felder began to assist him for the first time. Felder had met Chatoff through their work on disability issues and Felder had written an *amicus* brief in the Supreme Court on behalf of Amy in which he focused on the legislative history of the EAHCA. Like Chatoff, Felder agreed to work on the case on a pro bono basis.[78] Felder also unsuccessfully tried to help persuade the school district to retain an interpreter for Amy in fifth grade.

Rather than continue to fight the school district, Amy's family moved to New Jersey (where her father had been working for several years) while she was in sixth grade. For the first time, she was able to attend a school with other deaf children and an interpreter. Her brother was no longer harassed because there were lots of deaf children at the school. She describes the move as "truly the best thing that happened."[79] The move was also good for her father because it shortened his commute, but it was quite a financial strain as the New York school district put a lien on their house and it was very difficult to sell.[80] This lien was likely the result of an order from the Second Circuit Court of Appeals, dated October 13, 1983, awarding $4,582.00 in costs to the school district from the Rowley family.[81] The district court files reflect that the Rowleys paid the judgment on April 10, 1984. On January 19, 1984, the court closed the case because Amy was no longer attending school in the district.[82] There is also an entry on April 9, 1984, in the court of appeals files indicating that the appeal was withdrawn without costs and without attorney fees and with prejudice.[83]

Amy, along with many other children with disabilities, was hurt by the Supreme Court's decision that an IEP is appropriate so long as it is "reasonably calculated" to allow the child to receive "educational benefits." Under this standard, some children, like Amy, whose achievement falls well below their aptitude are held to be adequately educated simply because they are advancing from grade to grade. There is no right for a child with a hearing impairment to have "equal access" to verbal instruction, as one would expect under an equality standard.

Congress has amended the IDEA many times since *Rowley* was decided, arguably to raise the substantive standard established by that decision. "Interpretive services" are now listed as a "related service" in the regulations implementing the IDEA.[84] In the findings section, the statute now emphasizes the importance of "high expectations" for children with disabilities and "ensuring their access to the general education curriculum in the regular classroom to the maximum extent possible" and helping them to meet "to the maximum extent possible" the developmental goals and "challenging expectations" that have been established for all children. The current regulations state that a child with a disability should have a free and appropriate public education "even though the child has not failed or been retained in a course or grade, and is advancing from grade to grade."[85] Some hearing officers and courts would therefore place less weight on the fact that Amy could advance from grade to grade without an interpreter. They would question whether an education can be "adequate" when the child has minimal access to classroom oral instruction.

Nonetheless, as chapters 8 through 12 will demonstrate through a discussion of hearing officer decisions, *Rowley* still has an important impact on hearing officer decisions. Neither the courts nor Congress has ever overruled *Rowley*, and it is common for hearing officers to conclude that a child has made "adequate" progress even when it is clear that the child is performing significantly below his or her potential. The IDEA is not an equal opportunity statute—children with disabilities are not expected to receive an education comparable to that of their nondisabled peers. The IDEA merely provides the guarantee of an "adequate" education, which can be a quite limited education.

The continued shortcomings of the IDEA are apparent throughout the Rowley story. The school district's original position was that it would not offer Amy the particular service she needed to access oral communication unless she failed without it. Her parents did not want to have to wait for her to fail to get appropriate assistance.

Amy's parents hired experts to help them with the case and brought information to the attention of the hearing officer to educate him about Amy's situation. But they could never overcome the results of the two-week kindergarten trial even though the interpreter had qualified his conclusions as applying only to an informal kindergarten classroom. The school district also appeared to have virtually unlimited resources and sent many observers to Amy's classroom who could testify that she did well without an interpreter. Amy's parents never consented to this constant intrusion on Amy's school day and, despite hiring many experts of their own, could never sufficiently educate the court about the educational needs of a profoundly deaf child.

Although this case was decided long before the Supreme Court resolved the burden of proof issue in an IDEA case, it is clear that the hearing officer placed the burden of proof on the Rowleys. There was no way they could have more, individualized information than the school district without cameras in the classroom! There was also no way the Rowleys could have known the importance of the two-week kindergarten trial to the determination of appropriate services for Amy for the next five years. With hindsight, they would probably have counseled five-year-old Amy before the beginning of the two-week trial to expect a strange man to be in her classroom but to pay attention to him because he could provide her with a lot of help through interpreting. By the time Amy decided she desperately wanted an interpreter when she was eight years old, the school district was no longer collecting data.

The expense of this litigation was enormous. In 1982, Amy's lawyer, Michael Chatoff, submitted documents to the district court to try to recover attorney fees for the years he spent litigating the case and the successful result he obtained for two years.[86] In his attorney fee petition, he indicated that he worked on this case for no compensation for four years. He took no other clients during this time and supported himself by also working for West Publishing Company as an editor. He would work on the case in morning, evenings, and weekends and had no legal assistance from any other source until he became quite ill. He took the case on a contingency basis so that the Rowleys were responsible for only the costs that totaled $5,400. He spent 2,506 hours on the case outside the courtroom and 38 hours on the case inside the courtroom, incurring nearly $400,000 in legal fees (at a rate of $150 per hour outside the courtroom and $170 per hour inside the courtroom). Despite his success in acquiring an interpreter for Amy for two years, he recovered no attorney fees.

Michael Chatoff was a tireless, passionate, and devoted attorney for Amy Rowley. His passion can be found in many of the briefs and oral arguments. He objected to the notion that the school district thought it could teach Amy to "hear" by offering her extensive speech therapy and other services. He also strongly cross-examined the school district's witnesses, challenging their qualifications to suggest what accommodations were needed for Amy. After one testy exchange with a school district witness over the issue of whether all deaf people have some residual hearing, Chatoff asked for permission to testify. He explained to the court his wish to testify that he had no residual hearing at all. Although this was a side issue in the case, it reflected Chatoff's passion in trying to correct myths about deafness. Unfortunately, Michael Chatoff passed away in 2007, so I could not interview him for this book. But the court papers present a vivid picture of a tireless and passionate advocate for Amy Rowley. Even so, Amy's family had to leave the school district in order for Amy to receive an adequate education with an interpreter.

4

Michael Panico

Michael Panico began kindergarten in the fall of 1975 at the Memorial School in Burlington, Massachusetts, shortly after Congress adopted the EAHCA.[1] After three years of Michael's foundering in school and not receiving an educational plan that was likely to help him make adequate progress, his parents decided to send him to private school and seek reimbursement from the school district for their educational expenses. Although they eventually reached a favorable settlement with the school district, Michael's case reflects the sloppy way in which many school districts implemented the EAHCA in the early days of enforcement.

The case also shows the strain imposed on families as they seek to obtain an education for their child. Michael's parents initially paid for local counsel but soon found those expenses out of their reach. Like Amy Rowley's parents, Michael's parents were fortunate to receive the assistance of outstanding pro bono legal counsel. And, although theirs was a family of modest means, they were also fortunate to receive enough scholarship assistance to make it possible for Michael to attend private school while this litigation proceeded. Most parents cannot afford to pursue Michael parents' legal strategy—paying for their child to attend private school and then seeking reimbursement— because they do not have the funds for private school.

Michael struggled in school from the outset. Using Title I funds, the school provided him with remedial reading assistance in grades one and two. At the end of first grade (May 1977), the school district recommended that Michael be retained in grade one because of "overall immaturity." Even though the school district did not comply with the procedural requirements of the special education laws, by meeting with Michael's parents and creating an educational plan devised for Michael's special needs, it unilaterally instituted what it called an "educational plan" for Michael in May 1977 under which he received some reading tutoring.

At the end of first grade, Michael's parents requested an evaluation of their son. They shared with the school district an evaluation conducted by Michael's pediatrician in June 1977. The school district contended that it gave Michael's parents a three-page notice of "Rights to Parents" at that time; the parents disputed having received such a document. The school psychologist evaluated Michael in June 1977 and concluded that his performance was typical for a child of his age and that he had some "emotional issues" that should not affect his academic performance. He was found not to have any significant learning disability. At the end of first grade, he was found to be reading at "preprimer" to "primer" levels and performing at grade level in math. A formal IEP was not put in place although Michael's parents were sent copies of assessment reports and suggestions that a private reading tutor contact his teacher. It appears that the school district was not yet familiar with the procedural requirements under the special education laws because it did not make a formal determination of disability status.

During second grade, at the recommendation of his pediatrician, Michael's parents had him privately evaluated by a pediatric neurologist, Dr. Ira Lott, on December 16, 1977. Upon Dr. Lott's recommendation, Michael was also evaluated at the Cortical Function Test Laboratory in January 1978. The lab "found evidence of crossed dominance, left-right confusion, reversals and difficulties in sequential memory."[2] Michael's father provided the school with these neurological evaluations. The school system did not conduct its own neurological evaluations.

The school district wrote an IEP for Michael in March 1978, during the spring of second grade. The records do not indicate when the school district decided to identify Michael as disabled and whether school personnel met with the parents to devise the IEP. The school district relied on the private neurological examinations to write the IEP. In spring 1978, academic testing revealed that Michael was somewhat below grade level in reading and at grade level in math. Under the IEP, Michael was supposed to receive individual reading instruction and small and large group counseling. That IEP was in effect until June 1979 (the end of third grade) when the school district proposed a new plan.

The new IEP specified that Michael was to receive individual reading instruction for one hour per day. Nonetheless, during third grade, in fall 1978, a second child was assigned to the reading teacher, Ms. Black, for approximately half the period. Michael's parents did not learn of that change until May 1979. In spring of third grade, Michael was found to be at least a year below grade level in reading and only in the thirty-fourth percentile for math. The gap between Michael and his peers appeared to be growing.

Without notifying the parents or requesting consent, the school district conducted evaluations of Michael in spring 1979. Although the school district claimed that these evaluations were conducted for "retention" purposes rather than for special education purposes, the results were used in creating the next IEP—one that was proposed to begin in June 1979. The school shared various parts of these assessments with the parents at small meetings but did not meet with them to devise the educational plan, as required by the EAHCA.

The dispute in this case arose over the content of the IEP proposed by the school district on June 28, 1979, for the 1979–80 school year (fourth grade). The school district concluded that Michael was making "limited progress" and that the gap between his performance and grade level was growing with respect to reading. The school district proposed transferring Michael to the Pine Glen School within the school district and placing him in the classroom of John McAleer, who had many years of experience teaching special needs students, especially those with emotional disorders. The daily schedule for McAleer's class included one and a half to two hours of reading per day with additional time allotted for other related skills. There were seven children in the classroom, and an aide would be present during reading, so the student–teacher ratio would be approximately 4:1 during reading instruction. In addition, Michael would have, on average, at least fifteen minutes per day of one-to-one instruction in reading under the Helen Grush reading method. Michael's reading skills placed him at or near the bottom of the class. The proposed program offered the opportunity for Michael to integrate into a regular math class. The school day in McAleer's classroom was fifteen to twenty minutes shorter than the regular school day because of the transportation schedule of the students. The ages of the students in the class ranged from seven to eleven years. Michael would have been one of the oldest students in the class but one of the weakest readers.

Michael's parents rejected that plan in July 1979 because the other students had needs that were very different from Michael's and some of the other students would likely have been disruptive to Michael. The classroom was really not designed for a student with a very significant learning disability in reading, which is why Michael would have been one of the oldest students and one of the weakest readers. Michael's parents initiated a due process complaint in July 1979 and enrolled Michael in the Carroll School, a private day school, in September 1979 for fourth grade so that he could be in a school setting that really emphasized the needs of children with learning disabilities in reading. The Carroll School used the Orton-Gillingham method, which was the method usually recommended for students with learning disabilities and the one that had worked best for Michael in the past; it also grouped children according to age and skill level so that Michael could be in a classroom with other children who were his age and at his skill level. Individual tutoring as well as counseling was also available. In the due process complaint, Michael's parents sought reimbursement for their private medical testing and for tuition at the Carroll School.

Michael's parents hired a local attorney in solo practice, Gerald B. Gallagher, to handle the due process hearing. A failed mediation session occurred on August 17, 1979. A four-day hearing was held in the fall of 1979; an advocate from the Federation for Children also assisted Michael's parents. Two attorneys represented the school district. The hearing officer issued a decision on January 31, 1980, when Michael was in fourth grade at the Carroll School.

Michael's parents argued that McAleer's classroom would not be appropriate for their son. They believed that McAleer's classroom was designed for students with substantial emotional or behavioral problems and would not be an appropriate setting for Michael to work on his reading goals, especially because McAleer used the Helen Grush method rather than the Orton-Gillingham method for teaching reading. Michael had very serious attention issues, and they thought that McAleer's classroom would be too disruptive for him. Because Michael was described as a competitive child, they also believed he would be unhappy in a classroom in which he was one of the oldest children yet one of the weakest readers.

Various witnesses testified at the due process hearing, including the reading tutor who had worked with Michael at school and during an unpaid summer tutorial. She testified that McAleer's class was inappropriate for Michael because the needs of another child conflicted with his needs. Michael's father and the educational advocate observed McAleer's classroom. The educational advocate testified that the classroom was not appropriate for Michael because at least one child had needs and educational goals incompatible with Michael's and that the environment would not be academically stimulating for Michael, particularly in math.

The school district offered testimony that McAleer's classroom was appropriate—that he had many years of experience teaching children with disabilities and that he was prepared to respond to Michael's educational needs through the Helen Grush method reading program.

The hearing officer concluded that the program offered by McAleer would not be appropriate because Michael needed "a small group reading program composed of students with similar disabilities and achievement levels."[3] She concluded that Michael could not receive an appropriate education in that setting because of the wide skill variance among the students in McAleer's classroom. She also criticized the school district for failing to comply with state standards about the maximum range of ages in a classroom (thirty-six months). She was also concerned about the change in the reading method from Orton-Gillingham to Helen Grush. Both the reading tutor and McAleer testified that Michael would benefit from consistency in methodology. The tipping point for the hearing officer seemed to be the school district's record of procedural errors. She said,

> I might have acceded to Burlington's suggestion to try the new program, had the record supported Burlington's capacity to comply with educational and procedural mandates on Michael's behalf. On the contrary, I find substantive and continuing procedural irregularity. This circumstance combined with doubts that Mr. McAleer's classroom is an appropriate placement lead me to conclude that the IEP is inadequate to give reasonable assurance of Michael's educational progress. I further find the Carroll School is the least restrictive adequate program within the record."[4]

The hearing officer therefore believed that a record of procedural violations was relevant to the issue of whether the proposed IEP was "appropriate." She also thought an IEP could be invalidated based on "doubts" about a teacher's ability to implement a program. Finally, she thought that the correct legal standard for determining the appropriateness of a placement was whether there was "reasonable assurance" of educational progress. Because she was deciding this case before there was much case law on the EAHCA, she was not aware of the legal standards that would later develop.

Accordingly, the hearing officer ordered the Burlington Public Schools to pay for Michael's tuition and transportation to the Carroll School for the 1979–80 school year and to reimburse his parents for the cost of that placement dating from their rejection of the educational plan for 1979–80. The opinion makes no statement about what should be Michael's educational placement for any subsequent school year.

The hearing officer also determined that the parents were entitled to reimbursement for their medical expenses. The EAHCA provided that parents can be reimbursed for independent medical evaluations when they provide notice to the school district that the school district's evaluations are inadequate. In this instance, the hearing officer concluded that the parents were not informed about their right to be reimbursed for independent medical evaluations so the parents did not conform to the notice requirements. Also, the hearing officer concluded that the school district treated Michael's pediatrician as if he were a member of the school evaluation team. Because the school district relied heavily on those evaluations for its own reports, it was required to reimburse the parents for their expenses.

The case then underwent six years of subsequent litigation before reaching the U.S. Supreme Court. The first legal maneuver was the school district's requesting a federal district court judge to stay the hearing officer's order that it reimburse Michael's father for the cost of educating him at the Carroll School. Following a brief hearing at which no new evidence was presented, this request was denied on July 24, 1980 (at the end of fourth grade).[5] The school district appealed this decision, but it was not decided by the court of appeals until other matters involving this case also came to the court of appeals about a year later.

Without hearing additional evidence, the district court judge (Rya W. Zobel) then issued a ruling on November 19, 1980, while Michael was in fifth grade, on cross-motions for summary judgment on the appropriateness of the hearing officer's decision.[6] The school district sought to overturn the hearing officer's decision on three bases: (1) there was not substantial evidence in the record to conclude that the placement in McAleer's class was not appropriate, (2) the hearing officer's decision was tainted by consideration of inappropriate procedural issues, and (3) the private school was not the least restrictive placement that was adequate to meet Michael's needs.

Like the hearing officer, Judge Zobel was hampered by the fact that there was not yet much precedent in interpreting the EAHCA. She made some fundamental errors that were later reversed by the court of appeals.

Even though the EAHCA was a federal statute, Judge Zobel used state law rather than the federal special education law to determine the appropriate standard of review. Under state law, she deferred to the hearing officer's decision and determined whether there was "substantial evidence" in support of the hearing officer's decision, not whether she would have reached the same decision as an independent factfinder. Under that standard, she concluded that judgment should be entered for Michael. The school district was liable for the tuition and the costs of various medical professionals. By then, Michael was already in fifth grade at the private school. Following Judge Zobel's decision, the state of Massachusetts wrote to the school district threatening to freeze all of its special education assistance unless the school district complied with the original hearing officer's decision. Thus, Michael had the hearing officer, the district court judge, and the state of Massachusetts on his side.

The school district sought a stay of the district court's decision through an appeal to the First Circuit Court of Appeals. In a decision filed on January 28, 1981, the First Circuit denied the stay while Michael was in fifth grade.[7]

On February 9, 1981, the school district agreed to pay all of Michael's future tuition and transportation expenses to attend the Carroll School pending the determination of the appeals. But it persisted in refusing to reimburse Michael's father for the costs of Michael's attending the Carroll School in fourth grade in 1979–80.

Both parties sought clarification of the reimbursement rules before the district court judge. On February 12, 1981, Judge Zobel entered a decision ordering the school district to pay for Michael's tuition at the Carroll School during the pendency of the proceedings in the case.[8] She also ordered the school district to reimburse Michael's father in the amount of $8,837.97 for past educational expenses.

The school district appealed Judge Zobel's decisions to the First Circuit Court of Appeals, arguing that she had improperly granted summary judgment in favor of Michael because she improperly considered matters of state law in her ruling. They argued that the town was entitled to a stay of her ruling, and that Michael's father was not entitled to reimbursement for the 1979–80 expenses during the pendency of this litigation.

The First Circuit ruled for the school district on the first issue because Judge Zobel applied state law, rather than federal law, in reviewing the decision of the hearing officer. It found that the deferential "substantial evidence" standard was not the correct standard of review when a federal district court judge reviewed a state hearing officer decision because the EAHCA provided: "In any action brought under this paragraph the court shall receive the records of the administrative proceedings, shall hear additional evidence at the request of a party, and, basing its decision on the preponderance of the evidence, shall grant such relief as the court determines is appropriate."[9] Unlike the state standard, this rule allows the district court judge to hear additional evidence and evaluate it under a preponderance of the evidence standard. She is not required to defer to the hearing officer's decision under a deferential standard of review.

Even though the First Circuit remanded the matter to be heard by the district court under the appropriate standard, it did not overturn the refusal by the district court judge to stay the hearing officer's order. This matter was governed by a rigorous "abuse of discretion" standard. The First Circuit concluded, "We therefore cannot say that the district court abused its discretion in denying the Town's request for preliminary injunction."[10]

Nonetheless, the First Circuit reversed the district court's February 12, 1981, order that the school district reimburse Michael's father for the 1979–80 tuition. The rule governing the February 12, 1981, order was the statutory language that "the child shall remain in the then current educational placement" during review proceedings. The school district had agreed to pay for Michael to attend the Carroll School during the pendency of the proceedings. It had simply balked at reimbursing Michael's parents for the costs of Michael's attending Carroll School before the hearing officer decision was rendered. A different rule—the preliminary injunction standard—governed whether Michael's parents were reimbursed for the 1979–80 tuition during the pendency of the litigation. Because the district court judge had applied the wrong legal standard in determining whether the hearing officer decision should be affirmed, she could not have properly issued a preliminary injunction to give the basis for reimbursing Michael's parents for the 1979–80 tuition. Thus, Michael's current placement was the Carroll School—because that was the decision of the hearing officer that was in effect until the appeals were resolved—but there was no basis for reimbursing Michael's parents for the costs of his attending the Carroll School in 1979–80 because his parents had not demonstrated a likelihood of prevailing on the merits.

The First Circuit's decision was issued on June 18, 1981, remanding the case back to the district court judge under the correct standard of review. By this point, Michael had completed fourth and fifth grades at the Carroll School.

The case then returned to the district court judge for proper fact finding under the correct federal standard. This time, Judge Zobel concluded that she needed to conduct a trial. The Panicos' lawyer was not an experienced trial court lawyer in federal court, and he contacted another attorney, David Rosenberg, to see if he would assist him with the trial as a pro bono matter through his large law firm, Hill & Barlow.[11] Rosenberg had been doing this kind of work for more than a decade and also had the resources of his law firm to assist in the case, including the assistance of some junior associates. He agreed to handle the mater.

The district court judge conducted a four-day trial and rendered a decision on August 13, 1982, after Michael had completed sixth grade. Following the U.S. Supreme Court's intervening decision in *Board of Education v. Rowley*,[12] which had been decided on June 28, 1982, the district court judge considered whether procedural or substantive violations had occurred under the EAHCA's evolving legal standards.

With respect to procedural violations, the district court judge posed the question as "whether the *state* had complied with the procedures set forth in the Act"[13] in how it made the complaint process available to Michael's parents. Under that legal rule, the district court judge ignored arguments that the school district had failed to follow various educational rules by proposing a classroom population whose ages spanned more than thirty-six months, a shortened school day, and lack of notice to various aspects of the IEP process. Because the parents were "afforded the right to complain about the IEP proposed by the Town and have appealed to the state level" and the proposed IEP conformed to the federal statutory requirements, the district court judge concluded that "Massachusetts has fully complied with the Act's procedural requirements."[14]

With respect to substantive violations, the district court judge posed the legal issue as whether the "IEP was reasonably calculated to enable Michael to receive educational benefits."[15] She placed the burden of proof on the school district to demonstrate "by a preponderance of the evidence, that the placement in Mr. McAleer's class at the Pine Glen School was appropriate for the school year 1979–80."[16] She concluded that the IEP itself conformed to the special education law's requirements and that McAleer was able to implement the IEP because he was a highly experienced teacher who had taught three other children with similar problems over the previous five-year period. Because the school district had successfully demonstrated that the 1979–80 IEP was appropriate, the district court judge also ruled that "the parents have failed to meet their burden of showing that for subsequent years such placement would have been inappropriate."[17] Thus, the school district was not legally required to pay to send Michael to private school because it was offering him an adequate education.

Oddly, the district court judge based the right to subsequent reimbursement on the outcome of the decision about the 1979–80 IEP without consideration of whether Michael's educational situation might be changing. IEPs are supposed to be written on an annual basis, but that does not appear to have happened in Michael's case. This is similar to the assumption that permeated Amy Rowley's case—that the decision as to whether she needed an interpreter throughout her education should be made on the basis of a two-week trial with an interpreter in kindergarten.

The district court judge also decided the reimbursement for medical expenses differently from the way she had in the earlier hearing. This time, she followed more closely the federal statutory language and ruled that the school was responsible for the fees due to Michael's pediatrician but that Michael's parents had not met the required legal standard for reimbursement for another medical evaluation because there was "no evidence either that it was the equivalent of similar evaluations conducted by the Town with which the parents disagreed or that the parents gave the Town prior notice that they intended to seek further testing."[18]

This result—which was dramatically less favorable to Michael's parents than the 1981 decision by the same judge—shows how changing the legal standard of proof can very much alter the outcome. In the 1981 case, the judge was quite deferential to the hearing officer and seemed to be looking for evidence of what would be the best educational plan for Michael. In the 1982 decision, she weighed the evidence independently and asked only whether the program proposed by the school district was "reasonably calculated" to provide Michael with an adequate education.

This case also shows the high level of sophistication needed to challenge a school district's plan. Not many parents could discern the difference between two reading methodologies, take the time to visit both proposed placements, and pay for an expensive private placement. Michael's parents were very fortunate to find pro bono legal counsel when the case became too complicated for their local counsel. They also had the benefit of an educational advocate who visited the various options and could testify about them in the context of Michael's needs. Under existing Supreme Court jurisprudence, the costs of such experts are not recoverable even if the parents prevail, yet their work is critical to successful advocacy on behalf of the child. Poor parents usually cannot afford the services of such educational advocates.

Michael's parents were the victims of a legal whipsaw. They won before the hearing officer in 1980 and before the judge in 1981, but now they found themselves on the hook for Michael's private education for three academic years. Michael's parents were not wealthy, and these expenses were beyond their financial means.[19]

The district court's decision raised a new issue—whether Michael's parents were entitled to have the public school pay for Michael's education at a private school during the time period when it appeared that Michael was legally entitled to attend private school at public expense. On January 31, 1980, while Michael was in fourth grade, the hearing officer had ruled in favor of Michael's parents. The district court judge affirmed that decision on November 19, 1980, while Michael was in fifth grade. The district court judge did not overturn that decision until August 13, 1982, while Michael was in sixth grade. Even though the district court eventually ruled in August 1982 that the hearing officer decision from January 1980 was erroneous, was the school district financially responsible for Michael's private school expenses from January 31, 1980, to August 13, 1982?

Michael's parents went back to the district court and argued that they were entitled to reimbursement for tuition during the review proceedings. That issue also arose in two other cases pending in the district court. Those three cases were consolidated in one district court—not before the judge that had been hearing Michael's case. On March 7, 1983 (spring of Michael's seventh-grade year), Judge Bailey Aldrich ruled that Michael's parents were not entitled to reimbursement for these expenses.[20] Judge Aldrich said, "To permit reimbursement when the parents, without excuse, unilaterally transferred the child to a private placement during the review process could only serve to encourage parents to disregard the statutory scheme; they would have nothing to lose. The fact that in this case the transfer also ultimately proved incorrect only reinforces this conclusion."[21] The only silver lining in the decision was that the parents could seek to offset the sum they owed the school district for Michael's tuition by subtracting the amount the district received from the state for Michael's private school tuition expenses. The case was continued to determine that offset.

In light of Judge Aldrich's determination that the parents could request an offset for savings to the district, the case returned to Judge Zobel to determine the amount of that offset. Because the state had received some money from the state to pay for Michael's education in 1980–81 and 1981–82, that money was reduced from what Michael's parents had to repay the school district.[22] Judge Zobel reached that determination on May 9, 1983, as Michael was completing seventh grade.

Michael's parents appealed the resolution of the reimbursement issue to the Court of Appeals for the First Circuit. They argued that the school district had to pay private school tuition during the review proceedings. In addition, they raised the substantive question of whether the district court judge was correct in ruling that the 1979–80 IEP was valid. In other words, was Judge Zobel correct in ruling in August 1982 that the school district had offered Michael an adequate education under the EAHCA? In a lengthy decision, the First Circuit ruled in favor of the parents on nearly all grounds.[23] The First Circuit again concluded that Judge Zobel had made numerous errors.

First, the First Circuit ruled that Judge Zobel had used the wrong standard in reviewing the allegations of procedural violations, because she failed to consider how procedural violations affected substantive rights. The claims that the school district violated Michael's procedural rights "are material and relevant to the determination of whether the federal right to a free appropriate public education has been provided under the IEP."[24]

Second, the First Circuit concluded that the district court judge had not properly considered the violations of state substantive standards in determining whether Michael had been provided an appropriate IEP. It found that she had improperly ruled that the school district's violations of state regulations were irrelevant to the issue of whether the placement was appropriate. The district court judge should have considered that the school district was offering Michael an IEP that was in violation of state law in two respects: It required him to be in a classroom with children whose ages spanned more than a thirty-six-month period and it provided him with a school day that was shorter than that required under state law. The First Circuit also found that the district court judge improperly ignored various findings by the hearing officer as to why the placement was inappropriate for *Michael* rather than for disabled children *generally*. By definition, an IEP is supposed to be an "individualized" educational program.

Third, the First Circuit found that the district court judge made various evidentiary errors with respect to the weight she gave to the administrative record and the deference accorded the administrative findings. In round one, the First Circuit had reversed her decision as too deferential to the hearing officer's decision. In this round, the First Circuit reversed her decision as not sufficiently deferential. The district court judge treated her role as conducting a trial *de novo* under which she was "bound" to consider additional evidence.[25] Instead, the First Circuit found that she should have used discretion to allow additional evidence in such a way as not "to change the character of the hearing from one of review to a trial *de novo*."[26] Further, the First Circuit held that, although the district court judge was not supposed to apply the state's deferential review standard for reviewing a hearing officer's decision, she should have accorded deference to the hearing officer's decision under *federal law*. Because the state hearing officer had concluded that a proposed IEP did not meet "the state's substantive or procedural requirements pertaining to a free appropriate public education for a particular disabled child,"[27] the district court should have given weight to those findings. "[T]he district court should have circumscribed its review and accorded the state findings deference."[28] Thus, a district court judge who was reversed in 1982 for applying a deferential standard of review was reversed in 1984 for failing to apply a deferential standard of review! This complicated journey shows how difficult it is for lawyers and judges to understand the technicalities of the special education laws. Without the assistance of a pro bono lawyer who had the resources of a large law office, it is unlikely that Michael's parents could have pressed those technical arguments.

The First Circuit also reviewed the various lower court decisions about who should pay for Michael's attendance at private school during the 1979–80 school year and thereafter. This issue was enormously complicated because different time periods corresponded to different legal rules. It was also complicated by the fact that the First Circuit did not know how the district court would resolve the question of whether the proposed IEP met the *Rowley* standard for an appropriate IEP. It had merely held that the district court judge applied the wrong standard. It had not sought to dictate the result under the correct legal standard. Thus, the court of appeals had to render a decision with a rule of law that could be applied only after the second remand to the district court judge was completed.

The school district argued that a parent could never be reimbursed for tuition when the parent makes a unilateral transfer to a private school. The school district relied on the following section 1415(e)(3) of the EAHCA: "During the pendency of any proceedings conducted pursuant to this section, unless the State or local educational agency and the parents or guardian otherwise agree, the child shall remain in the then current educational placement of such child, . . . until all such proceedings have been completed."[29] It argued that Michael's parents were precluded from receiving reimbursement because they did not allow Michael to remain in his "then current educational placement." The First Circuit rejected the school district's argument, saying, "We cannot in good faith condemn the parents for moving the child from the 'current placement' all parties had agreed to be insufficient. As we have emphasized, Congress valued consistency in a disabled child's education, but not foolish consistency."[30] Thus, the First Circuit ruled that a unilateral parental move does not constitute a bar to reimbursement for the parents "if their actions are held to be appropriate at final judgment."[31] The issue of whether the parents could be reimbursed for the 1979–80 school year would depend on the resolution on remand of whether the education offered to Michael by the school district met the *Rowley* educational adequacy standard.

The next issue was the school district's responsibility to pay for Michael's education in 1980 and beyond when Michael's parents were acting in reliance on a hearing officer order that held the school district responsible for that education (an order that was later overturned). Because the school district had paid for Michael's private education for several years, the issue was whether Michael's parents should be expected to reimburse the school district for the private school tuition it paid. Michael's parents argued that they should not have to reimburse the school district when they acted in reliance on the hearing officer's decision, even if that decision was eventually overturned. The district court judge (in the consolidated action) had concluded that Michael's parents could not make this "reliance" argument—that they were responsible for the cost of the private school placement if the hearing officer's decision was overturned on appeal.

After considering the Act's objectives and interests, the First Circuit held that "where the final state administrative decision rules a town's proposed IEP inappropriate and orders the town to fund placement, and the parents have complied with and implemented that decision, a town or local educational agency is estopped from obtaining reimbursement for the time period, usually one year, covered by the state agency decision and order."[32] Nonetheless, the court also held that the parents cannot rely on that rule until the hearing officer decision is issued. Because the hearing officer decision was rendered in January 1980, that rule would give Michael's parents the right to reimbursement for only the spring semester of 1980 (if they did not prevail on remand).

That discussion resolved only the matter of the 1979–80 school year. The school district also sought reimbursement from Michael's parents for their payments for the 1980–81 and 1981–82 school years. Because the district court judge overturned the hearing officer decision in August 1982, Michael's parents could not use a reliance argument to have the public school pay for private school education after August 1982.

The issue of how to handle the 1980–81 and 1981–82 school years was complicated by the fact that the school district was not properly following the special education law. The First Circuit found that "pending review of an earlier IEP, local educational agencies should continue to review and revise IEPs in accordance with applicable law, at least in the absence of a stipulation between the parties providing for how the outcome of the suit will affect later years."[33] However, that process was not followed in this case. The school district did not prepare IEPs during the subsequent years of the litigation. And "the State ordered the Town to continue funding the Carroll School placement after 1979–80, despite the lack of IEPs or state substantive reviews for those years."[34] These facts left the case in an "unusual posture." In ordinary cases in the future, the First Circuit contemplated that school districts would continue to prepare IEPs and parents would seek state review of those IEPs. But this was not an ordinary case. The First Circuit therefore remanded the issue of subsequent payments to the district court to consider under its equitable jurisdiction.

Rather than return to the district court for further consideration, the case next went to the U.S. Supreme Court. The Court did not review all the matters considered by the First Circuit—it considered only the issue of whether a court can order reimbursement to a parent who unilaterally moves a child to a private placement during the review proceedings when the parent ultimately persuades the court that the private placement was appropriate.[35] Hence, it sought to resolve whether Michael's parents could be reimbursed for the 1979–80 school year if they prevailed on remand. The Supreme Court concluded that such reimbursement was within the equitable jurisdiction of the lower courts. Recognizing that a final decision in most cases challenging IEPs will not come within a year of the complaint's being filed, the Supreme Court held that retroactive reimbursement is the only way to provide a child with a *free* appropriate public education. Otherwise, "it would be an empty victory to have a court tell [parents] several years later that they were right but that these expenditures could not in a proper case be reimbursed by the school official."[36]

Thus, on April 29, 1985, when Michael was in eighth grade, his parents learned that *if* they won on remand, the school district would be responsible for Michael's tuition for fourth grade. Given the First Circuit's ruling, the school district was at least responsible for tuition while the appeal of the favorable hearing officer decision was proceeding in the courts. But a lot of matters were still within the discretion of the district court judge who had now decided this case twice and was presented with a third opportunity to follow the conflicting guidance from the First Circuit.

On remand, the case finally settled. The district court judge congratulated the Panicos' lawyer for his victory before the First Circuit and the Supreme Court. The Panicos' lawyer indicated that his firm had taken the case on a pro bono basis and was prepared to go forward with another trial even if the case did not settle. Although the terms of the settlement are confidential, Michael Panico was able to stay in private school through graduation and go on to attend college. The story seems to have had a happy ending despite the peaks and valleys of more than six years of litigation.

The Panicos were fortunate that their local lawyer was able to persuade the law firm of Hill & Barlow to take the case on a pro bono basis for nearly three years. They were also fortunate that the school district had been ordered to pay Michael's private tuition while the case was under review. Even with the victory, the case brought enormous stress to their lives.

Unfortunately, all the "lawyering" in the case did not develop many useful precedents for other parents and their children because the ultimate victory for Michael was the result of a settlement. The only "law" established by the case is that parents who ultimately prevail on the merits can get reimbursed retroactively for the costs of private schooling. For Michael's parents, that was only a very small part of the ultimate cost of educating Michael. And that victory would be possible only for parents who had the resources to front such tuition money. The broader question—whether the school district could insist that Michael attend a special education class with children who had vastly different disabilities, with a shorter school day, and with a different reading program from the one he had been using—was never answered.

* * *

This chapter and the preceding one have told the stories of special education students whose parents were fortunate enough to retain counsel on a pro bono basis to take their cases all the way to the U.S. Supreme Court. Amy eventually lost, Michael eventually won, but neither had a smooth journey. More important, the publicity about their legal challenges received absolutely no attention in Congress, as the next chapter will reveal.

5

Post-1975 Amendments

Chapter 2 revealed that Congress disregarded predictions that the EAHCA would disproportionately fail to serve the needs of poor and minority children. Then, the U.S. Supreme Court decision in *Rowley* set a very low bar for the kinds of services that a school district must offer any student—saying that mere advancement from grade to grade was sufficient evidence of progress, irrespective of the child's cognitive aptitude. And the fortunate parents, like the Panicos, who were successful in taking their cases all the way to the Supreme Court faced enormous expenses that few parents could afford.

During the 1990s, as this chapter will demonstrate, some special education advocates warned that the special education law (now renamed the Individuals with Disabilities Education Act) was not serving the needs of poor and minority students. The evidence clearly reflected that certain disability categories were "white" and others were disproportionately "minority," with inadequate services also flowing to those in the minority classifications. Although Congress responded to descriptions of this inequity, its response has been largely ineffectual.

1977 Amendments

Because the original funding formulas lasted only through July 1, 1977, Congress had to enact its first amendments by that date. On June 17, 1977, it enacted a two-page public law to set new appropriation levels for some discretionary grant programs.[1] The 1977 amendments reflect quite modest increases in funding levels for certain projects. Congress made no substantive changes to the Act.

The 1977 amendments reported out of committee did not include reauthorization of appropriations for Part G of the EAHCA: Special Programs for Children with Specific Learning Disabilities, on the grounds that such children were by then covered under the general definition of disability and did not need specialized funding. Nonetheless, under a floor amendment, the committee's bill was amended to provide for the continuation of model specific learning disability projects under Part E: Research.[2] Congress therefore continued its special sensitivity to children with learning disabilities. The learning disability lobby had sufficient resources to essentially "undo" the Part G deletion by adding Part E.

1983 Amendments

The 1983 amendments made some minor substantive changes. The term "speech impaired" was amended to read "speech and language impaired." This change was made upon the recommendation of speech and language pathologists who reported that many of the children they served had significant language impairments.[3] The purpose of this change was not "to change or expand the population being served, but merely to make this term consistent with that which is being used by many state and local educational agencies as a way of accurately identifying communicatively handicapped children and youth."[4]

The 1983 amendments also broadened the right of children attending private schools to receive special education resources.[5] Some states, such as Missouri, prohibited a state from providing any funding to children in private schools, thereby making it impossible for them to receive government-funded special education services.[6] The 1983 amendments authorized the Secretary of Education to bypass the state educational agency in order to provide special services to children with disabilities in private schools. Because private schools are disproportionately available to middle-class children, this change increased the class disparities under the EAHCA.

The House Report also recommended changing the term "seriously emotionally disturbed" to "behaviorally disordered." [7] Congress did not adopt that change; instead, it directed the Secretary of Education to study whether the terminology should be changed.[8]

Finally, the House Report recommended amending the term "special education" to clarify that services provided should be designed to meet only the unique "educational" needs of the child with a disability. The purpose of that change would be to make clear that school districts do not have to provide services beyond what is considered "educational."[9] Congress did not adopt that recommendation; hence, school districts continue to be required to provide students with access to the entire school day, not merely its strictly educational components.

What is probably most important about the 1983 amendments is what Congress did *not* do. As discussed in the previous chapter, the U.S. Supreme Court decided *Board of Education v. Rowley*[10] in 1982, holding that a school district need not provide a sign language interpreter to a girl with a hearing impairment because she could make "adequate" educational progress in kindergarten and first grade without an interpreter. This case set a very low bar for the level of services that a school district must provide a child with a disability, suggesting that mere advancement from grade to grade is sufficient progress. This case has had a huge impact on the special education laws and has never been directly repudiated by Congress by amending the statute to change that rule of law. It received no mention during the deliberations concerning the 1983 amendments.

1986 Amendments

Congress was quite busy in 1986 with respect to the special education laws. On August 5, it enacted an amendment to the EAHCA to provide for attorney fees.[11] Then, on October 8, it amended the EAHCA to provide for a new title that would cover infants and toddlers with disabilities.[12]

Attorney Fees

Although Congress ignored the devastating impact that the *Rowley* case was having on the law of special education by imposing a nearly insurmountable burden of proof on parents who challenged the adequacy of IEPs, it repudiated a different decision in 1986. In *Smith v. Robinson*, the Supreme Court held in 1984 that school districts need not reimburse parents when they prevail in EAHCA proceedings.[13] Congress partially repudiated that decision through the 1986 amendments.

The *Smith v. Robinson* case involved Tommy Smith, a Rhode Island child with emotional disabilities. In November 1976, Tommy was scheduled to begin school in a day program at Emma Pendleton Bradley Hospital in East Providence.[14] A variety of laws governed his situation. Under Rhode Island state law, the state's Division of Mental Health, Retardation and Hospitals (MHRH) was responsible for a student's education if the student was found to be an "emotionally disturbed child."[15] If MHRH was responsible for Tommy's education, then the state of Rhode Island expected his parents to participate in "the costs of his care and treatment."[16] In other words, his education would not be free. In addition, Tommy was covered by the EAHCA.[17] By the time the case reached the U.S. Supreme Court, all the lower courts had ruled that federal law preempted state law so that Tommy was entitled to a *free* public education. His parents did not need to contribute financially to his education. The only question before the Supreme Court was whether his parents could recover their attorney fees. Because the EAHCA did not contain an attorney fees provision, the presumption was that Congress did not intend parents to be able to recover their attorney fees directly under the EAHCA pursuant to the "American Rule," which precludes awards of attorney fees to the prevailing party unless specified by law.[18]

In a 6–3 opinion written by Justice Harry Blackmun, the Court concluded that prevailing parties under the EAHCA could not recover attorney fees. He also ruled that parents could not simply bypass the cumbersome EAHCA procedural requirements and seek attorney fees under another statute— section 504 of the Rehabilitation Act.[19] In dissent, Justice William Brennan argued, "It is at best ironic that the Court has managed to impose this burden on handicapped children in the course of interpreting a statute wholly intended to promote the educational rights of those children."[20] He predicted that Congress would overrule the Court's decision, but, in the meantime, parents who sought to pursue litigation on behalf of their children would bear significant costs.[21]

Congress partially repudiated the holding in *Smith* by enacting P.L. 99-372, the Handicapped Children's Protection Act of 1986. The 1986 Act provided: "In any action or proceeding brought under this subsection, the court, in its discretion, may award reasonable attorneys' fees as part of the costs to the parents or guardians of a handicapped child or youth who is the prevailing party."[22] The Act made it possible for the prevailing party to obtain attorney fees for the costs of participating in a due process hearing but not for the costs of expert witnesses or the costs of IEP meetings or mediation that preceded the due process hearing. Thus, only parents who had the financial resources to get as far as the due process hearing could benefit from this rule, and even those parents could not get reimbursed for their expert witness fees. Few poor parents can take advantage of the attorney fees rule.

The structure of the attorney fees provision in the 1986 amendments to the EAHCA is also quite cumbersome. The provision refers to the authority of a "court" (not a hearing officer) to award attorney's fees. A parent who prevails before a state-level hearing officer cannot collect attorney's fees from that officer. He or she must bring a separate action (with a filing fee) in federal district court to obtain attorney's fees if the school district does not agree to resolve the case voluntarily. Such a case could easily take two years, given the backlog in most federal courts.

The attorney fees rules are reflective of the generally ill-thought-out structure of the IDEA. Why make a lawyer proceed in a separate legal action to attain attorney fees? If the attorney was successful before the state administrative hearing officer and wants to recover fees, he or she must instigate a separate proceeding just for that purpose. The federal judge will have no familiarity with the case and will have to examine the proceedings closely to evaluate the attorney's fees request. It would make more sense for the hearing officer who is already familiar with the case to make that determination.

Finally, while Congress repudiated the holding in *Smith* by providing for attorney's fees under the IDEA (or EAHCA), it did not broadly repudiate the reasoning underlying the *Smith* decision—that one cannot circumvent the IDEA's extensive procedural requirements by filing directly under section 504. That aspect of the *Smith* holding results in great harm to children with disabilities because their parents are forced to use the expensive and inefficient EAHCA administrative process rather than the section 504 enforcement scheme. Under section 504, parties can file directly in federal court when they believe they are victims of disability discrimination; they need not exhaust an administrative process. Relying on language from the *Smith* decision, most courts insist that parents exhaust their IDEA remedies before filing under section 504 even though section 504 has no exhaustion requirement for any kind of disability claim, such as a school district employee's alleging workplace discrimination.

That exhaustion requirement has become even more significant since 2008, when Congress broadly amended section 504 to cover a much larger class of individuals with disabilities. Section 504 now explicitly covers individuals who are substantially limited in speaking, learning, reading, concentrating, thinking, and communicating.[23] The EAHCA (now renamed the IDEA) covers only a student who fits a limited list of classifications and "who, by reason thereof, needs special education and related services."[24] Students with ADHD or even hearing impairments who need accommodations but not special education should be able to proceed directly under section 504 (and recover attorney fees) without first exhausting the cumbersome

administrative process of the EAHCA or IDEA. The *Smith* decision, however, continues to stand in the way of that option.

Thus, the 1986 amendments to the EAHCA seem like a real victory for
poor parents. On closer examination, however, it is clear that few poor parents can use that provision to be able to afford legal action. The 1986 amendments do not permit recovery of expert witness fees or expenses incurred
before the due process hearing. Further, the Act's enforcement structure
is expensive to implement because parents have to attend many meetings
long before they can file a due process complaint. The attorney fees provision merely helps parents with significant financial resources who can afford
those other expenses of EAHCA enforcement.

Coverage of Infants and Toddlers with Disabilities

Public Law 99-457, also enacted in 1986, reflects one of the most important changes to the EAHCA. Following extensive testimony and recommendations from many experts, Congress determined that it needed "to more
adequately address the needs of handicapped infants and toddlers (aged
birth to two, inclusive) and handicapped pre-schoolers (aged three to five,
inclusive)."[25] As the House Report noted, "Studies of the effectiveness of
preschool education for the handicapped have demonstrated beyond doubt
the economic and educational benefits of programs for young handicapped
children. In addition, the studies have shown that the earlier intervention is
started, the greater is the ultimate dollar savings and the higher is the rate
of educational attainment by these handicapped children."[26] In response to
these studies, Congress created Part H, which provides funds for state programs in early intervention services for infants and toddlers with disabilities
from birth through two years of age. (Children who are three to five years
of age were already covered under Part B—the school-age provisions for the
EAHCA.)

In providing financial assistance to the states to serve this population,
Congress used a much broader and more flexible definition of disability than
it had under the EAHCA. For infants and toddlers, it covered all children

who need early intervention services because they—(A) are experiencing developmental delays, as measured by appropriate diagnostic instruments and procedures in one or more of the following areas: cognitive
development, physical development, language and speech development,
psychosocial development, or self-help skills, or (B) have a diagnosed
physical or mental condition which has a high probability of resulting in

developmental delay. Such term may also include, at a State's discretion, individuals from birth to age 2 inclusive, who are at risk of having substantial developmental delays if early intervention services are not provided.[27]

Unlike the school-age definition for eligibility, this definition allows any child to receive early intervention services merely because he or she is experiencing developmental delays, or is at risk of experiencing those delays. Children do not need a diagnosed medical condition and do not need to be put in one of nine categories (like school-age children). It is consistent with the approach suggested by Professor Reynolds and Balow, when the EAHCA was adopted in 1975. As discussed in chapter 2, they proposed covering children who, for any reason, are handicapped in their ability to proceed with their schooling under ordinary arrangements.

Nonetheless, the programs made available under the infant and toddler program are not necessarily free of charge. The public law provides that early intervention services "are developmental services which . . . are provided at no cost except where Federal or State law provides for a system of payment by families, including a schedule of sliding fees."[28] The House Report offers no explanation for why states can charge a fee for these services. The requirement that the fees be on a "sliding scale," however, does mitigate the impact on poor families. And, as with the school-age program, Congress intended these programs to be available to all infants and toddlers with disabilities in a state.[29]

The programs offered to children under this new provision are also quite different from the programs offered for school-age children. This new provision provides services to the child with a disability as part of a family unit. Instead of an Individualized Educational Program (IEP), the child receives an Individualized Family Service Plan (IFSP). As the name suggests, services are provided to the family unit, as appropriate.

Congress also increased the funding for children ages three to five but did not change the definition of disability for that group. Prior to the 1986 amendments, states were not required to serve this age group if they were to receive funding. The 1986 amendments specified that states would lose all their funding for three- to five-year-olds if they did not agree to serve *all* three- to five-year-old children with disabilities. Although the children in that age group would receive an IEP (for a school-based program) rather than an IFSP, the House Report noted that

[t]he Committee received overwhelming testimony affirming the family as the primary learning environment for children under six years of age and

pointing out the critical need for parents and professionals to function in a collaborative fashion. Therefore, the Committee expects that whenever appropriate and to the extent desired by the parents, the preschooler's IEP will include instruction for parents so that they can be active and knowledgeable in assisting their child's progress.[30]

Nonetheless, Congress created (and has never changed) a system whereby there is a marked change in how services are provided at age three as children transition from a family-based IFSP to a school-based IEP. Typically, parents lose helpful family-based intervention when their child is three years old and transitions to a preschool program.

The infant and toddler program is probably the best special education program ever adopted by Congress because its sliding scale cost structure makes services affordable for low-income families. In the various books and articles written on the negative impact of special education on minorities and the poor, no one ever criticizes the IFSP model itself, although there are some criticisms of its implementation. In fact, by avoiding discrete disability labeling and taking the services to the family, the IFSP model responds to many of the criticisms of the IDEA.

This is not to say that the IFSP model is perfect. A lack of state funding and overextended social workers can make it a difficult system to implement effectively. But its basic structure is one that can work for a wide range of families without demeaning stigmas. Congress made some changes to the IFSP model in 1991, as described below, so that it can better reach both the urban and rural poor. As will be discussed below (the section "1991 Amendments"), that client population remains a challenging one to fully reach and serve under the IFSP model.

1990 Amendments

The 1990 amendments were both substantive and technical. In order to align the special education laws with the recently enacted Americans with Disabilities Act, the statute changed all references to "handicap" to "disability." The 1990 amendments also changed the definition of disability to include "traumatic brain injury" and "autism." As explained in the House Report, autism had been included under "other health impaired," but it now had its own category. The report explained this decision as follows: "The Committee has further determined that autism has suffered from an historically inaccurate identification with mental illness. This inclusion of autism is meant to establish autism definitively as a developmental disability and not as a form of mental illness."[31]

As the data in chapter 1 reflected, autism has disproportionately been a category for identifying white children as disabled. Whereas 56.7 percent of children identified as having an "emotional disturbance" in 2010 were white, 69.7 percent of those identified as having autism were white. In fact, "autism" was the category with the highest percentage for white children. By contrast, whereas 28.5 percent of children identified as having an "emotional distur- bance" in 2010 were black, 14.0 percent of those identified as having autism were black. Inclusion of the "autism" category helped reduce the percentage of whites identified as having an "emotional disturbance" from 67.1 percent in 1987 to 56.7 percent in 2010. By contrast, it had no effect on the number of black children identified as having an emotional disturbance. The percentage of blacks identified as having an "emotional disturbance" actually increased from 1987, when it was 25.1 percent, to 2010, when it was 28.5 percent. Thus, the committee's intentions may have been met for whites, but they were not met for blacks. Inclusion of the "autism" category did not cause a decline in the number of blacks identified as having an "emotional disturbance." Thus, one can understand the addition of the "autism" category as disproportion- ately meeting the needs of white, but not black, children.

Congress added "traumatic brain injury" (TBI) to the list of covered dis- abilities because it "is one of the leading causes of disability in children and youth." It listed this category separately to help overcome misunderstandings about it: "Too often, educators have been poorly informed and untrained in TBI; therefore, they inappropriately classify these students as mentally retarded, emotionally disturbed, or learning disabled, or some other cat- egory equally inappropriate."[32] Despite Congress's assertion that TBI is one of the leading causes of disability, it is not a frequently used category under the IDEA.

The House Report also focused on attention deficit disorder. It recognized the importance of this category, but the report did not recommend listing it as a separate disability. Instead, the report said it should be considered a type of "other health impairment" as indicated by existing regulations.[33]

The House Report also included a significant discussion of racial issues. It noted that "the overrepresentation of minorities continues to be one of the problematic issues in special education."[34] It decided to respond to this problem by encouraging more African Americans and Hispanics to become special education teachers.[35] The data from chapter 1 reflect that increasing efforts to recruit minority students to become special education teachers has had no impact on the overrepresentation of racial minorities in certain dis- ability categories. This is not surprising because special education teachers have little influence on which children are identified as disabled. The regular classroom teacher is the person most likely to make the referral because he or she is the person who has experience with the child. The school psychologist is usually the person who makes the classification recommendation. The special education teacher becomes involved only after the child has been identified as disabled and requires services. Some research supports the argument that regular classroom teachers who are African American are less likely than white teachers to refer African American children to special education.[36] But no data support the argument that having more African Americans work as special education teachers would solve the overclassification problem.

At a more basic level, though, one might want to discard the assumption that racial minorities, when they enter a profession, can really be expected to solve problems involving racial disparities. Over the years, I have had many phone calls from school personnel who feel powerless to persuade their school districts to follow the rules created by the IDEA. They worry they will lose their jobs if they are strong advocates for children. And these are often people with many years of seniority within a school system. I cannot imagine how a new employee who is also a racial minority can be expected to be a "watchdog" to avoid racial overrepresentation in certain disability categories. Such responsibility needs to be on the shoulders of school district superintendents, not on those of newly hired minority employees.

1991 Amendments

The 1991 amendments[37] revised Part H, the Infants and Toddlers with Disabilities Program, which was created by the 1986 amendments. Under the 1986 amendments, states were supposed to have plans that would go into effect by July 1, 1991, to deliver services to all infants and toddlers with disabilities or lose their funding for this category of service. Because of budget issues, many states contemplated dropping out of the program until their financial picture improved. Hence, the 1991 amendments created a mechanism whereby "[s]tates facing serious financial or administrative problems would be allowed to continue to participate in part H for a limited period of time, even if not in accordance with the timelines in the Act, if the States seeking the extension met certain conditions established by the Congress."[38]

Congress heard testimony that poor and minority children were unlikely to participate in Part H programs unless special efforts were made to reach out to them by culturally competent professionals. The Senate Report concluded that "few states have made more than piecemeal efforts to overcome the barriers created by poverty, language, geographic location and cultural differences."[39] It recommended that states recruit more "culturally competent" professionals to reach this client base. The 1991 Act tried to achieve that goal with the following language:

> [B]eginning in fiscal year 1991, [each state receiving funding must] provide satisfactory assurance that policies and practices have been adopted to ensure meaningful involvement of traditionally underserved groups, including minority, low-income, and rural families, in the planning and implementation of all the requirements of this part and to ensure that such families have access to culturally competent services within their local areas.[40]

Although difficult to enforce, this provision promotes equity by requiring states to consider the needs of their entire client population as a condition of receiving federal funding.

It is difficult to gather data on the effectiveness of the IFSP model, but some researchers have concluded that it works fairly well for low-income families. Others have concluded that this client population is still not receiving adequate services. In a 1997 study, Lyke Thompson found that lower-income families in Michigan reported receiving significantly higher numbers of early intervention services than higher-income families although they also reported lower scores on measures of family-level implementation than higher-income families.[41] In other words, poorer families received a higher quantity of services but were not satisfied with how those services were implemented within the family unit. The researchers explained this finding by speculating that "many of the respondents reporting lower [satisfaction] scores simply did not understand that [program] components had, in fact, been implemented for their families."[42] That conclusion, however, is counterintuitive. How could they not be aware of services implemented for their families? Another explanation is that they did not receive the services they thought they needed. More services therefore may not have correlated with more satisfaction.

In a 2003 longitudinal study, a group of researchers found a consistent pattern of lower-quality services for low-income minority families than middle-class white families during the initial early intervention process.[43] Families who were interviewed in Spanish were most likely to report that they did not understand the IFSP process.[44] Low-income families, as compared with middle-class families, were more likely to report that great effort was required to find out about early intervention services, and great effort was required to get services started.[45] The hallmark of the IFSP process is working with the family to achieve services. Higher-income households, as well as white families, were more likely to report that service decisions were jointly made between care providers and families.[46] Whereas white families tended to be satisfied with their level of participation in decision making, minority families were likely to report that they desired more involvement in decision making.[47] Minority families were less likely to think services were individualized, to rate the quality of nontherapy early intervention services lower, to conclude that professionals did not respect their values and cultural backgrounds, to believe that professionals ignored their opinions, and to observe that professionals did not make them feel hopeful about their child's future.[48] Minority families were more likely than white families to report that their children were receiving more therapy than needed.[49] Similar patterns were found based on income and education levels.[50]

Although the researchers were troubled by these differences on the basis of race, caregiver education level, and household income level, they also reported that none of the differences were large.[51] Nonetheless, they concluded, "[T]he persistence of these relationships across so many different items suggests that the process of entering early intervention services is not as supportive for families who are minority, less well educated, or low income." They recommended "models, practices, and professional skills that are more supportive of families who are poor or less well educated and who come from diverse ethnic backgrounds."[52]

Paula Sue Lalinde conducted a thoughtful examination of IFSP programs in a northeastern state with a reputation for providing high-quality services.[53] She studied families' experiences by socioeconomic group, using the factor of insurance type—whether they were covered by Medicaid or commercial insurance—to define socioeconomic status. She also had a racially diverse population. She concluded that "neither family race/ethnicity nor socioeconomic status (captured by insurance type) was associated with quality of services."[54] These positive results may be attributable to the overall high-quality program offered by the surveyed state. The service coordinator–to–family ratio was quite low: 1:7. The person providing family intervention services also acted as the service coordinator. Other studies have found that this model leads to high levels of contact with families and correlates with positive outcomes.[55]

One problem with generalizing from Lalinde's study to other states is that her study focused on a state with high levels of family-based intervention. The 2003 longitudinal study suggests that these results are not likely to be replicated in states with less effective family-related service models where poor and minority parents have trouble accessing effective services.

The Lalinde study, however, does suggest that high-quality IFSP services can be effective in reaching both poor and middle-class families when delivered through an effective model in which the service coordinator also serves as the intervention specialist. The family-based approach under the IFSP model is one that might achieve more equity across race and class lines than the school-based approach found for older children under the IEP model.

1994 Amendments

In 1994, Congress adopted the Improving America's Schools Act.[56] Disability was not a major topic addressed by this statute. Nonetheless, it merged funding for chapter 1 Handicapped Program with part B funding under the IDEA. It also gave school districts the discretion to remove children with disabilities to an interim alternative educational setting for up to forty-five days when such children bring a weapon to school.[57] This measure was included in a section entitled "Local Control Over Violence," but this one provision amended the Individuals with Disabilities Act (section 1415(e)(3)). Congress further amended this provision as part of the broader set of amendments adopted in 1997.

1997 Amendments: A Major Rewrite

After two years of deliberations, the Individuals with Disabilities Education Act Amendments of 1997[58] became law on June 4, 1997, marking the first major revision to the special education laws since 1975. This significant overhaul reorganized the IDEA so that, for example, the definitions are alphabetized and Part H became Part C. Eligibility requirements and procedural safeguards were consolidated. These changes made the statute easier to understand and use. The 1997 amendments also require states to include children with disabilities in statewide assessments (with accommodations). The IEP must indicate how assessments will be modified so that the student can fully participate in them. If students cannot participate in regular assessments, then schools were directed to develop alternative assessments by the year 2000.

The 1997 amendments were passed during Bill Clinton's second term as president, but Republicans controlled both the House and Senate. Thus, some of the changes reflected conservative attempts to save school districts money and allow them to exclude disruptive children from regular classrooms. Other changes increased the ability of parents to participate in the

IEP process and made it more likely that a child would participate in the regular education program.

Eligibility and IEPs

FINDINGS AND PURPOSE

There is language in this amendment that may have reflected an attempt to overturn the low substantive standard set by *Board of Education v. Rowley*.[59] As discussed in chapter 3, the U.S. Supreme Court rejected the conclusion reached by the lower courts in *Rowley* that the school district must seek to "maximize the potential of each handicapped child commensurate with the opportunity provided nonhandicapped children." Instead, the Court concluded it was sufficient to provide the child with an education that was "reasonably calculated to enable the child to achieve passing marks and advance from grade to grade." An education needed to be merely "adequate."

Congress updated the findings to reflect its disappointment with the progress made by children under the IDEA under this "adequate" standard. The findings state, "[T]he implementation of this [Act] has been impeded by low expectations, and an insufficient focus on applying replicable research on proven methods of teaching and learning for children with disabilities."[60] The findings also provide:

> Over 20 years of research and experience has demonstrated that the education of children with disabilities can be made more effective by—(A) having high expectations for such children and ensuring their access in the general curriculum to the *maximum* extent possible . . . (E) supporting high-quality, intensive professional development for all personnel who work with such children in order to ensure that they have the skills and knowledge necessary to enable them—(i) to meet developmental goals and, to the *maximum* extent possible, those challenging expectations that have been established for all children; and (ii) to be prepared to lead productive, independent, adult lives, to the *maximum* extent possible.[61]

In three different places, the findings refer to children's receiving programs and services to the "maximum extent possible." That standard is similar to the standard overturned by the Supreme Court in *Rowley*. Nonetheless, the *Rowley* decision is not mentioned in either the House or Senate reports.[62]

The findings also reflect a concern about educational inequity along both race and class lines. The findings state, "The Federal Government must be responsive to the growing needs of an increasingly more diverse society. A more equitable allocation of resources is essential for the Federal Government to meet its responsibility to provide an equal educational opportunity for all individuals."[63] The findings also reflect an awareness of the problem of misidentification of minority children:

> (A) Greater efforts are needed to prevent the intensification of problems connected with mislabeling and high dropout rates among minority children with disabilities. (B) More minority children continue to be served in special education than would be expected from the percentage of minority students in the general-school population. (C) Poor African-American children are 2.3 times more likely to be identified by their teacher as having mental retardation than their white counterpart.[64]

These findings are consistent with the statement of Senator Tom Harkin of Iowa during the committee hearings that the number one priority for the special education laws should be establishing "high expectations" for all children.[65]

What steps did Congress take to achieve these enhanced goals? Greater equity in implementation depended on modification of the Child Find and Individualized Education Program sections of the statute. Congress did modify those sections but not in ways that were likely to help achieve those goals.

CHILD FIND

Overview

The 1997 amendments create a new section entitled "Evaluations, eligibility determinations, individualized education programs, and educational placements."[66] The first three parts of this section deal with evaluations and eligibility determinations. In contrast with past procedures, schools are required to begin the evaluation process by reviewing existing evaluation data on the child and then, as appropriate, determine what new data are needed. (This change was intended to save school districts some money by avoiding unnecessary evaluations.) Evaluations must meet new, rigorous requirements such as using "technically sound instruments that may assess the relative contribution of cognitive and behavioral factors, in addition to physical or developmental factors."[67] Evaluation instruments must be "selected and administered so as not to be discriminatory on a racial and cultural basis."[68] Parents must be allowed to provide input about their child during the evaluation. (Previously, school districts were not required to give parents that option.) And, the evaluation process now serves two purposes:

determining the child's eligibility for special education and related services *and*, if the child had previously been found eligible for special education, considering what additions or modifications the child will need to his or her special education. Finally, the 1997 amendments clarify that "a child shall not be determined to be a child with a disability if the determinant factor for such determination is lack of instruction in reading or math or limited English proficiency."[69]

The House Report explains that "this provision will lead to fewer children being improperly included in special education programs where their actual educational difficulties stem from another cause and . . . this will lead schools to focus greater attention on these subjects in the early grades."[70] In theory, this rule could lead to less improper classification, but there is nothing in the 1997 Act to ensure that these children will receive academic support in some other way. This is the problem that has plagued the special education laws from the outset—poor and minority children who do not perform well academically can receive extra help if they are misclassified as disabled; if not, they may avoid the stigma of a disability label but are unlikely to get extra academic support.

Racial Disproportionality

The 1997 amendments also create a mechanism to track racial disproportionality in disability identification. Congress heard evidence about the problem of racial disproportionality in its hearings for the 1997 amendments. On behalf of the Clinton administration, Thomas Hehir, the Director of the U.S. Department of Education's Office of Special Education programs, testified,

> [W]hat we know about IDEA implementation at this point is that minority kids are more apt to be put in segregated environments; they are less apt to be included in assessments of educational progress. We also know through some research that at times, there are incentives to put kids into special education to avoid accountability. We have proposed in the past, and we certainly are likely to be proposing in the future, that these practices not be allowed to continue.[71]

Hehir, however, failed to specify how these practices could or should be stopped. Hehir was the only Senate witness who talked about racial educational equity in the Senate hearings.

In the House hearings, Representative William Goodling of Pennsylvania, a key Republican sponsor of the IDEA, asked Judith Heumann, the Assistant Secretary of the Office of Special Education and Rehabilitation Services at the U.S. Department of Justice, about the problem of racial overidentification. She responded with the following explanation:

> I think on the issue of overidentification there are two issues that we need to look at. One is the fact that as poverty is a link to disability, it wouldn't be surprising that we see more minority children who have been identified as having special education needs.
>
> We obviously have a concern if children are being identified if they don't have those needs. But I would say we are equally concerned about the fact that in too many cases students who have legitimate disabilities are being removed from the more inclusive educational setting to a more restrictive setting without appropriately doing assessments, without appropriately developing the IEP, without appropriately assuring that interventions are first being tried in the classroom that the children are currently in.[72]

Later in the hearings, Heumann testified, "I think for minority children one of our concerns really has been that once these children have been identified, it hasn't resulted in better services but, in many cases, has resulted in their not participating in the general curricula or receiving appropriate teachers, and many of these children wind up dropping out of school."[73] In other words, the executive branch was aware that special education was not serving poor and minority children very well, as a result of problems with disability classification and inadequate services for those children identified as disabled.

Despite recognizing these problems, Heumann did not suggest any changes to the IDEA as a means of addressing them. Instead, she suggested that the federal government would "monitor the States every few years" and place "a focus on the issue of overidentification and the issue of placement of children."[74]

Consistent with Hehir's and Heumann's testimonies, the approach of the 1997 amendments was data collection rather than structural change. The 1997 amendments require that each state "provide for the collection and examination of data to determine if significant disproportionality based on race is occurring in the State with respect to—(A) the identification of children as children with disabilities, including the identification of children as children with disabilities in accordance with a particular impairment described in section 1401(3) of this title; and (B) the placement in particular educational settings of such children."[75] As a result of the 1997 amendments, we have the kind of data summarized in chapter 1. There continues to be a wide divergence in disability classification on the basis of race. The 1997 amendments allow us to collect more data on the existence of the problem but provide no means to resolve it.

Writing in 2002, Thomas Hehir, who strongly backed the data collection effort, admitted that attempting to resolve the problem of racial disproportionality through federal enforcement has been insufficient and ineffective.[76] Rather than propose new solutions, though, Hehir simply expressed confidence that measures introduced in the 1997 amendments can help overcome these problems. For example, he expressed confidence that "the new requirement that parents must be involved in decisions about the placement of their children" will benefit African American parents who "have frequently objected to the placement of their children in special classes."[77] That, of course, is an unrealistic expectation for parents who do not have the time, expertise, and advocacy skills to challenge school district decisions. Hehir was seemingly aware of that problem when he touted the potential for "Community Parent Training Centers"[78] to be a valuable resource for minority communities, but there is no evidence that these centers have solved the power imbalance for most minority families under the IDEA. Thus, even when faced with evidence about the failure of the 1997 amendments to address the problems of racial disproportionality in classification and inadequacy of services to racial minorities, the proponents of the 1997 amendments offer no viable alternatives.

Individualized Education Programs

The 1997 amendments add more requirements to the definition of an IEP. As reflected in its interest in research-based standards, the 1997 amendments require that annual goals be "measurable" and include "benchmarks or short-term objectives."[79] Despite the reference to "maximum" progress in the findings section of the IDEA, there continues to be no clear substantive goals in the IEP section of the statute. The 1997 amendments require that the child be "involved in and progressing in the general curriculum" without defining how much progress is enough.[80] The purpose of this change was to encourage school districts to increase participation in the regular education curriculum. Similarly, the Act requires an explanation of the extent to which children who qualify for special education will not be participating with nondisabled children in the general education classroom. The 1997 amendments also specify that the child "advance appropriately toward attaining the annual goals" without stating how one determines what is "appropriate."[81]

The 1997 amendments also expand the description of who should be a member of the team that writes the IEP. Prior to 1997, the statute required that the following people attend the IEP meeting: a school district representative, the teacher, the parents or guardian, and, when appropriate, the child. The 1997 amendments add to that list: a special education teacher, "an individual who can interpret the instructional implications of evaluation results," and "other individuals who have knowledge or special expertise regarding the child."[82] The second requirement was intended to supplement the research-based requirements of the 1997 amendments. The amendments also clarify the parent's right to be involved in placement decisions.

The 1997 amendments also emphasize periodic review of the IEP. Schools must report the progress of students under an IEP as often as they report progress for nondisabled children. If it becomes evident that a child is not making progress toward the IEP goals, then the team must meet and revise the IEP. The 1997 amendments therefore give parents enhanced opportunities to communicate with school districts about the development and implementation of the IEP. These kinds of changes particularly benefit parents who are already active in their children's school life and can understand the special education process.

Discipline

The 1997 amendments also enhance the ability of school districts to discipline children with disabilities by removing them to an alternative educational setting. Discipline was the most heavily discussed topic at the hearings, with many witnesses asking Congress to increase the authority of school districts to remove disruptive children from the classroom, even those with disabilities. Nonetheless, some witnesses did testify that children with disabilities were no more likely to cause discipline problems than other students and that changes to the discipline rules were unnecessary.

The House committee explained the balance sought by Congress with the new discipline provisions: "[T]he Committee has attempted to strike a careful balance between the [school district's] duty to ensure that school environments are safe and conducive to learning for all children, including children with disabilities, and the LEA's continuing obligation to ensure that children with disabilities receive a free and appropriate public education."[83] This "balance" gave school districts greater authority to exclude children with disabilities from regular educational programs. Prior law had mentioned alternative educational placements if children brought weapons to school. The 1997 amendments give school districts more opportunities to place children in alternative education environments irrespective of the disability-related nature of their conduct. For children who are not engaged in activities

involving drugs, weapons, or potential danger to others, the 1997 amendments create a more rigorous set of rules to avoid suspensions that would last
more than ten days when the behavior was disability-related.

The enhanced discipline rules are in tension with Congress's stated objective in the 1997 amendments to keep children with disabilities in school and
avoid having them drop out at a young age. In the findings sections, the 1997
amendments state that "[t]he drop-out rate is 68 percent higher for minorities than for whites" and "[m]ore than 50 percent of minority students in
large cities drop out of school."[84] The enhanced discipline rules, however,
increased the likelihood of students with disabilities, when they are minority
students, being suspended and then dropping out of school. The late Representative Donald Payne of New Jersey, a past chairman of the Congressional
Black Caucus, made that connection when he stated, "And I do think the
area of cessation of services, where a school district has the right to suspend,
presents a number of problems, because we do find that there are children
of color disproportionately in these classes."[85] However, Payne made no concrete suggestions to correct this problem.

Thomas Bloom, Inspector General, U.S. Department of Education, shared
the results of an audit of special education funding that resulted in recommendations for dramatic changes to better serve the needs of poor children.
Rather than base special education funding on the number of children classified as disabled, he recommended "the use of two factors in the Special
Education fund allocation: total population of persons aged 3 through 21
and poverty levels." He explained: "Because this method uses objective data
derived for other purposes, it eliminates any possible financial incentives for
manipulating student counts, including retaining students in special education just to continue receiving special education funds."[86]

Bloom provided data to support this recommendation. First, he noted
that the current classification system is quite inconsistent and unreliable.
One piece of evidence of this unreliability is that "states, including those
which border one another, reported widely divergent counts in the propor-
tions of children in each disability category, calling into question their reliability and the reliability of the total disabled child count."[87] Second, he noted
that "there is a strong correlation between poverty and the level of disabilities
within a community."[88] Hence, a fair and objective system would have to consider both the overall population and, more specifically, the population of
poor children if it were to be equitable.

Although Congress did not adopt Bloom's suggestion that a poverty
increment be added, it did follow his recommendations about tying funding
to the number of children in the state rather than to the number of children

classified as disabled. Prior to 1997, funds were disbursed to states based on "the number of children with disabilities in the State, aged 6 through 21, who are receiving special education and related services."[89] The 1997 Act provided (with various exceptions) that "the Secretary shall first allot to each State an amount that bears the same ratio to the amount of such remainder as the number of infants and toddlers in the State bears to the number of infants and toddlers in all States."[90] In theory, this change should have given states a disincentive to overclassify children as disabled in order to receive federal funding. But it did nothing to change the problems between categories—the pattern of minority children's being overclassified as mentally retarded or emotionally disturbed and then being placed in segregated classrooms. And, if poverty is linked to disability, it did nothing to provide poor school districts with ample resources to fund special education programs.

Attorneys/Mediation

In 1997, the IDEA was amended to allow attorneys to collect their fees from the school district if they attend a meeting that is scheduled as a result of a successful due process hearing. The 1997 amendments say: "Attorneys' fees may not be awarded relating to any meeting of the IEP Team unless such meeting is convened as a result of an administrative proceeding or judicial action, or, at the discretion of the State, for a mediation described in subsection (e)."[91] This rule, however, would benefit only those parents who had managed to get through due process. Few poor parents have the financial resources to take advantage of this new rule.

The change in the attorney fees rules is a bit surprising in light of the testimony heard by Congress. Many witnesses criticized the role that lawyers play in special education matters and spoke heavily in favor of mediation (without lawyers). In fact, no witness testified in favor of this change, and it received no mention in the various reports.

The 1997 Act also increased the amount of information available to parents from the school district. The value of this information, however, would depend on a parent's ability to understand it.

In addition, the 1997 Act increased the emphasis on mediation, requiring each state to make mediation available and bear the cost of it. School district representatives strongly supported this increased emphasis on mediation because they thought it would reduce their litigation costs. They wanted mediation to occur without attorneys, but that suggestion was not incorporated into the statute. Nonetheless, parents cannot get reimbursed for their attorney expenses for attending mediation irrespective of the outcome. By contrast, parents can get reimbursed for their attorney expenses when they are successful at a due process hearing. The 1997 Act therefore made it unrealistic for most parents to afford an attorney for mediation (but did not preclude a school district's bringing an attorney to mediation). Many witnesses from states that already had mediation testified that it sharply reduced the number of due process hearings. Everyone seemed to assume that those results suggested that mediation was a positive contribution to the IDEA process.

There is, however, another way to understand those mediation results. Because mediation is an informal process, one might expect that the results reflect the power relationships of the two parties. Parents who pursue mediation, especially without an attorney, may agree to a "settlement" that is quite favorable to the school district. The fact that a due process hearing does not occur does not necessarily mean that the school district compromised in a way that is beneficial to the child. Because mediation is a confidential process, there is no way to collect evidence about mediation results. As reflected in chapters 8 through 12, many states today have few due process hearings because most cases are resolved through mediation. In other states, mediation has a weaker record of resolving cases voluntarily. There is no way to know whether Congress's assumption in 1997 that the proliferation of mediation and the absence of due process hearings really produce better results for the child. Instead, the mediation results may simply reflect the power imbalance between parents and school districts, especially when the parents cannot afford to retain a lawyer.

Private School Education

The 1997 amendments also provide some benefits to parents who send their children to private schools. The 1997 amendments provide that school districts may offer the special education and related services funded under Part B on the premises of private—including parochial—schools. The 1997 amendments also specify that parents may be reimbursed for the cost of a private educational placement when the school district has not made a free appropriate public education available to the child. These reimbursement rules assist only parents who can afford to pay for private education.

* * *

The 1997 amendments were quite extensive. In theory, they should assist a child in receiving a free and appropriate education that better reflects his or her abilities and disabilities. Congress's increased attention to racial disproportionality should also have helped equalize disability classification and programming. Unfortunately, the amendments actually made the statutory benefits even more out of reach for poor and minority parents by increasing the resources needed for effective advocacy. And the increased availability of discipline for children with disabilities made it easier for school districts to segregate and exclude children with disabilities, who were often poor and minority children.

2004 Amendments

President George W. Bush signed the 2004 amendments into law on December 3, 2004. The House had approved the Conference Report by a vote of 397 to 3, and the Senate agreed to it by unanimous consent. Thus, these amendments continued to reflect strong bipartisan support for the IDEA. Many of the changes aligned the IDEA with No Child Left Behind (NCLB) by requiring that special education teachers meet various standards for "highly qualified teachers." Thus, the impetus for some changes was the political realities underlying NCLB rather than concern for the special education law.

The racial disproportionality rule was strengthened to require the states to have in effect policies and procedures designed to prevent the inappropriate overidentification or disproportionate representation by race and ethnicity of children as children with disabilities.[92] Congress's ambivalence about challenging the problem of racial disproportionality, though, was captured in Bush's signing statement. He said that the executive branch shall construe that provision of the Act in a manner consistent with the First Amendment and the Fifth Amendment "to afford equal protection of the laws."[93] In other words, the Bush administration (like many members of Congress) did not approve of race-specific solutions to problems of equal protection, consistent with their opposition to race-based affirmative action. The administration might go along with data collection, but there was no reason to think it would support any race-specific solutions to the problems of racial inequality in special education.

One of the most important changes made by the 2004 Act (which will be discussed extensively in chapter 13) stipulates that a school district can no longer be required to use the "discrepancy model" in determining whether a child has a specific learning disability. Under the discrepancy model, a child is deemed learning disabled if there is a significant discrepancy between aptitude and achievement. Because it is easier to show a discrepancy between aptitude and achievement when a child has a high aptitude, this model has disproportionately identified as learning disabled students who have an above-average IQ. The 2004 amendments allow school districts to use a "response to intervention" (RTI) model to classify students as learning disabled.[94] Under the RTI model, students could be classified as learning disabled merely on the basis of consistent low achievement in a subject (even after attempts at intervention) without the necessity of showing a discrepancy between achievement and aptitude. In theory, this rule should have made it easier for students to be classified as learning disabled, when they are struggling in school and do not have a high IQ, because they would no longer have to show a discrepancy between aptitude and achievement. As chapter 13 will reflect, the 2004 amendments have not solved the learning disability mess. These changes have led to enormous delays in reaching students with disabilities as states use an amorphous and unscientific RTI model for months or even years before offering students special education and related services.

The 2004 amendments also expanded the notice requirements. Within ten days of receiving a parent's objection to the school district's evaluation of his or her child or the proposed IEP, the school district must send to the parent (1) an explanation of why the agency proposed or refused to take the action raised by the complaint; (2) a description of other options that the IEP team considered and the reasons why those options were rejected; (3) a description of each evaluation procedure, assessment, record, or report the school district used as the basis for the proposed or refused action; and (4) a description of the factors relevant to the school district's proposal or refusal.[95]

The 2004 amendments also increased the emphasis on alternative dispute resolution options. Prior to the opportunity for a due process hearing, the parties must engage in a resolution session or mediation, unless they agree in writing to waive such a meeting. The school district can bring an attorney to the resolution session only if an attorney also accompanies the parent. A resolution meeting, unlike mediation, does not involve the presence of a neutral third party. It is similar to another IEP meeting. These rules should reduce the frequency of due process hearings by essentially requiring parents to participate in one more step before going to due process.

The 2004 amendments also changed the attorney fees rules to make them more favorable to school districts. They gave a court the authority to grant attorney fees to the school district when the plaintiffs' claims are deemed frivolous or without foundation, or when brought in bad faith. It also clarified that a parent is not entitled to attorney fees for successfully resolving the matter at a resolution meeting.

The 2004 amendments gave school districts more authority to discipline students with disabilities. It also allowed them to suspend children for a longer period before determining if their behavior was a manifestation of their disability. Whereas the old rules referred to "10 days" or "45 days," the new rules referred to "10 school days" or "45 school days." The 2004 amendments limited school districts to two situations in which they could conclude that the conduct was a manifestation of the child's disability: (1) when the conduct in question was caused by a *direct and substantial* relationship to the child's disability or (2) the conduct in question was the *direct result* of the school district's failure to implement the IEP.[96] The conferees explained that these "direct" requirements were intended to ensure that "the conduct in question was caused by, or has a direct and substantial relationship to, the child's disability, and is not an attenuated association, such as low self-esteem."[97]

The 2004 amendments gave hearing officers more authority to place a child in an alternative educational setting for up to forty-five days. Prior language had required the hearing officer to consider many factors before making that determination. The 2004 Act merely requires the hearing officer to conclude that "maintaining the current placement of the child is substantially likely to result in injury to the child or others."[98] The "substantially likely" rule is vague and gives hearing officers increased discretion to approve an alternative educational placement.

The result of the changes in the discipline rules has been to make it disproportionately more likely that African American students will be subject to suspensions lasting at least ten days. Table 2, drawn from U.S. Department of Education data, tracks the percentage of students in each racial category who have faced at least a ten-day suspension and are classified as disabled under IDEA.[99]

The Department of Education has modified some if its definitions over time so that data are not entirely comparable year to year. But the overall pattern reflects that, since 2002, the percentage of African American students facing suspension has been higher than that for any other racial group, and the difference between African Americans and whites increases over time. This is a very important trend because suspensions are highly disruptive to any child's education. It is hard to see how we are educating "all" students with disabilities if more than 4 percent of African American children with disabilities are receiving suspensions for more than ten school days. It makes one wonder how far we have come since the days when African American boys were excluded from school on the pretense that they were "mentally retarded." Now, they are admitted to school and then disproportionately excluded on the basis of discipline rules.

Table 2

Percentage of Students with Disabilities by Race Suspended from School

	American Indian/ Alaska Native	Asian/ Pacific Islander	Black (Not Hispanic)	Hispanic	White
1998–99	0.56%	0.4%	0.36%	0.49%	0.2%
2002–3	1.5%	0.5%	2.38%	1.13%	0.74%
2005–6	1.69%	0.39%	2.78%	0.8%	0.67%
2007–8	1.78%	0.52%	4.11%	0.98%	1.09%

Conclusion

The IDEA has an unusual legislative history. While Congress fiercely fought over other spending programs, it has reauthorized the IDEA in recent years through strong bipartisan votes.

The strong bipartisan support reflects a number of factors. First, and most important, it reflects the benefits of the IDEA to families who have a lot of political capital and can take advantage of the parent-centric nature of IDEA advocacy. Second, it reflects the ability of school districts to use the "school discipline" card to make it easier to discipline students with disabilities who do not follow school rules. The latter movement was part of a national infatuation with "zero tolerance" school discipline policies and harsh criminal sanctions for young people.[100] Both of these developments harm poor and minority families while placing an even greater advocacy burden on any family whose children seek to benefit from special education.

Various legislative factors have caused the special education laws to be less effective for poor and minority children than for middle-class white children, but inadequate funding has certainly played a salient role. When the EAHCA was enacted in 1975, Congress promised to increase the level of federal funding to 40 percent by 1982. That did not happen. Instead, funding has usually hovered in the 8 to 12 percent range. As a result, resource-rich school districts simply have more options with respect to special education programming, as they do with all programming. Inadequate funding has made it easier for Congress to reauthorize the IDEA every few years. Although we think of the IDEA as being a federally funded program, the limited nature of that funding means that it is more a "bill of rights" rather than a federally funded program. And that bill of rights is most available to children who attend resource-rich schools. As President Bush's signing statement made clear in 2004, there is no commitment to offer additional resources on a racially defined basis.

Over time, the IDEA has increased the burden on parents to act as effective advocates in order for their children to receive adequate educational programs. In 1973, Professor Oliver Hurley argued for new special education laws under which children would have an "advocate" to avoid mislabeling. Describing the existing system, he said that the labeling/placement process "is an institutionalized extension of society's discriminatory responses to an outgroup, the Black and Brown minorities and the poor."[101] Hurley hoped the requirement that there be a written program and frequent reevaluations would make the system more equitable. Unfortunately, the lack of effective advocacy for many children, including poor and minority children, has precluded the realization of those aspirations.

6

Brian Schaffer

The next two chapters tell the story of Brian Schaffer and Joseph Murphy. Neither child came from a low-income family; their cases help reveal how difficult it is for any child to prevail under the IDEA. Their cases were brought after Congress amended the IDEA in 1997, and again in 2004, in various ways that were supposed to benefit students with disabilities. Yet, as with Amy Rowley (chapter 3) and Michael Panico (chapter 4), these stories reveal a cumbersome legal process that rarely produces success even for children with highly involved parents and qualified legal counsel.

Brian Schaffer's case is crucial for all parents challenging an IEP for two reasons. First, the U.S. Supreme Court has held that the burden of proof should fall on parents when challenging the adequacy of their child's IEP. Second, the lower courts that handled this case interpreted the *Rowley* adequacy standard as creating a very low threshold for a school district despite the 2004 IDEA amendments, discussed in chapter 5. The hearing officer candidly refused to give any weight to the parents' experts because these experts were likely to be seeking more than the "basic floor of opportunity" required by the IDEA. In other words, so long as a school district offered some expert testimony, parents were unlikely to be able to meet their burden of proof to demonstrate that an IEP does not even create a "basic floor of opportunity." Congress's statement in its findings to the 2004 amendments that school districts should have "high expectations for [disabled] children . . . ensuring their access to the general education curriculum in the regular classroom, to the maximum extent possible, in order to . . . meet developmental goals and, to the maximum extent possible, the challenging expectations that have been established for all children"[1] has been rendered a legal fiction by the Supreme Court's decision in the *Schaffer* case.

Brian Schaffer was born on May 13, 1984.[2] At seven years of age, he was diagnosed with attention deficit hyperactivity disorder (ADHD) and began taking medication for that condition. Starting in preschool, Brian attended Green Acres School, a private institution with classes from preschool to eighth grade. The cost of tuition is not in the record but, as of 2011, the school's website indicates that the annual cost of tuition is around $30,000. Although it is not a school designed for students with disabilities, the staff will make accommodations for students based on consultation with an educational expert. The average class size is around thirteen students.

Brian's educational problems began to surface in second grade, when he was found to be only pretending to read during silent reading time. The school began to offer him extra assistance, but he was not able to read at grade level. By seventh grade, he was on probationary status and was not able to perform at grade level despite "individual attention from classroom teachers, a peer buddy to ask for clarification of direction, priority seating, extra time on class assignments and standardized tests, tutor rewriting of essay questions on his test to multiple choice or short answer, assignments not penalized if turned in late, and exclusion of Spanish from his educational program."[3] With these extensive accommodations in place, Brian received passing grades in all of his subjects during the third trimester of the 1997–98 school year, but neither his parents nor the school considered his performance to be satisfactory.

Because of his continuing difficulties despite considerable assistance, in October 1977 the Green Acres staff informed Brian's mother, Jocelyn Schaffer, that Brian needed more assistance than they could provide, and the Schaffers should try to find Brian a school better designed to address his learning difficulties. On November 7, 1997, Brian's mother contacted Linda Brand, the special education teacher at the local public school, Herbert Hoover Middle School, to request that Brian be identified as a child with a disability. She also sought help from Brand in locating an appropriate private school for him. Brand informed Brian's mother that the public school system might have a program that would meet Brian's needs.

Brian's mother then contacted Dr. Carol A. Kamara, a speech-language pathologist/audiologist, for the purpose of arranging a communication assessment of Brian. Kamara conducted a three- to four-hour assessment on December 9, 1997, and concluded that Brian's "auditory processing of words was so severely impaired by discrimination issues that his ability to execute any auditory tasks should be considered possibly compromised by this one feature." The report said that Brian's "serious needs in reading, writing, spelling, and probably math indicate that he should be placed in a self-contained, full-day special education program."[4] Kamara also recommended individual speech/language therapy for Brian.[5]

Brian's mother also arranged for her son to be evaluated by a psychologist, Dr. Ruth B. Spodak, and her staff for a complete psycho-educational evaluation, which was subsequently undertaken on January 5, 1998. The report concluded that Brian "will do best in a small, structured setting, where expectations are clear and consistent."[6]

In December 1997, Brian's parents also submitted an application for him to be admitted to the McLean School and to the Lab School in Washington, D.C. Both are private schools. They were notified on March 1, 1998, that he had been admitted to the McLean School for the 1998–99 school year. The Schaffers made a deposit on March 16, 1998, to secure a spot in the McLean School. This school offered classes taught by certified special education teachers in class sizes of six to twelve for students with moderate, but not severe, learning disabilities.

Meanwhile, the public school system began to evaluate Brian. On February 26, 1998, the school team tentatively concluded that he had a speech-language disability and/or learning disability but also agreed to reconvene after studying Spodak's and Kamara's reports, and collecting further information.

The school district assigned the task of evaluating the Spodak and Kamara reports to Pamela Zahra, a speech-language pathologist. Brand, the public school's special education teacher whom Brian's mother had originally contacted, and Zahra conducted some additional assessments. Finally, the school psychologist, Barbara Butera, conducted an observational and psychological assessment of Brian. The parents gave permission for school district personnel to contact both Spodak and Kamara, but no such contact ever occurred.[7]

The school team (including Brian's parents and their attorney) met on April 6, 1998, to determine if Brian was disabled and, if so, what educational program would be appropriate for him. School personnel were willing to identify Brian as having a speech-language disability and a learning disability. Zahra indicated that she did not agree with Kamara that Brian had "severe auditory processing difficulties related to discrimination at the word level" and "auditory dyspraxia."[8] She made that determination based on personal observation. She did not readminister the audiology diagnostic testing conducted by Kamara.

The school district proposed that Brian be placed at Herbert Hoover Middle School for eighth grade. For three of his classes (world studies, science, and English), he would be in a classroom with twenty-four to twenty-eight students and two teachers. Brian would be one of five to six students in the class who would be on IEPs and would receive additional assistance from a special education teacher. Instead of attending a foreign language class, he would receive additional assistance with his writing and other subjects in a self-contained special education classroom with six to eight students. Additionally, he would receive one weekly forty-five-minute session of speech-language therapy in a group of two to five students. He would be in a regular classroom for math, physical education, and the arts rotation.

Brian's parents objected to this educational plan because of the large class sizes. The school district then offered to place Brian at the Robert Frost Middle School, where there were smaller self-contained special education classes. Brian's parents visited the Frost School and learned that for two of Brian's classes (world studies and science), he would be in a class with twenty-eight to thirty students and two teachers. Brian would be one of four students in the class on an IEP receiving additional instruction. He would have special education classes for both English and writing with a class size of eight to twelve students. Speech/language therapy would be in a group of two to five students. Math, gym, and the arts rotation would be in regular classes with as many as thirty-two students. Thus, his parents realized that they would be forced to consider a tradeoff between Robert Frost Middle School and Herbert Hoover Middle School, with the Frost School having larger general class sizes but offering two, instead of one, opportunities for small, self-contained special education classes. In both settings, Brian would attend math in an entirely regular classroom.

Following their visit to the Frost School, Brian's parents sent a letter to the school district objecting to that placement and advising the school district of their intention to send Brian to the McLean School. They said that the proposed placement (at the Frost School) "would be insufficient to meet [Brian's] identified needs" and "is too large, not structured enough, has insufficient services and does not include required related services."[9] They also complained that the school district had not properly identified Brian's "complete disability."[10] The latter statement referred to the fact that the proposed placement did not take into account Brian's auditory processing disorder.

Brian's parents filed a request for a due process hearing on May 26, 1998, and a hearing was held on June 16, June 23, July 2, 1998, before the state's hearing officer—Administrative Law Judge (ALJ) Stephen J. Nichols. Legal counsel represented both the parents and the school district. The school district produced six expert witnesses and the parents produced four witnesses, including Brian's mother and three experts. The school district's experts accepted many of the conclusions of the parents' experts but disagreed with the recommendation of Brian's experts that Brian had a central auditory processing disorder (CAPD) and should attend the McLean School.[11]

One procedural issue that perplexed the hearing officer was that of who should bear the burden of proof in this case. He described the assignment of the burden of proof as "critical" in this case because both sides offered testimony from expert witnesses with "impressive" credentials.[12] After reviewing the case law from other jurisdictions, as well as Congress's intentions, he concluded that it was appropriate to place the burden of proof on the parents. He decided that Congress intended the courts to defer to the expertise of local education authorities in all IDEA cases involving the appropriateness of the educational program devised by the school district.[13] Such deference was consistent with placing the burden of proof on the parents because the school district would prevail in the event of a virtual tie on the strength of the evidence.

The hearing officer's determination about who should bear the burden of proof was also influenced by the parents' conduct in this case. Because the parents had already applied to the McLean school and paid a deposit to hold Brian's spot before even attending the school district meeting to devise an educational plan, the hearing officer described their participation as a "mock effort" to create a public school placement. Their failure to request any specific additional services for Brian within the public school setting when they objected to the school district's plan "strongly suggest[ed] a design by the Parents to simply obtain funding from [the school district] for their predetermined decision to have the Child enter the 8th Grade at the McLean School of Maryland."[14] The hearing officer concluded that the parents' refusal to enter into discussions with the school district as a "partner" meant that their conduct was "inconsistent with the congressional intent behind the statute."[15] Therefore, the hearing officer found, they should bear the burden of proof in challenging the school district's proposed placement.

The hearing officer was faced with two key issues at the hearing with regard to the proposed IEP for eighth grade. First, did Brian have a significant central auditory processing problem that needed to be addressed in order for him to receive an adequate education? Second, could Brian's educational needs be met in an inclusive classroom with twenty-four to thirty students?

The hearing officer answered the first question in the negative by discounting audiologist Kamara's testimony for two reasons. First, Kamara primarily relied on the SCAN-A test to diagnose Brian's CAPD, but she acknowledged on cross-examination that, as an audiologist, she could not determine if his low scores were the result of CAPD or ADHD. The hearing officer credited speech pathologist Zahra's opinion, based on informal observations, that Brian did not have a CAPD even though she had not conducted diagnostic testing. Second, the hearing officer found Kamara to be "evasive" when she refused to quantify the seriousness of Brian's speech-language disability as mild, moderate, or severe. Thus, the hearing officer was willing to accept a placement for Brian that did not take into account the CAPD diagnosis even though he did conclude that Brian had "moderate" CAPD.

The hearing officer answered the second question, concerning class size, in the affirmative by discounting the educational placement recommendations of the parents' experts. Although Kamara had recommended that Brian be placed in a self-contained, full-day special education program, she had also stated that Brian "demonstrated many average and borderline average skills that might seem to allow him to be placed appropriately in a regular education setting with some special education support."[16] The hearing officer therefore concluded that Kamara was equivocal on the subject of an appropriate placement. Further, Kamara acknowledged that she had not visited the inclusion models suggested by the school district, thereby lessening, in the hearing officer's view, the "probative value" of her opinion about the inappropriateness of an inclusive placement.[17]

The hearing officer discounted Kamara's recommendation that Brian receive individual, rather than group, speech-language therapy. Because her report said that one of Brian's two weekly thirty-minute therapy sessions could "be addressed in a small group of students who have similar issues," the hearing officer concluded that it would be appropriate for all of Brian's therapy to occur in a group setting.[18]

The hearing officer also discounted the value of psychologist Spodak's recommendations at the hearing with respect to educational placement because Spodak herself had met with Brian for only ten minutes. Two members of her staff who also held Ph.D. degrees had conducted the actual evaluation. While their report had included the statement that Brian "will do best in a small, structured setting, where expectations are clear and consistent," it failed to include the statement that Brian "must" be educated in such an environment in order to receive educational benefits.[19] Those factors caused the hearing officer to question "the probative value of Dr. Spodak's opinion that the Child could receive only minimal educational benefit in anything other than small, self-contained special education classes."[20]

Finally, the hearing officer gave weight to the fact that Brian earned all passing grades in his third trimester at the Green Acres School when he was in a regular classroom for all his subjects and receiving extensive classroom and testing accommodations. This fact led the hearing officer to be "skeptical" "that the Child's educational environment must shift from a fully mainstreamed regular education setting in all academic subjects in a private school to a very restrictive special education setting in all academic subjects during the 1998–1999 school year in order for the Child to receive anything other than minimal educational benefit."[21]

The hearing officer gave weight to Brian's record of "success" in the third quarter at Green Acres even though the school considered Brian to be performing so unsuccessfully that it refused to continue educating him. Further, the hearing officer failed to give weight to the fact that the classroom at the Green Acres School had only thirteen students. The inclusive placement recommended by the school district had between twenty-four and thirty-two students, a very different educational atmosphere.

The hearing officer's decision shows how little evidence a school district must produce to meet the *Rowley* "adequate education" standard if the burden of proof is placed on the parent. He recognized that it is nearly impossible for parents to prevail when they bear the burden of proof under the *Rowley* standard:

> There is an inherent concern in evaluating testimony from experts such as Dr. Spodak and Dr. Kamara. Their knowledge of special education law is extensive. Their testimony during the instant hearing is couched in terms taken from the case law. Their testimony purports to be consistent with the recommendations listed in their written assessment of the Child. Those written assessments were created before the Parents requested a due process hearing. It is common sense to expect that recommendations from a private consultant, who conducts an assessment of student with disabilities, and who is privately paid on behalf of that student, would be, and should be, designed to maximize that student's potential, not simply to allow "educational benefit" to the student with disabilities so that the student receives the "basic floor of opportunity" provided for by the IDEA. *Board of Education v. Rowley*, 458 U.S. at 200-01, 102 S.Ct. at 3048.[22]

In other words, it does not matter if the parents' experts testify that the school district's proposed plan is not likely to provide their child with "appropriate" or "adequate" educational benefit (the relevant legal standard). The hearing officer will presume that the parents' experts *really* mean that the school district is not "maximizing" the child's educational potential—an impermissible standard under *Rowley*. Thus, the hearing officer discounted the testimony of both Spodak and Kamara that Brian would not receive even minimal educational benefit unless he were placed in a small, self-contained classroom for all of his instruction.

In considering the supposed biases of the parents' experts, the hearing officer did not consider the possible biases of the school district's experts. They were employed by the school district and had a strong financial interest to offer testimony sympathetic to their clients' position—that Brian could receive an adequate education within the school district and did not need to attend an expensive private school in order to obtain an adequate education.

Given the skepticism that the hearing officer expressed with regard to the parents' experts and his conclusion that that they had made a "mockery" of the school district meeting by predetermining that they wanted their son to attend the McLean School, it is not surprising that he concluded that the two placements offered by the school district were "reasonably calculated" to "provide educational benefit and to meet the Child's educational needs" so that Brian "would obtain significant, measurable, educational benefit during the 1998–1999 school year if he attended either of those schools."[23]

Nonetheless, the hearing officer did note that this was a close case in which the burden of proof issue was "critical," setting up an appeal by the parents of the burden of proof issue to a federal district court judge. The judge concluded that the burden of proof in such a case should fall on the school district, not the parent, when the dispute is over the initial IEP.[24]

> To acknowledge the expertise of school officials is not the same as saying that they should not have to demonstrate to an impartial fact-finder, at least in the first instance, that the proposed goals and objectives of the IEP address the student's needs, or that the IEP delivers services to those needs in a way that will provide progress towards those goals and objectives, or that the proposed criteria to evaluate the child's progress are in place and can actually measure the extent to which the objectives are obtained.[25]

Hence, the judge concluded that it was appropriate to place the burden of proof on the school district in a dispute over an initial IEP even if the burden of proof might be on the parents in other instances, such as when the parents want the school district to change an existing IEP.

Brian's case involved high-income parents who had already paid for him to attend private school for seven years and were now paying experts and a lawyer to persuade a court that the school district should pay for their son's private schooling. In concluding that the burden of proof should fall on the school district in such a case, the judge acknowledged Congress's seeming concern for economically disadvantaged minorities. He concluded that the burden of proof had to be on the school district because low-income parents might not be able to afford any expert witnesses. If the school district did not have the burden of proof, then it could win "without having to produce any evidence of justification of the IEP."[26] He asked whether such a result "is fair, apart from whether Congress could have intended it."[27]

Because the hearing officer was found to have imposed the wrong burden of proof, the district court judge remanded the case back to the hearing officer for reconsideration. With the burden of proof on the school district, the hearing officer issued modified findings of fact and concluded that the school district had not proposed an adequate educational plan for Brian. Giving greater weight to the parents' experts, he concluded that Brian "experiences highly significant difficulty with auditory processing skills."[28] He also criticized the school district for proposing only group speech/language therapy when the plaintiffs' experts recommended only individual therapy. He also concluded that the inclusion model was not appropriate for Brian because "the presence of a special education teacher sitting near the Child in class . . . is likely to add to his distraction."[29] The hearing officer then concluded, "The Child's learning disability, his distractibility, and his auditory processing skills deficit dictate that he be in small classes for all his academic subjects; large classes are not appropriate for the Child."[30]

The crux of the case on remand was whether the hearing officer should credit the testimony of the plaintiffs' audiologist that Brian had a CAPD or the testimony of the school district speech-language pathologist that he did not. This time, the hearing officer concluded that "an audiologist is more qualified to diagnose auditory processing problems than a speech/language pathologist" and that, as even the speech-language pathologist acknowledged, the audiologist had administered a "formalized standard objective measure of central auditory processing."[31] The hearing officer, however, was willing to give greater weight to the audiologist's recommendation only when the burden of proof shifted to the school district.

Because the school district's IEP "had no goals to address the Child's severe auditory deficit (perception of sound), which is responsible for his reading

problem, and no goals to address his articulation problem,"[32] the hearing officer concluded that the IEP was deficient. But the hearing officer emphasized
repeatedly that the burden of proof was decisive because the case otherwise
rested in "equipose [sic]."[33] In other words, a school district can rely on its
speech-language pathologist to take the position that a diagnosis of a CAPD
is not appropriate, without using scientifically accepted diagnostic tools, and
devise an IEP that ignores a qualified audiologist's CAPD diagnosis so long
as the school district does not have the burden of proof.

The school district appealed the hearing officer's second decision to the
federal district court. The federal court judge affirmed the decision to assign
the burden of proof to the school district in a case involving the challenging of an initial IEP.[34] Further, the judge affirmed the finding of the hearing
officer that the school district had not offered Brian an adequate educational
plan. The judge also awarded the parents full reimbursement for the cost of
sending their son to a private school despite their supposed "predetermina-
tion" with respect to private schooling. He noted: "The critical consideration,
as the Court sees it, is not whether the parents have their minds set on private school, but whether they have cooperated in good faith to attempt to
develop an IEP to the maximum extent possible."[35] Nonetheless, the judge
did not award the parents reimbursement for educating their child at a private school for the following two years (1999–2000 and 2000–1) because
they had failed to independently challenge the IEP for each of those years.[36]
Quoting a Fourth Circuit opinion, the judge found that when "parents of a
disabled child challenge multiple IEPs in court, they must have exhausted
their administrative remedies for each academic year in which an IEP is
challenged."[37] Despite having retained legal counsel for more than four years,
Brian's parents had made a fatal procedural error in not challenging each IEP
in which the school district insisted on placing Brian in a large classroom
within the public school.

Two more years passed before the case was heard in the Fourth Circuit
Court of Appeals. Reversing the district court, the Fourth Circuit concluded
that the burden of proof should be placed on the party initiating a proceeding—in this case, the parents. To reach this result, the court emphasized:
"Because Congress took care in specifying specific procedural protections
necessary to implement the policy goals of the Act, we decline to go further,
at least insofar as the burden of proof is concerned."[38]

In a strongly worded dissent, Judge J. Michael Luttig concluded that the
decision in this case was unfair to typical parents who are much less sophisticated than Brian's parents:

I fear that, in reaching the contrary conclusion, the majority has been unduly influenced by the fact that the parents of the disabled student *in this case* have proven to be knowledgeable about the educational resources available to their son and sophisticated (if yet unsuccessful) in their pursuit of these resources. If so, it is regrettable. These parents are not typical, and any choice regarding the burden of proof should not be made in the belief that they are. For the vast majority of parents whose children require the benefits and protections provided in the IDEA, the specialized language and technical educational analysis with which they must familiarize themselves as a consequence of their child's disability will likely be obscure, if not bewildering. By the same token, most of these parents will find the educational program proposed by the school district resistant to challenge: the school district will have better information about the resources available to it, as well as the benefit of its experience with other disabled children. With the full mix of parents in mind, I believe that the proper course is to assign the burden of proof in due process hearings to the school district.[39]

Judge Luttig failed to note that these supposedly sophisticated parents made a crucial mistake in not challenging each IEP developed by the school district during the pendency of this litigation. This failure reveals that even parents with sophisticated legal counsel can find the IEP process "bewildering," thereby further highlighting the risks of which Judge Luttig warned.

Brian's parents appealed the Fourth Circuit decision to the U.S. Supreme Court, which affirmed the decision of the Fourth Circuit. Emphasizing that the IDEA is an example of "cooperative federalism," Justice Sandra Day O'Connor concluded that the burden of proof falls on the parents in this kind of matter.[40] Even one of the more liberal members of the Court, Justice John Paul Stevens, concurred in the majority's opinion "because I believe that we should presume that public school officials are properly performing their difficult responsibilities under this important statute."[41] The Supreme Court remanded the case for reconsideration based upon its determination of the correct burden of proof.

The Supreme Court acknowledged that by placing the burden of proof on the party seeking relief, it was usually placing that burden on the parents. Nonetheless, it acknowledged that the burden can be on the school district when it is the moving party seeking "to change an existing IEP . . . or if parents refuse to allow their child to be evaluated."[42] Further, the Court emphasized the crucial importance of school districts' following the statute's procedural requirements, particularly the right of parents to review all the educational records and obtain an independent educational evaluation at school district expense so that "they are not left to challenge the government without a realistic opportunity to access the necessary evidence, or without an expert with the firepower to match the opposition."[43] As chapters 8 through 12 will demonstrate, hearing officers often do not sufficiently protect parents' rights to the statute's procedural safeguards such that they do not have the "firepower" to match the opposition when they have the burden of proof. Few parents have the kind of economic resources of the Schaffer family to pay private tuition and hire both lawyers and experts.

The Supreme Court issued its opinion on November 14, 2005, and the district court held a remand hearing on September 17, 2007.[44] Brian was twenty-three years old by then, so information was available about how he had fared in high school. After a difficult time in eighth and ninth grades at the private McLean School, Brian's parents transferred him back to the local public high school, where he attended the kind of small special education classes that his parents had always sought for him. The school district offered this program to Brian because, following the district court decision assigning the burden of proof to the school district in 2000, it thought it could be found legally responsible for Brian's private education if it did not offer an appropriate public education. Thus, it offered an education plan consistent with the recommendations of the experts retained by Brian's parents. Brian did well in these special education classes and managed to transition to regular classes for twelfth grade and graduated from the public high school with a 3.4 grade point average in his final term.[45]

At the district court hearing, Brian's parents argued that the hearing officer was wrong to conclude that the case had been in equipoise when the hearing officer was determining the sufficiency of the eighth-grade IEP. First, they argued that the hearing officer, in the first decision, had given insufficient weight to the views of their audiologist that Brian's primary disability was a CAPD and that he therefore needed much smaller classrooms than those provided by the school district. Second, they argued that subsequent developments demonstrated the seriousness of Brian's CAPD and his need for smaller classrooms and that the school district itself eventually came to that realization two years later.

Despite these arguments, the district court judge ruled for the school district. He refused to consider the post-hearing developments which demonstrated that Brian could make adequate educational progress only in small, self-contained special education classrooms. The district court judge insisted, "The appropriate inquiry is whether the Board's IEPs at the time of creation were reasonably calculated to provide some educational benefit to the student. Courts should not judge an IEP in hindsight. . . . Ultimate success is not the touchstone of the inquiry. Reasonable calculation is all that is required under the law."[46] Finally, the district court judge decided to defer to the hearing officer's conclusion that the case was in equipoise so that the assignment of the burden of proof was determinative. He granted the defendant's motion for summary judgment.[47] The Fourth Circuit affirmed the district court, concluding this matter on January 29, 2009,[48] six years after Brian's graduation from high school.[49]

The amount of money Brian's parents spent on legal fees is extraordinary. They had two administrative hearings, several district court hearings, several court of appeals hearings, and one Supreme Court hearing. They also paid for private school tuition in both eighth and ninth grades for which they did not receive reimbursement.

This case has created a high burden of proof for parents who challenge IEPs, making it virtually impossible for them to win. Nonetheless, Brian received some benefit from this litigation. There was a brief window when the school district thought it had the burden of proof in these kinds of cases and might have to reimburse Brian's parents for his private school education if they could not offer an adequate educational program. That litigation pressure induced the school district to offer Brian a special education placement in tenth grade consistent with his experts' recommendations. And that plan was highly successful for Brian, allowing him ultimately to graduate from high school with little special education support.

Unfortunately, that door has been closed to other students like Brian because they usually must bear the burden of proof in such cases. In a handful of states, such as New Jersey (which will be discussed in chapter 10), the state legislatures have imposed the burden of proof on the school district. Brian's school district chose to spend thousands of dollars in legal fees rather than offer him an educational program consistent with the recommendations of his experts. Brian was very fortunate that the school district thought it was likely to lose when the burden of proof was placed on them and therefore provided him with an appropriate educational program in tenth grade. That program enabled him to achieve educational success for the first time. Meanwhile, other children with a CAPD and ADHD who also need a small, more structured class setting in order to attain academic success are unlikely to be able to argue successfully for such programs given that that they now bear a difficult burden of proof.

The difficulty with assigning the burden of proof to parents in these kinds of cases is the problem of speculation. How can a parent demonstrate that a program is not "reasonably calculated" to attain academic success in the future if it has not yet been put in place? In this case, the parents had expert witnesses with good grounds for insisting that Brian could not get an adequate education in classes with twenty-four to thirty-two students irrespective of the level of support found in those classes. Because Brian had not yet attended a classroom with that exact program, there was no way to "prove" that that program was inadequate.

I have spoken with many attorneys around the country since the Supreme Court decided Brian's case. They tell me that they are extremely reluctant to take cases challenging an IEP because they find the burden of proof to be insurmountable. Chapters 8 through 12 will examine hearing officer decisions from four states and the District of Columbia. The data from these states confirm these anecdotal reports. Even in New Jersey, where the state has assigned the burden of proof to school districts, parents rarely win cases in which they challenge the adequacy of IEPs because, in practice, the hearing officers have imposed a very light burden of proof on school districts.

Ironically, one of the few cases in which I have seen a parent successfully challenge an IEP is my own, the case in which I successfully challenged my son's IEP (as discussed in chapter 1). My victory has led me to reflect on why I, but not Brian's parents, was able to prevail.

Like Brian, my son, Sam, had ADHD and a CAPD, and the school district had classified him as having a "learning disability." As in Brian's case, Sam's audiologist concluded that he had a CAPD and the school district's speech-language pathologist insisted that he had ADHD and not a CAPD. At the due process hearing, the school district's approach was to attack the audiologist (even though the school district had retained her for many years to conduct their audiology evaluations). And, as in Brian's case, the school district wanted to place Sam in an inclusive classroom with a special education teacher as well as offer him one class period per day during which he would be in a setting limited to children on IEPs, so that he could get extra support.

Unlike Brian's situation, though, we never sought private schooling or a full-time special education environment. As recommended by the audiologist, we requested a personal listening device to allow Sam to better access classroom instruction. Evidence from a thirty-day fourth-grade trial demonstrated that such a device was effective. The trial period evidence was crucial to our success. It allowed us to demonstrate that Sam attained educational success only when he had that kind of accommodation. Thus, we did not have to rely entirely on speculation to prove what kind of program would be effective.

From my conversations with other attorneys, I have learned that my son's situation is exceedingly rare. Because of the success of the thirty-day trial of the listening device in fourth grade, we were able to meet our burden of proof. Without that evidence, we would have had mere speculation about the beneficial effects of the listening device in the future. It is rare to have prior evidence that can be used to rebut the "reasonably calculated" decision by the school district.

In fact, the importance of data from a trial can be seen in the *Rowley* case itself (which was discussed in chapter 3). The two-week trial from kindergarten, during which Amy Rowley supposedly did not benefit from a sign language interpreter, was determinative of the outcome of her case even as she advanced in school. As a deaf child, she was expected to attend fourth grade with a teacher whose thick moustache and strong accent made him impossible to understand through lip reading, because she had refused to pay attention to an interpreter in a kindergarten classroom when she was five years old. Unfortunately, parents have no ability to influence how those trials are conducted. I was not even aware that my son was having a thirty-day trial while it took place. I had no control over the school's sloppy record keeping during the trial. Amy's parents were not able to prepare her so that she would try to take advantage of the sign language services when they were offered. With the burden of proof on the parents, the school district can do sloppy trials and still meet their burden of proof. I was lucky that the fourth-grade teacher had written a couple of e-mails to us about the success of the thirty-day trial and mentioned it on my son's report card. Otherwise, we would have had no way of demonstrating the success of the trial, because the school district had not followed scientifically accepted data collection practices before, during, and after the trial to assess whether the intervention (i.e., listening device) was helpful.

Another factor that seemed to influence Brian's case was the perception of the hearing officer that his were greedy parents who were not acting in good faith. The hearing officer concluded that Brian's parents wanted the school district to reimburse them for private school rather than offer Brian an adequate public school education. In fact, the hearing officer's prediction was wrong. Brian's parents did send Brian to public school when he was offered an appropriate education. By contrast, the fact that I was requesting for my son only a listening device that could be purchased for about $1,000 may have made my request seem more sympathetic to the hearing officer. Although the expense of the parents' proposed remedy should not influence the determination of whether the school district's proposed program is adequate, it probably does so.

In sum, the Supreme Court's decision in Brian's case is discouraging for all parents because few parents can meet the high burden of proof required to successfully challenge an IEP. Judge Luttig was right to speculate that this decision is particularly troubling for poor parents who cannot afford expert witness testimony at all. Both Brian and my son eventually benefited from appropriate educational plans. The empirical data from the hearing officer decisions that will be discussed in chapters 8 through 12 reflect that Brian's and Sam's experiences are highly unusual.

7

Joseph Murphy

This is the story of a child who foundered in school, despite receiving special education services, for about ten years before his parents gave up on the public school system and sent him to a private school. Joseph's parents tried to make economical choices—initially proceeding without a lawyer and going along with the school district's recommended program. It eventually became clear to Joseph's parents, through the assistance of Marilyn Arons, who acted as both an educational consultant and a lay advocate, that the school district was misclassifying Joseph's disability and providing him with inappropriate services. With Arons's dogged assistance on a pro bono basis, they were able to persuade a hearing officer that the school district had not provided Joseph with an appropriate educational plan and should be responsible for the costs of Joseph's private education.

The Murphys' case highlights the need for parents to have an educational consultant and a lay advocate assist them to help ensure that their children receive appropriate services. Few parents have the expertise to negotiate with school districts about their children's educational plans without such assistance. Unfortunately, the U.S. Supreme Court ruled in the *Murphy* case[1] that school districts need not compensate parents for the expense of an educational consultant or a lay advocate even when that individual helps the parents demonstrate the inadequacy of the school district's IEP.

Joseph Murphy began his education in 1989 at LaGrange Elementary School in the Arlington Central School District in Poughkeepsie, New York. He displayed signs of attention deficit problems as early as kindergarten and was diagnosed with a moderate attention deficit and a "fragile ego" in second grade.[2] By the end of second grade, standardized tests suggested he was about a year below grade level despite having an average IQ. He was not referred to the school district's special education committee until November of fourth grade even though, by then, he had repeated third grade. By this time, he had also been diagnosed as having ADHD and was taking Ritalin to control his symptoms.

The special education committee compiled information in fourth grade for Joseph. His biggest deficit appeared to be in speech and language, where he was found to be 1.5 standard deviations below the mean for children in his age group. His academic scores showed deficits in arranging puzzles, strategies for decoding unfamiliar words, and dictation. Classroom observation revealed that he was "unable to determine what was relevant to solve a mathematics problem."[3]

The school district classified Joseph as learning disabled and implemented an IEP in January of fourth grade. He received two thirty-minute sessions of group speech/language therapy and extended time on tests. His regular classroom teacher received two hours of consultative services per week from a special education instructor. A new IEP was prepared in May of fourth grade for the following academic year that offered essentially the same services.

The school district conducted further speech/language testing in June of fourth grade. Concluding that Joseph had a "moderate communication disorder," the evaluator recommended that he receive individual speech/language therapy twice per week (in addition to the group therapy) and be placed in a language-enriched educational program with a low student-to-teacher ratio. The IEP was amended in July to reflect these recommendations.

When the special education team met at the end of fifth grade, the school district claimed that Joseph had standardized test scores in the normal range. His speech/language therapist reported that he had made excellent progress. The IEP prepared for sixth grade provided minimal extra assistance and included no further speech/language therapy.

Because of Joseph's academic difficulties in sixth grade, the IEP team reconvened in November and drafted a new IEP that placed him in a collaborative classroom with a 15:1 child-to-adult ratio for instruction in English, social studies, science, and study skills. A special education teacher assisted the teacher in this collaborative classroom.

Joseph continued to struggle in sixth grade. By the end of three-quarters of the school year, his overall average was slightly under 70. His mother requested that he receive home instruction for the final quarter because, according to his physician, Joseph had been incorrectly classified as learning disabled rather than as having ADHD and had developed a phobia about his present placement. He was home tutored for the rest of sixth grade and ended the year with grades ranging from 65 for modified mathematics to 74 for modified science.

For seventh grade, Joseph transferred to a different middle school within the district. He was reclassified as "other health impaired" (with ADHD) and received one period of resource room services per day as well as extra time on tests. Joseph continued to receive grades around 70. The school district agreed to have Joseph evaluated by a private psychologist, who concluded that Joseph exhibited "signs of a moderate to severe developmental aphasia" (a type of language impairment) and that he should be evaluated by "a speech pathologist with training and experience in childhood aphasic and language disorders."[4]

Joseph's IEP remained unchanged for eighth grade until his parents provided the results of further testing. In September of eighth grade, an independent speech-language evaluator concluded that Joseph was "severely functionally language disordered." A neuropsychologist found that Joseph had a "near total incapacity to process continuous language, written or oral." She suggested that Joseph needed to be in a very small class and that an alternative placement should be considered. She considered it to be "imperative" that Joseph receive "cognitive-linguistic" therapy from the independent speech-language evaluator.

The school district refused to pay for the independent speech-language evaluator to provide therapy to Joseph but did modify his IEP so that he would receive forty minutes of individual speech/language therapy from a school district therapist three times per week. (Joseph's parents paid for the independent speech-language evaluator to continue to work with Joseph after this request was denied.) The school district's therapist concluded that Joseph needed to continue to receive these services in ninth grade and also needed daily assistance for organizational and functional language skills by a special education teacher and a speech pathologist. Joseph's private speech-language evaluator continued to recommend that Joseph receive more intensive assistance, including enrollment in a residential school for language-impaired students. Joseph continued to be educated in regular education classes. Despite these interventions, the achievement tests administered by the school district documented significant deficits in listening comprehension, word attack, word comprehension, spelling, and vocabulary. Other than in a computer class, Joseph's grades ranged from 58 (technology) to 70 (English and earth science).

For ninth grade, the school district recommended that Joseph be placed in a special education program for English, global studies, mathematics, physical science, and study skills and enroll in regular education classes for electives and physical education. In addition, the school district recommended that he receive three forty-minute sessions of individual speech/language therapy per week.

Joseph's parents rejected this IEP because they believed it did not provide Joseph with the highly intensive therapy with specialists he needed for his particular kind of disabilities in order to make educational progress that he had not been making. They filed a due process complaint, notifying the school district that they wanted to send their son to Kildonan School at public expense. They also sought reimbursement for their expenditures for services provided by the independent speech-language evaluator. A nonlawyer expert, rather than a lawyer, assisted them at the due process hearing. A hearing occurred in two parts over an extended period of time. The first set of hearings occurred on October 28; November 2, 18, and 20; and December 9 and 10, 1998.[5]

On February 26, 1999, the hearing officer rendered a decision in which he concluded that the school district had not met its burden of proof to demonstrate that Joseph would receive some educational benefit from the proposed IEP. He concluded that the classroom with twelve to fourteen special education students was "a distracting environment far removed from the one-on-one tutoring indicated to deal with his executive functioning deficit."[6] (An executive function deficit is an inability to engage in step-by-step planning to solve problems; the deficit is usually exacerbated by a distracting environment.) Further, he concluded that school staff had insufficient experience "in teaching a student with an executive functioning deficit or other disabilities similar to those of this student."[7] Hence, the hearing officer found that the school district's proposed IEP was not adequate because it "satisfies neither the academic nor social needs of this student."[8]

One reason that Joseph's parents were able to prevail was that the hearing officer concluded that the school district bears the "burden to demonstrate that the educational program recommended by its [educational committee] is reasonably calculated to allow the child to receive educational benefits in the least restrictive environment."[9] Applying that burden of proof, the hearing officer ruled for the parents, finding that the recommended educational program was "*not* reasonably calculated to allow this student to receive educational benefit in the least restrictive environment."[10]

This decision was rendered before the U.S. Supreme Court concluded in Brian Schaffer's case (discussed in chapter 6) that the burden of proof should lie with the parents, not the school district.[11] (Nonetheless, New York enacted legislation in 2007 that generally places the burden of proof on the school district when the parent is challenging the validity of an IEP.[12]) The assignment of the burden of proof was crucial to the parents' ability to prevail under the *Rowley* standard for an adequate education (discussed in chapter 3). Because Joseph had not yet attended the school district's special education classes, it would have been very difficult under the *Rowley* standard for the parents to demonstrate that that program would offer no educational benefit, if the burden of proof were on them. Nonetheless, the school district, which had the burden of proof, could not demonstrate that the proposed IEP *would* provide educational benefit because the program was inconsistent with the experts' recommendations for Joseph.

Additionally, the hearing officer ruled that Joseph's parents should be reimbursed for the private speech therapy services because they "went beyond the speech pathology available from the school district to deal with the student's executive functioning deficit and other neurological problems."[13]

Because the hearing officer had concluded that the school district's IEP was not reasonably calculated to provide educational benefit, he held additional hearings on April 12, May 13, and June 2, 1999, to determine if Kildonan School was an appropriate placement for Joseph. At this stage of the deliberations, the parents had the burden of proof to demonstrate the appropriateness of that placement. The hearing officer issued a decision on July 7, 1999, concluding that Kildonan was an appropriate placement and that the school district should reimburse Joseph's parents for the cost of sending Joseph to Kildonan School for the 1998–99 school year.

The hearing officer reached this conclusion after first determining the precise nature of Joseph's disability. He concluded that Joseph had both an executive functioning disorder as well as a discourse deficiency that made it difficult for him to process information quickly. The most appropriate placement for Joseph in light of these disabilities was a small classroom structure that provided "one-on-one teaching, a comfortable relationship with the therapist in the school, and teachers skilled in dealing with students who have language problems."[14]

The hearing officer also considered evidence about Joseph's performance at the Kildonan School because he had spent an entire academic year there before a decision was rendered. While recognizing that Joseph was still struggling in school, the hearing officer also concluded, "[O]bservations of the student's behavior, communication, and peer interaction indicate improvement during his attendance at Kildonan."[15]

An appellate state-level hearing officer reviewed the original hearing officer's decision. (Like Ohio, as discussed in chapters 1 and 8, New York has a two-step state-level review process before a case can be appealed to a state or federal judge.) The state-level review officer affirmed the original hearing officer's decision, although on different grounds. Emphasizing the school district's burden of proof, he found it had failed to demonstrate that Joseph would be grouped with other students having similar needs and had failed to establish that Joseph's IEP's annual goals and objectives were achievable in the recommended class.[16]

Even though Joseph's parents had the burden of proof to establish the appropriateness of the Kildonan School, the review officer affirmed the determination that that school was appropriate for him. Joseph's educational performance continued to be weak, but the review officer found that, in contrast to previous years, the teachers' "year-end reports indicated that his effort and achievement improved as the school year came to an end."[17] After considering equitable matters involving public policy principles of fairness, the review officer concluded that Joseph's parents should be reimbursed for the cost of sending Joseph to Kildonan School.[18] Nonetheless, the review officer concluded that they should not be reimbursed for the cost of private speech pathology services because of the "vague accounting" offered for these services by the private speech pathologist. Again, burden of proof was important to this determination, with the review officer stating, "I must therefore find that respondents failed to meet their burden of proof about the appropriateness of the services provided by the speech pathologist."[19]

The review officer's decision was rendered on December 14, 1999, and the school district sent Joseph's parents a check for $20,750 about five weeks later to reimburse them for the 1998–99 school year tuition. The school district, however, appealed the review officer's decision to a federal court.[20]

The successful review officer decision was binding on only the 1998–99 school year. Joseph was also enrolled in the Kildonan School for 1999–2000, and his parents wanted the courts to conclude that Kildonan was his appropriate placement for that year as well. The review officer decision regarding the 1998–98 school year was rendered during the middle of the 1999–2000 school year.

On January 7, 2000, Joseph's parents filed a due process complaint with a state hearing officer in which they argued that the school district's proposed placement for 1999–2000 was also inappropriate and that they should be reimbursed for the expense of sending Joseph to Kildonan School for that year as well. Meanwhile, they also brought in federal district court an action to determine if Kildonan School was their stay put educational placement so that they would receive reimbursement for tuition payments until the hearing officer resolved their new due process complaint. They brought this action without a lawyer, continuing to rely on their educational expert for assistance. As in Michael Panico's case, discussed in chapter 4, they were arguably entitled to have the school district pay for their son's education starting from the date of the state-level review officer decision regarding the 1998–99 school year irrespective of whether that decision was reversed on appeal.

The legal rules about such payments were confusing (and the Murphy family was proceeding without legal counsel). The IDEA specifies that "in the absence of an agreement with the state or local school district, parents who unilaterally change their child's placement are financially responsible for their child's education unless and until that placement is deemed appropriate by administrative decision or a court."[21] The school district had complied with the hearing officer's order and reimbursed the parents for the 1998–99 school year even though it still had the right to appeal that decision. The district court judge needed to decide whether the parents should be reimbursed for the first half of the 1999–2000 school year (before the decision of December 14, 1999) and whether the school district should be considered financially responsible for the period from December 14, 1999, to the date of the legal action.

The issues for these two time periods were different. During the first half of the 1999–2000 school year, Joseph's parents were sending him to a private school before they had been successful on the merits before the state review officer. As such, they were acting at their own risk and were entitled to reimbursement only if they prevailed at the end of the entire litigation process. Because an appeal of the review officer's decision was still pending, it was premature for them to be reimbursed for those payments. The district court judge held that plaintiffs "are not entitled to reimbursement for this period until the SRO [state review officer] decision is upheld in court or it is certain that the District does not intend to appeal the SRO decision."[22]

The different rule of law, however, governed the time period of December 14, 1999, to the date of the legal action. Once the state review officer rendered a decision on December 14, 1999, that decision became Joseph's "then-current" placement for stay put purposes.

> From that date forward, the District is responsible for maintaining that placement. . . . This does not mean that the District must fund Joseph's

tuition at Kildonan for the remainder of his education. However, until a new placement is established by either an actual agreement between the parents and the District, or by an administrative decision upholding the District's proposed placement which Plaintiffs choose not to appeal, or by a court, the District remains financially responsible.[23]

Because the review officer's decision was delayed for two months for reasons beyond the parents' control, the judge actually set the date for the district's financial responsibility at September 17, 1999.[24] In other words, the judge created the legal fiction that the review officer had ruled on September 17, 1999, rather than on December 14, 1999, so the earlier date was used for determining when the school district was responsible for payments until the litigation process ended.

The policy behind requiring the district to pay for the Kildonan School was that otherwise the stay put provision would be rendered meaningless. It would not be much of a "right" if the parents could have their child "stay put" at the private school only pending the federal appeal if they bore the expense of implementing that right. Also, the judge made clear that, even if the school district prevailed on appeal, the parents would not have to reimburse the school district for the cost of Kildonan School from September 17, 1999, until that appeal was decided.[25] Again, that is similar to the rule that governed Michael Panico's case, as discussed in chapter 4.

The school district appealed this decision to the Second Circuit Court of Appeals. In a decision rendered on July 16, 2002, the three-judge panel, in an opinion written by then–Circuit Judge Sonia Sotomayor, affirmed the district court decision. The school district had two main grounds for appeal. First, they argued that the plaintiffs had failed to exhaust their state remedies before bringing suit in federal district court. Second, they argued that the decision should be vacated because the parents had proceeded *pro se* on behalf of their child in conflict with rules of the court.[26]

The Second Circuit ruled for the parents on both counts in a case in which the parents did secure legal counsel for the first time. (The U.S. Department of Justice also participated as *amicus curiae* on the side of the parents.) First, the Second Circuit found that appealing a denial of a child's stay put rights is an exception to the rule requiring parents to exhaust their state remedies before proceeding in federal court because it is otherwise impossible to have a timely resolution of that issue. Second, it found that the parents should have been required to find counsel in the district court but that the failure to use legal counsel was not a reversible error. Because the purpose of the rule to require legal counsel is to make sure that children have adequate counsel, "it is hardly in the best interest of Joseph Murphy to vacate an injunction that inures to his benefit so that he may re-litigate this issue below with licensed representation in order to re-secure a victory already obtained."[27] (The Supreme Court eventually tackled in the *Winkelman* case[28] (discussed in chapter 8) the issue of whether parents can proceed *pro se* on behalf of their children in federal court.) Because the parents had been reimbursed for the 1998–99 school year and the district's responsibility under stay put began on September 17, 1999, this decision was very positive for the parents.

One reason Joseph's parents were able to prevail was that they hired a well-known educational consultant and lay advocate, Marilyn Arons. Their next step was to request that the school district compensate Arons for her services: $29,350 in fees and $7,847.14 for her transportation expenses.[29] Arons had taken the case on a contingency basis with the understanding that the parents would seek to have the school district pay for her services if they prevailed.[30]

The kind of work that Arons did on behalf of parents and their children raised two distinct legal issues: Should nonlawyer advocates be entitled to fees for their advocacy work and should experts, in general, receive fees from school districts when parents prevail?

The IDEA provides that a district court can award "reasonable attorneys' fees as part of the costs . . . to a prevailing party who is the parent of a child with a disability." Those fees, however, are limited to preparation for the due process hearing because the IDEA also states that "[a]ttorneys' fees may not be awarded relating to any meeting of the IEP Team unless such meeting is convened as a result of an administrative proceeding or judicial action, or, at the discretion of the State, for a mediation described in subsection (e)."[31] The IDEA also provides that a child is entitled to a *free* and appropriate public education. Hence, Joseph's parents argued that their child's education would not be "free" if they were responsible for all the costs of hiring experts to assist them in their IDEA case.

The IDEA is unusual in its provision allowing parents to use lay advocates in roles similar to those usually reserved for lawyers. It permits parents to use a lay advocate to assist them at IEP meetings and even at due process hearings, although one might otherwise consider that kind of work, when practiced by a nonlawyer, as the unauthorized practice of law. The IDEA states that parents have "the right to be accompanied and advised by counsel and by individuals with special knowledge or training with respect to the problems of children with disabilities" at due process hearings.[32] Marilyn Arons made a career out of advocacy on behalf of parents and their children and had a record of remarkable success. For example, in *J.S. v. Ramapo Central*

School District, she was retained by J.S.'s parents after they could not come to an agreement with the school district about an appropriate placement for their son. After three days of representing the parents at a due process hearing, Arons was able to negotiate the outcome desired by the parents—placement of their son at an out-of-state educational facility at state expense.[33] Similarly, in *Connors v. Mills*, the parents were able to attain reimbursement for sending their child to a private school after receiving extensive assistance by Arons.[34] Arons has successfully represented dozens, if not hundreds, of parents since the passage of the special education laws in the 1970s.[35]

In the first two rounds of their seeking expert fees in this case, Joseph's parents were able to convince the district court and court of appeals that they should be reimbursed for the time that Arons spent on their case as an educational consultant (but not as a lay advocate).[36] In other words, she should be paid for her educational services but not for her work that was quasi-legal in nature, like writing briefs or other legal memoranda. The lower courts awarded $8,650 to Arons out of the $29,350 that the Murphys had sought on her behalf. The primary basis for the Second Circuit's conclusion that the school district should pay those expert fees was a statement in a Conference Committee Report on the IDEA: "The conferees intend that the term 'attorneys' fees as part of the 'costs' include reasonable expenses and fees of expert witnesses and the reasonable costs of any test or evaluation which is found to be necessary for the preparation of the . . . case."[37] Further, the Second Circuit noted that it would be inconsistent with the purpose of the IDEA for the statute to specify that people with "special knowledge" can accompany a parent and then bar any reimbursement for such an individual's service.[38]

In a 6–3 opinion in 2006 (eight years after Joseph's parents challenged the appropriateness of Joseph's eighth-grade education plan), the Supreme Court overturned the Second Circuit, concluding that the term "costs" does not include expert witness fees unless Congress explicitly provides that rule in the statutory text.[39] It refused to allow the language in the Conference Committee Report to overturn the general default rule in American jurisprudence—that the term "costs" does not include expert witness fees. As Justice Ruth Bader Ginsburg noted in her concurrence, "The ball, I conclude, is properly left in Congress' court to provide, if it so elects, for consultant fees and testing expenses beyond those IDEA and its implementing regulations already authorize, along with any specifications, conditions, or limitations geared to those fees and expenses Congress may deem appropriate."[40]

Congress has not overturned the Supreme Court decision. Bills have been repeatedly introduced to reimburse parents for the cost of expert witness fees (but not for the services of nonlawyer advocates). These bills have never made it out of committee.[41] Thus, parents who pursue due process claims can receive compensation only for attorney fees, not for experts or non-attorney advocates, despite the supposed guarantee that parents can use non-attorney advocates at due process hearings and the fact that parents cannot possibly prevail without using experts. Thus, children get a *free* and appropriate public education only when parents and school districts agree about the content of an IEP. If there is any disagreement and the parents hire private experts or nonlawyer advocates, the parents cannot expect to receive any reimbursement for those services.

Murphy was a huge blow to the ability of low-income parents to pursue IDEA claims. But to be clear: Even if the Supreme Court had affirmed the Second Circuit's decision in *Murphy,* low-income parents would still find it quite difficult to pursue IDEA claims. The Second Circuit had awarded only about $9,000 to Arons for her hundreds of hours of work on behalf of the Murphys as an educational consultant. The Murphys did not even seek to attain reimbursement for expenses borne before the due process hearing because the statutory language is clear that those expenses (including attorney fees) are nonreimbursable even if the parents eventually prevail in the due process hearing. Further, the courts had not awarded any money to Arons for the hours she spent as a lay advocate at the due process hearing and in federal court. Thus, even the favorable Second Circuit opinion awarded Arons only a small fraction of what she sought to charge for her work and expenses on behalf of Joseph Murphy.

As reflected in chapters 8 through 12, successful parents nearly always hire experts who offer their independent evaluations of children's disabilities and need for individualized education programs. Further, successful parents often use an advocate, in some cases during the IEP process itself. Finally, successful parents typically have experts testify at the due process hearings. Most of these hearings last several days, and the entire saga often lasts years. Even if the parents prevail, there is no way the parents will spend less than several thousand dollars on experts because no insurance policy compensates a parent for medical professionals who testify at hearings. At best, a parent's health insurance policy may pay for some underlying tests. Of course, many parents have little or no insurance for their children.

The fact that Congress could continue to insist it is requiring school districts to provide children with a "free" and appropriate public education while continuing not to overturn *Murphy* is evidence that it has an insufficient commitment to extending the benefits of the IDEA beyond the upper-middle-class parents who can afford expensive litigation. Hence, it is not surprising that nearly all the Supreme Court cases brought under the IDEA are for claims of tuition reimbursement when parents unilaterally send their children to private schools, because only parents who can afford to front the costs of private schooling can also afford to hire the various experts necessary to pursue a successful IDEA claim. And, even if proposed congressional bills were to become law, parents would still not be able to hire nonlawyer advocates to assist them at IDEA hearings or get reimbursed for advocacy expenses before the due process hearing.

Joseph's parents were able to help their son obtain an appropriate education at public expense only because of what might be considered a "perfect storm." They happened to live in a jurisdiction that placed the burden of proof on the school district to demonstrate that the educational plan was appropriate. And they happened to receive the pro bono assistance of an extremely effective nonlawyer advocate. Arons took the case with the understanding that she would be paid only if Joseph's parents prevailed *and* if the school district agreed to compensate her. Few parents are sufficiently fortunate to get the services of such a highly qualified expert and advocate for free. Thus, the promise of a free and appropriate public education is elusive for many children.

8

Ohio

U.S. Supreme Court cases tell only a small part of the story of what it means for parents to challenge IEPs through the hearing officer system. Few parents and their children make it to that level of the litigation process. The IDEA creates cumbersome administrative procedures that parents must navigate before they can even file a complaint. This chapter and the following four report hearing officer results from the early stages of the litigation process. They will demonstrate the difficulties that parents have in using that process and how unlikely they are to succeed, especially if they do not have a lawyer.

Before proceeding, it would be helpful to have an overall sense of how the hearing process operates. Parents and school districts sometimes disagree about whether a child should be identified as disabled or whether the educational plan is sufficiently individualized or appropriate. When disagreements occur, a parent can invoke a series of procedural protections.

Typically, the parent will express his or her disagreement at the eligibility meeting or at the IEP meeting by refusing to sign the document proposed by the school district. When the school district learns of the parent's disagreement with these conclusions, it must then provide the parent with an explanation for why it took that position in a document that the statute calls "written prior notice."[1] Upon receiving that information, the parent may decide to challenge the school district's recommendation by filing what is called a due process complaint.

A parent who files a due process complaint must be given an opportunity to resolve the dispute voluntarily by attending a meeting with the school district or by mediation. If the attempt at a voluntary resolution is unsuccessful, then the parent is entitled to a due process hearing before an impartial hearing officer.

Although the hearing is called a due process hearing, the parent can actually complain about both procedural and substantive violations of the statute. Procedural violations might involve problems such as the wrong people being invited to meetings or parents' not receiving information in a timely manner. Substantive violations might involve issues like an inappropriate IEP or an incorrect disability classification.

Because typically an IEP is valid for only one year, parents who disagree with the content of an IEP can file a complaint on an annual basis. The fact that an IEP, for example, is valid for first grade does not mean that the same IEP will necessarily be valid for second grade. Each IEP is supposed to be developed on an individualized and annual basis to reflect the child's current level of performance.

Some states have two levels of hearing officer decisions that a parent must pursue before he or she can appeal to a state or federal court. Other states have only one level of hearing officer decisions. Ohio—whose hearing officer decisions will be discussed in this chapter—has two levels of hearing officer decisions.

Chapter 1 presented two stories from Ohio—one involving my son and one involving the child of another parent, whom I called Marilyn. Both of those cases involved parents who pursued the first step of Ohio's two-step administrative process. Although I was able to hire a lawyer to help me file a due process complaint and obtain needed services for my son, Marilyn, who was a low-income mother, was unable to maintain the schedule of an expedited hearing process or file any kind of brief on behalf of her son, who faced suspension from school. To have been successful, Marilyn would have needed to hire both experts and legal counsel—unreasonable expectations to place on low-income parents of a child with disabilities. There were no resources in place to help her meet what is typically an insurmountable burden of proof for parents trying to assist their children with disabilities.

To give the reader a stronger sense of how difficult it is to pursue both rounds of Ohio's administrative process, this chapter will discuss the story of one family—the Winkelmans—who pursued five years of administrative complaints and took their case to the U.S. Supreme Court on a procedural ground, before securing a victory.

With the assistance of two teams of pro bono lawyers, the Winkelmans challenged their son's IEP in first grade, second grade, third grade, and fourth grade, while also appealing an adverse decision from kindergarten. They also secured scholarship assistance to make it possible for Jacob to attend a private school during much of this litigation. Finally, in 2008, a hearing officer concluded in a 210-page opinion that the school district had violated the IDEA by not offering a proper transition program for Jacob from the private school to the public school. That victory cost the school district $174,000 in legal fees and $64,500 per year in private school tuition. Only by virtue of the Supreme Court's taking the Winkelmans' case on a procedural issue were they able to attain competent and free lawyers who persevered with their case until they prevailed. And these are white middle-class parents. As you read this story, imagine how the results might have differed if the family had not had the time, energy, and finances to pursue this case with the assistance of legal counsel.

Jacob Winkelman was born on May 25, 1997.[2] He was the youngest of four children; his sister Jenna had been previously diagnosed with autism and received an adequate education in the public schools. By age two, Jacob was also diagnosed with autism and soon began receiving home therapy. At age three, he began to attend a school district preschool program that his sister had successfully attended. After a year in that program, it became clear to both the parents and the school district that the program was not working well for Jacob. He was regressing and engaging in quite aggressive behavior. The school district agreed to pay for Jacob to attend the Achievement Centers,[3] a special preschool for children with autism. He started that program in July 2001, at the age of four, attending for the 2001–2 and 2002–3 school years. The Achievement Centers serve children only until age five; hence, Jacob needed a different program for the 2003–4 school year, when he was ready to start kindergarten.

The school district held an IEP meeting on June 2, 2003, to discuss Jacob's placement for kindergarten. The school district recommended a placement in the public school where Jacob would be in a self-contained classroom for six hours at the outset but then would have opportunities to transition into a regular education kindergarten as appropriate. Jacob's parents refused to consent to that placement because they thought it would be similar to the placement that had not worked well during Jacob's preschool years. They wanted Jacob to attend the private Monarch School,[4] which they believed offered a program similar to one that had been successful for Jacob at the Achievement Centers. They had been pleased with the public school option for their daughter but felt it would not work for Jacob because his autism was much more severe. Based on the advice of Jacob's physician, they were concerned that Jacob might have to attend a residential program if school-based intervention was not successful.

When the school district refused to agree to the placement at the Monarch School, Jacob's parents filed a due process complaint on June 9, 2003. (As explained above, parents can file a due process complaint to contest procedural and substantive matters. In this case, they were contesting the setting in which Jacob would receive his services.) The Winkelmans participated in mediation with the school district without a successful resolution. They also hired a lawyer, Dr. Donald R. Menefee, who had a Ph.D. in education administration, was a former principal at Kenston Middle School, and had had a private law practice since 2001.[5] In a radio interview, Jacob's mother described Menefee as an inexperienced and ineffective lawyer but the only one whom they could afford.

Before the due process hearing was held, the Winkelmans requested that the independent hearing officer (IHO) designate the Achievement Centers or the Monarch School as their stay put school during the pendency of the litigation. (An independent hearing officer is the first-level review officer in Ohio.) The IHO designated the Achievement Centers as the stay put school on August 28, 2003, even though it had no kindergarten program. Unfortunately, the Winkelmans did not ask for reconsideration or clarification of that decision because it could not be implemented. (It appears that Jacob's mother thought that Menefee was not a competent lawyer because he mistakenly requested that the IHO rule that the Achievements Centers was Jacob's stay put option even though it was not possible for Jacob to continue to attend that program because of his age.) The IHO might have reconsidered that decision and determined that the Monarch School had the program most like that of the school Jacob had previously attended under an IEP if Jacob's parents had sought timely clarification.

Given the IHO's impractical ruling that Jacob should attend the Achievement Centers during the pendency of the litigation, the Winkelmans decided to enroll Jacob at the Monarch School. Tuition was $56,000, which they were able to pay with the help of some financial aid. On February 19, 2004, while Jacob was enrolled in kindergarten, the IHO ruled in favor of the school district, concluding that the IEP offered at the public school was adequate under the IDEA.[6] A state-level review officer (SLRO) affirmed the IHO decision on June 2, 2004.[7] Because Ohio has a two-step administrative process, the Winkelmans needed to exhaust both steps before they could appeal their case to a state or federal court.

By this time, the Winkelmans were dissatisfied with their lawyer and running out of money. Nonetheless, they wanted to pursue this matter aggressively at both the federal court and administrative levels. They decided to proceed without the assistance of legal counsel on two fronts—to appeal the administrative decisions concerning Jacob's kindergarten IEP to a federal court and to challenge all future IEPs written by the school district on behalf of Jacob through the administrative process. Jacob's mother had decided to make pursuing his case a full-time job. As noted above, an IEP typically lasts for only one year. Thus, Jacob's parents could challenge the school district's proposed IEP on an annual basis, bringing new facts before the hearing officer with each challenge.

Although the IHO had not designated the Monarch School as Jacob's stay put school during the administrative appeal process of Jacob's kindergarten IEP, the Winkelmans sought to have the district court make that designation. They requested a temporary restraining order in federal court to keep Jacob in the Monarch School pending resolution of their federal case. On August 24, 2004, shortly before the first day of first grade, District Judge Ann Aldrich denied that request. She designated the public school as the stay put school during the appeal.

Soon after, the Winkelmans therefore learned that they had been unsuccessful before the district court judge with respect to Jacob's kindergarten IEP. But the school district had a responsibility to have a valid IEP in place for first grade as well. Following Judge Aldrich's ruling, the Winkelmans therefore filed a due process complaint on August 24, 2004, arguing that the school district was in violation of the IDEA because no IEP was in place for Jacob on the first day of first grade. They also argued that the private Monarch School should be designated as the stay put school pending resolution of this new complaint. On September 20, 2004, the IHO ruled that the public school was the stay put school during the pendency of the case. On the same day, the school district convened an IEP meeting, which the parents did not attend, to write an IEP for Jacob for first grade. That IEP specified that Jacob would be educated at the public school, not the Monarch School.

Faced with three decisions failing to designate the Monarch School as the stay put school, the Winkelmans decided to home school Jacob for first grade. They also asked Judge Aldrich to reconsider her decision that the public school be the stay put school. Because of a personal issue, Judge Aldrich recused herself from the case, but a new federal judge ruled in December 2004 that Judge Aldrich's decision was correct. Thus, four decisions had now determined that the Monarch School was not Jacob's stay put school pending the outcome of litigation.

The stress on Jacob's family was enormous. They were trying to appeal the adverse kindergarten decision, pursue a new complaint regarding first grade, and home school Jacob. Despite their efforts, Jacob was regressing while being home schooled.

On June 2, 2005, at the end of first grade, the Winkelmans learned that they had lost in federal court on the merits with regard to Jacob's kindergarten IEP.[8] Because Jacob had engaged in a "great deal of regression"[9] during a year of home schooling, his parents were determined to have him educated at the Monarch School. Jacob was described as "impulsive with a high activity level, sometimes oppositional and defiant, and . . . flopped on the floor if he refuses to do something."[10] On one occasion, he needed to be restrained because of the potential risk of injury to himself.[11] Jacob's doctors stated in their medical reports that in their "strong opinion" Jacob would need to be "institutionalized" or "placed outside the home" if he did not receive what they considered "medically necessary services" that could be provided only at the highly intensive program offered at the Monarch School.[12]

Still proceeding without an attorney, the Winkelmans pursued an appeal to the Sixth Circuit regarding Jacob's placement in kindergarten, but no decision had been rendered by the time second grade was ready to begin. The school district devised a new IEP on August 18, 2005, that again designated the public school as Jacob's educational placement. The school district's lawyer attended this meeting even though legal counsel did not represent the Winkelmans. The meeting became quite heated, and the Winkelmans refused to sign the IEP.

At this point, matters became confusing for all parties. Second grade was scheduled to begin on August 23, 2005, and the school district was not sure if it could implement an IEP without the parents' consent. The Winkelmans were strained financially and were not sure they could obtain sufficient scholarship assistance to send Jacob back to the Monarch School. They were still handling all the legal matters without assistance of counsel. Tuition was now $62,000 for the Monarch School. Jacob's parents decided that they should let the school district pick up Jacob on August 23 and be responsible for his education. The school district, however, did not schedule transportation for Jacob on that date as a result of its own confusion about the status of Jacob's IEP. When no transportation arrived, Jacob's mother decided to take Jacob back to the Monarch School, where she arranged a tuition agreement while they pursued scholarships for Jacob. On August 26, 2005, the Winkelmans filed another due process complaint, alleging that the school district did not have a valid IEP in place when Jacob started second grade.

The school district responded to the Winkelmans' complaint concerning second grade by arguing that the complaint did not meet the "sufficiency" requirements that Congress had added to the IDEA in 2004. A complaint could be deemed "insufficient" if it did not meet highly specific pleading requirements. An IHO ruled in favor of the school district, finding that the complaint was insufficient, but allowed the Winkelmans to re-file their complaint. (As we will see below, school districts frequently argue that complaints are "insufficient" and get them dismissed without a hearing officer's ever considering the merits.) The Winkelmans filed a new complaint on September 9, 2005, which the school district again challenged as legally insufficient. The IHO, however, ruled that the new complaint was mostly sufficient, allowing the case to go forward.[13] At this time, the Winkelmans had two due process complaints pending in Ohio—one for the 2004–5 school year (first grade) and one for the 2005–6 school year (second grade). Meanwhile, their kindergarten case was still pending on appeal in the Sixth Circuit.

Shortly after the beginning of second grade, on September 20, 2005, they learned that they had lost their kindergarten case before the Sixth Circuit Court of Appeals on the technical ground that parents are not allowed to bring cases *pro se* on behalf of their children.[14] The Sixth Circuit did not reach a decision on the merits as a result of this procedural error on their part. The result was that the adverse district court decision was the binding legal decision with regard to the validity of the kindergarten IEP. In order to have an opportunity to overturn that decision, they needed to appeal the adverse Sixth Circuit decision to the U.S. Supreme Court. If the Supreme Court ruled in their favor on the procedural issue, then they could seek resolution of the substantive decision on remand to the Sixth Circuit.

The Winkelmans' legal problems had therefore greatly increased in complexity. The only way they could get a decision on the merits from the Sixth Circuit on their kindergarten case was if the Supreme Court reversed the Sixth Circuit's decision that parents could not appear *pro se* in an IDEA case. In that event, they could return to the Sixth Circuit for a decision on the merits regarding the kindergarten IEP. They also needed to continue to pursue their administrative cases involving first and second grades. They could also anticipate challenging an IEP for third grade. They faced these legal battles amidst the challenges of raising four children, two of whom were autistic.

Because of the publicity that ensued when they lost in the Sixth Circuit on procedural grounds, they began to receive offers of free legal assistance. Two teams of lawyers began to take over the work they had been attempting to do on their own. The first team worked on their challenges to the new IEPs. The second team worked on their appeal of the Sixth Circuit's decision to the Supreme Court. Ironically, the publicity regarding their failed attempt to proceed *pro se* in the Sixth Circuit resulted in free legal assistance so that they would not have to proceed *pro se* in the future, irrespective of how the

Supreme Court resolved the question of whether they were entitled to proceed on a *pro se* basis.

At the end of second grade, the school district again developed an IEP that placed Jacob in the public schools for third grade. On June 6, 2006, the Winkelmans filed another due process complaint. Mediation was unsuccessful, but they now had the assistance of legal counsel. Once again, they filed a motion for the Monarch School to be designated the stay put school during the pendency of the litigation and lost that motion.

On December 1, 2006, before the prior cases were resolved, the Winkelmans also filed a due process complaint alleging that the recently devised 2006–7 IEP was inappropriate. A new issue they emphasized in the December 2006 complaint was that Jacob would need a transition plan if he were to move from the private school to the public school. With the assistance of counsel, they had begun to pursue the administrative complaints much more aggressively and pressed the importance of an appropriate transition plan.

On March 30, 2007, during the spring of Jacob's third-grade year, the IHO ruled on the complaints regarding the 2004–5 (first-grade) and 2005–6 (second-grade) school years.[15] In a seventy-one-page opinion, he found that the school district was responsible for nine days of tuition and transportation because of the confusion at the beginning of the 2005–6 school year about the implementation of the IEP. Otherwise, he concluded that the school district had offered Jacob an adequate education. The school district appealed that decision and the SLRO ruled in September 2007[16] that the school district was responsible for only one day of tuition and transportation.

In a separate sixty-page opinion, another IHO ruled for the school district regarding the December 2006 complaint.[17] He ruled that a school district does not have the legal responsibility to put a plan in place for the sole purpose of transitioning a student from private school to public school. This decision was affirmed by an SLRO on June 28, 2007.[18] Thus, by the beginning of Jacob's fourth-grade year, the Winklemans had not attained any significant victories in the administrative process despite the assistance of counsel. The kindergarten, first-grade, second-grade, and third-grade IEPs had all been found to be legally adequate. The hearing officer also rejected the argument that, after several years at the private school, Jacob would regress tremendously if he transferred from the private school to the public school unless he received extensive support to make that transition successful. Because parents can file a new IEP challenge each year, based on current circumstances, the Winkelmans tried to insist that the hearing officer consider how Jacob's needs had changed as a result of his having spent so many years in a private school. That argument was unsuccessful at that time.

Meanwhile, Jean-Claude André, a California lawyer, was taking their kindergarten case to the U.S. Supreme Court on a pro bono basis. André successfully argued to the Supreme Court that parents should be allowed to bring IDEA cases on a *pro se* basis because the parents' rights are also being vindicated in such matters through tuition reimbursement.[19] Even though it is true that parents are not allowed to represent their *children* on a *pro se* basis, the Supreme Court recognized that a claim for tuition reimbursement is also a claim of the *parents* themselves. Thus, the Court held that parents could pursue tuition reimbursement cases without assistance of legal counsel (on a pro se basis). This decision was rendered on May 21, 2007, amidst the unfavorable administrative law decisions on the subsequent IEPs, near the end of third grade.

This Supreme Court decision, however, was only a procedural victory about the right of parents to proceed *pro se*. The Winkelmans still needed to convince the Sixth Circuit to rule for them on the merits with regard to the kindergarten IEP. Given that they had already lost at two levels of administrative hearings regarding the kindergarten IEP as well as in the district court, the odds were slim that they could prevail on an appeal of the original administrative law decision. When the case returned to the Sixth Circuit for a decision on the merits (this time with the Winkelmans having the assistance of legal counsel), the Sixth Circuit rendered a decision on October 2, 2008, that affirmed the original district court's decision from 2005.[20] Hence, in the fall of Jacob's fourth-grade year, the Sixth Circuit decisively determined that the kindergarten IEP was valid.

Nonetheless, the Winkelmans persevered; they were entitled to challenge the proposed IEP on a yearly basis. On June 6, 2007, the school district prepared an IEP that established the public school as Jacob's IEP for fourth grade. Once again, the Winkelmans challenged this IEP with a due process complaint. They brought in national experts to argue that Jacob would need an elaborate transition plan to move from the private school to the public school because he had by this point been in the private school for more than five years. His needs had also changed as he began to approach puberty. As a ten-year-old, he was 5 feet 2 inches tall and weighed more than 200 pounds. Jacob had also threatened to kill himself if he could not return to Monarch.[21] Although Jacob's behavior was good at the private school, it was reasonable to expect that significant assistance would be needed for him to transition successfully to a larger and more chaotic environment at the public school, especially because he had been diagnosed with an oppositional defiance disorder.

On March 7, 2008, an IHO issued a 210-page opinion[22] in which he concluded that the school district had offered Jacob an adequate IEP, but he also found that the transition plan was legally insufficient. The key factor after weeks of hearings was the testimony of Angela Kress, an aide in the Parma City school district. Kress was assigned to be the one-on-one assistant/aide on Jacob's first day at the public school. By now, Jacob had been diagnosed as having an oppositional defiance disorder in addition to autism and, as noted, weighed more than 200 pounds. Nonetheless, Kress had received no special training for providing services to Jacob. She was a high school graduate who had attended a two-day autism workshop several years earlier and testified that she could not recall the content of the workshop and did not know the characteristics of an autism disorder. Although Jacob was supposed to receive social skills reinforcement and practice with the aide, she testified that she had no training in sensory integration or a sensory diet and did not know what those terms meant. When asked how she would have helped Jacob on the first day of school, she testified, "I don't know. I was never told anything about [the student], so I don't know." When asked if she was prepared to be Jacob's aide tomorrow if he were to start school, she said, "No."[23] In light of such testimony, the hearing officer could not possibly rule that the transition plan to the public school was "adequate," even though he had otherwise concluded that the IEP was adequate.

The school district did not lose before the IHO because its various IEPs were ever found inadequate. It did not lose because of the team of national experts that testified on behalf of the Winkelmans. It lost because it did not put in place a proper transition plan to transfer a child from a highly structured private setting to a public setting. Had the school district properly trained Kress to handle Jacob's transition, it is unlikely that the Winkelmans would have prevailed, even with the assistance of two highly skilled teams of lawyers and many experts.

In August 2008, an SLRO affirmed the IHO's opinion.[24] The hearing officer ordered the school district to cover the $68,500 Monarch School tuition for the 2007–8 school year. A federal court later awarded more than $174,000 in attorney fees to the Winkelmans. According to Jacob's mother, the public school agreed to continue to pay Jacob's tuition at the Monarch School after the 2008 decision.

Following these decisions, Jacob's mother, Sandee Winkelman, has made a career of advising parents how to deal with school districts if they believe the education being proposed for their child is inadequate. She advises parents that they must (1) take their role seriously, (2) be fully prepared before attending meetings, (3) assert themselves, (4) start as early as possible in advocating for their children, and (5) pay for full independent evaluations at least three times in their children's schooling. If they conclude that litigation is necessary, they should expect devoting time and resources to the due process hearing to become a full-time job.

Even if one follows that advice, the *Winkleman* case reflects how difficult it is for parents to prevail under the IDEA. So long as the school district had an IEP in place, not even a team of experts could persuade the hearing officers of its manifest inadequacy. Their only other option—which the Winkelmans had tried when Jacob was three years old—was to allow him to attend the public program and wait for him to fail. They were understandably reluctant to go that route. Instead, they kept pouncing on every technical error by the school district—failing to have transportation for Jacob's first day of second grade, allowing the school district's lawyer to attend an IEP meeting, and hiring an inexperienced aide to handle Jacob's transition to public school in fourth grade. That strategy of pure doggedness finally succeeded.

One might wonder why the school district kept fighting the Winkelmans, because the litigation costs were higher than the cost of Jacob's private school tuition. One explanation may be that the school district chose not to capitulate to Jacob's parents because their lawyers advised them that their legal position was correct. Under existing Supreme Court precedent (the *Rowley* decision[25]), they were entitled to insist that Jacob attend the public school program so long as it was "adequate." And no court ever concluded that their IEPs were not adequate. The school district's position was the legally correct position. Unless Jacob returned to the public schools and regressed, the school district was entitled to argue that the IEPs it proposed were adequate. The school district lost only when it hired an inexperienced aide and failed to develop a proper transition plan that could plausibly be effective for a severely autistic child with behavioral issues who had been attending a highly structured private school for five years. Few parents have the doggedness to persevere for enough years to make that sophisticated legal argument even possible.

* * *

The Winkelman case represents one family's attempt to survive the hearing officer process and obtain an adequate education for their son. This chapter and the following four chapters will survey the hundreds of stories that can be gleaned from hearing officer decisions. Most of these parents did not have the resources of the Winkelmans. According to the IDEA, parents are supposed to be able to navigate this process on their own and prevail under an informal system of litigation. The state administrative process is supposed to help resolve disputes for the benefit of children. Parents are often too intimidated by this highly complex process to pursue it. Even if they do, and even if they eventually prevail, long delays typically still deprive their children of an adequate education. Although some children may benefit from the stay put rules during these proceedings, most children experience wholly inadequate educational plans while this process unfolds. Unlike Jacob, they do not have two teams of lawyers arguing for their rights.

* * *

As explained at the beginning of this chapter, Ohio has a two-level administrative process for due process complaints. The first stage is before an independent hearing officer (IHO) and the second stage is before a state-level review officer (SLRO). Only after exhausting these two stages can a party appeal a decision to state or federal court.

Ohio special education cases include sufficiency determinations and due process decisions decided by IHOs, state-level review determinations decided by SLROs, and state and federal court cases decided by judges. Unlike the other states investigated, the investigation of Ohio was from a slightly earlier time period—2002 through 2006—because this work was done at the beginning of this research project. The Ohio cases, like those of other states, reflect that parents were unlikely to win special education cases when they proceeded on the merits. And, like Florida, which will be discussed in chapter 9, and California, which will be discussed in chapter 11, parents of children with autism brought a disproportionate number of cases.

Thirty-five cases in this database are sufficiency determinations—the hearing officer was resolving a claim by the school district that the parent's due process complaint did not meet "sufficiency" standards with regard to the required specificity for a complaint. (That was one of the arguments made in the Winkelmans' case by the school district.) Parents won fifteen of these thirty-five (42.8 percent) sufficiency determinations. Unlike in Jacob Winkelman's case, parents who lost these cases did not amend their complaints and re-file; instead, this decision was the end of the process for them. Prevailing in a sufficiency determination is a limited victory for parents—it simply means that they can file a due process complaint. All the parents who lost were proceeding on a *pro se* basis. These cases reflect that parents without legal counsel can find it difficult to meet the technical requirements of filing a due process complaint. Several complaints were dismissed for small matters like failing to include the child's residence address. Although sufficiency determinations happen in every state, Ohio was the only state in which my survey of decisions included that kind of matter.

Fifty-five cases in this database are first-level hearing officer decisions. Parents won eighteen of these fifty-five (32.7 percent) cases. Thirty-one cases reflect appeals to SLROs. Parents prevailed in eight of these thirty-one (25.8 percent) cases. There are also nine court challenges (that are appeals from the SLRO decision through the state or federal court systems). Parents prevailed in two of these nine (22.2 percent) cases. Because of the further appeals that took place, not all the parents who prevailed at the first level of hearing officer decision ultimately prevailed. For example, in *Kings Local School District v. Zalazny*[26] the parents won a case before both the IHO and the SLRO but lost at both the district court and court of appeals levels. Both federal courts concluded that the education offered by the school system was adequate and the procedural errors did not cause substantive harm, thereby overturning decisions that would have made the local school district responsible for the child's placement at a private school. Similarly, a mother who was proceeding on a *pro se* basis prevailed before a hearing officer in a case against the Northwest Local School District.[27] The mother was challenging the school district's decision to declassify her daughter, Amanda,[28] as disabled under the IDEA. The hearing officer found in the mother's favor, but that decision was overturned by the SLRO, who concluded that the mother's witnesses, who did not appear in person and who were not necessarily knowledgeable about the IDEA's legal standards for a disability classification, were less persuasive than the school district's witnesses. The mother could not meet her burden of proof without assistance of legal counsel or medical experts. The strongest evidence of an adverse educational impact was Amanda's recent high rate of absenteeism. Absenteeism is often related to depression and can predictably have an adverse impact on educational performance. But the mother did not make those causal connections through testimony and, thus, the SLRO ruled in favor of the school district.

In one of two cases in which the parents prevailed in federal court, they merely persuaded the judge to defer to the hearing officer's decision that a student with leukemia meets the definition of "other health impairment."[29] The other case involved highly complex procedural matters that wound through the courts for several years after the parents refused to comply with the school's request for medical records for a child with a specific learning disability and the school district tried to make a unilateral change in their child's IEP.[30] There were no cases in which a parent persuaded a federal or state court to reverse an adverse hearing officer decision on the merits.

Unlike the other states reviewed, many Ohio parents experienced difficulty having their children declared eligible for special education services. In other states, parents were more likely to challenge the adequacy of the IEP or whether it was being implemented. When Ohio parents successfully raised procedural violations, the harm was often found to be insignificant, so no remedy was ordered. Thus, the victory was not meaningful.

Several of the Ohio cases reflect how difficult it is for a parent to proceed on a *pro se* basis and attain the required burden of proof. In another case, against the Northwest Local Schools,[31] the school district had completed two evaluations in which they concluded that a child did not qualify as an individual with a disability under the IDEA. The mother did not at the time file a due process complaint against those evaluations. Several years later, when her son was in high school, she filed a due process complaint. The hearing officer was quite frustrated with how the mother handled the complaint because she was vague in her allegations and did not understand how to submit evidence. The hearing officer presumed that the mother wanted to allege her son was not receiving an appropriate IEP, but in order to do that, the mother would have to first establish that her son was eligible for an IEP as a child with a disability. The mother did not understand how to establish eligibility in order to make that argument.

Establishing that a child is eligible for special education services is not a simple matter under the IDEA because the parent has to establish that the child has a disability *and* that the disability produces an adverse educational impact. In this case, the mother was able to demonstrate that her son had various disabilities—asthma, vision problems, thyroid condition, depression, and possibly a sleep disorder. But the mother appears not to have understood that she also needed to demonstrate that these conditions produced an adverse educational effect. The lengthy hearing officer opinion does not mention any test scores or grades to reflect whether the child was having difficulty attaining grade-level performance, although there is some reference to difficulties with statewide proficiency exams. Because the parent had the burden of proof on establishing that her child should be classified as disabled, the lack of evidence meant that the parent could not prevail. The mother appeared to be unable to interpret standardized scores and had not known how to use the available resources to gain that knowledge. Hence, the burden of proof was insurmountable.

As in many *pro se* cases, the hearing officer noted that the mother proceeded without legal counsel and tried to assist her child, but could not meet the required burden of proof. The case record did not disclose the race or class background of the parent, but she was a single mother who did not have the financial resources to pay a medical expert to testify at the due process hearing. She used a one-paragraph letter from her child's doctor as her only proof about her son's medical condition. The hearing officer bent over backward to assist the mother by repeatedly extending deadlines, inferring claims that were not made precisely, and allowing informal evidence to be used as proof. The hearing officer even went outside the complaint to order the school district to conduct a new multi-factor evaluation of the child despite the fact that the lack of a recent evaluation was not part of the mother's complaint. But the hearing officer was bound by the law and could not conclude that the mother had met her burden of proof on the question of whether her son, who had never been classified as disabled, had an adequate IEP.

In sum, it is nearly impossible for parents to prevail in Ohio without the assistance of highly sophisticated legal counsel. The two-step administrative process simply reflects additional hurdles for parents who want to seek a remedy in state or federal court. Highly technical requirements for filing a complaint combined with a high burden of proof mean that few parents prevail. The Winkelmans may have been unusual with respect to the amount of resources they used to bring five due process complaints, but, unfortunately, parents seem to need the Winkelmans' high level of doggedness to prevail. Requiring parents to have superhuman doggedness and extensive legal assistance, like the Winkelmans, imposes unreasonable barriers on parents intent on ensuring that their disabled children are provided with effective educations.

9

Florida

As one of the nation's largest states, and a state with a diverse population, Florida was an important jurisdiction in which to examine due process hearings. Florida also has an unusually small number of due process decisions, suggesting perhaps that it has a pro-child educational system in which numerous due process decisions are unnecessary. The results from Florida's due process hearings suggest otherwise.

Before looking at the overall results from Florida, it will be helpful to examine two stories—that of a boy whom I will call Johnny and that of Derek Hughes. Johnny's case reflects the lack of assistance to parents who are proceeding *pro se* even when they are unable to participate meaningfully in the process because of other stresses in their lives. Johnny's case (with its adverse outcome for a child with behavioral issues) is similar to that of Marilyn's son from chapter 1. The Hughes case reflects the continuing difficulty of arguing that a school district's IEP is inadequate under the *Rowley* standard despite the 2004 amendments to the IDEA. Like Amy Rowley's, Derek's parents had to move to a new school district in order for him to receive an adequate education. But the challenges faced by many families are far larger than the assigning of the burden of proof. The school district had the burden of proof in Johnny's case and no difficulty prevailing.

* * *

Johnny was a first-grade student eligible for special education who had been classified as having autism spectrum disorder and language impairments.[1] He was also eligible for occupational therapy. He began kindergarten in the Broward County school system in 2008 and was assigned to Mary Whalen's classroom. Whalen teaches in a self-contained classroom for students with autism spectrum disorder who have what are described as "more complex needs." Christine Orlando, an autism coach, and J. Mehlman, a speech-language pathologist, assisted her in the classroom for part of the day.

Because of behavioral issues that were interfering with Johnny's ability to learn, the school district prepared a functional behavior assessment (FBA) for him in preschool, kindergarten, and first grade. Marian Klinger was the leader of the team that developed the FBA, including the first-grade FBA. In first grade, Johnny's behavior was described as: kicking objects/people, throwing objects, screaming/crying, pulling adults' hair, attempting to bite, dropping to the ground, hiding under furniture, and running away from an assigned area. Klinger developed a daily data collection form in the fall of first grade and asked Whalen to record Johnny's behavior and how he responded to various kinds of sensory stimulation that was sought to decrease his negative behavior. The data sheets were shared with Johnny's parents; they were asked to provide input from Johnny's private behavior analyst but they never provided that input.

The collected data reflected that Johnny engaged in tantrum/aggressive behaviors three to six times per day that could last from fifteen minutes to three hours. Avoidance behaviors occurred from two to ten times per day and could last from five to thirty minutes. Following this data collection and various interviews with relevant people, the school district developed a behavioral intervention plan.

On March 24, 2010, Johnny's mother stated at an IEP meeting that she was not in agreement with the behavior plan and wanted an independent evaluation. Klinger was present at that meeting but did not communicate that request to the school district. It also appears that she did not explain to Johnny's mother that she was entitled to file a due process complaint in order to challenge the content of the IEP and the behavior intervention plan. Johnny's mother repeated her disapproval of the evaluation and behavior plan in an e-mail sent to Klinger on May 12, 2010.

In response to the May 12 e-mail, the school district sent two follow-up e-mails to Johnny's mother asking her to clarify whether she was requesting an independent FBA at public expense. Johnny's mother wrote a reply in which she was sharply critical of the school district's evaluation and its behavioral intervention plan, questioning Klinger's qualifications to devise a plan. She criticized Klinger as someone who "is not capable of writing a behavior plan that is not an environmental control plan. . . . This is why I want a professional who knows how to do an FBA and develop a [behavioral intervention plan]."[2] She described the intervention plan as only an environmental control plan rather than a behavioral intervention plan because it sought to change Johnny's environment rather than teach him to modify his behavior. She alleged that the school district abused Johnny instead of providing him with a behavioral plan that used an applied behavior action (ABA) plan to address his behaviors that stem from his autism. ABA is a well-recognized teaching technique for children with autism. It uses a proactive, constructive educational approach rather than a punitive approach when dealing with disruptive or even destructive behaviors associated with autism. Johnny's mother further claimed that the school district was refusing ABA to all children with autism. She was clearly upset with both the evaluation and the behavioral plan that had been developed by the school district.

When the school district received her response, it had two choices. It could agree to pay for an independent evaluation or it could deny that request and file a motion for a due process hearing to defend its decision. If it filed a motion for a due process hearing, it had the burden of proof to demonstrate that its evaluation was appropriate and adequate. The only issue at the due process hearing would be the adequacy of the school district's evaluation; the merits of the behavioral plan itself would not be an issue. The only way for the merits of the behavioral plan to be at issue would be if Johnny's mother filed a due process complaint herself.

The school district decided to defend its evaluation rather than agree to pay for independent professionals to conduct their own evaluation of Johnny. It filed a request for a due process hearing on June 10, 2010, nearly three months after Johnny's mother had first noted her objection to the evaluation and the behavioral plan. The school district decided to hire a lawyer to conduct a several-days due process hearing rather than accede to the mother's request and gather additional information for a child who the school district's own data showed was having great difficulty in school. It chose a contentious rather than a cooperative response.

It is important to note that this kind of issue arises disproportionately for poor parents who cannot afford to hire experts to conduct their own evaluation. The Rowleys, the Winkelmans, and many of the middle-class families discussed in this book were able to use a team of experts to assist them on their cases, but they often needed reduced-fee or donated services in order to pursue their cases effectively. Johnny's mother had virtually no available resources to gather independent information. Johnny was seeing a private therapist, but it is unlikely that Johnny's mother had the resources to hire that person to create a school-based behavioral intervention plan. Further, that person might not have had the expertise to create such a plan. Johnny's mother was seeking an independent evaluation so that qualified individuals not employed by the school district could make professionally appropriate recommendations. Without that information, Johnny's mother could not successfully bring a due process complaint to challenge the behavioral plan itself.

Like the case brought by Marilyn in Ohio, discussed in chapter 1, Johnny's mother was not able to successfully navigate the due process hearing rules. Even though it was clear from Johnny's mother's e-mails that she also objected to the behavioral intervention plan, she was never assisted in filing a due process complaint to challenge that plan. She clearly thought that issue would be considered at the due process hearing requested by the school district, but she would soon learn that that was not the case.

The due process hearing was supposed to begin on June 25, 2010. Ten days before the hearing was to occur, the school district requested a continuance because some of its staff could not attend the June 25 hearing. The hearing was rescheduled for July 13, 2010—nearly four months after Johnny's mother had initially requested an independent evaluation.

Not only did the school district request a continuance, but it also asked the hearing officer to rule in its favor on requests being made by Johnny's mother regarding the preparation for the hearing. It objected to her requests that the school district provide her documents to the hearing officer, that the school district provide her with a free electronic transcript in Microsoft Word format at the end of the hearing, and that the hearing also include the issue of the appropriateness of the behavioral intervention plan. Johnny's mother did not respond to these arguments by the school district, and, on June 25, 2010, the hearing officer granted the first and third requests and deferred resolution of the second objection until the hearing. The hearing officer offered no basis for his second ruling; the IDEA specifies that the school district is responsible for providing the hearing officer transcript to the parent.

Rather than reply to the school district's objections in a timely manner before the hearing officer, Johnny's mother filed a complaint in federal court and sent a copy of the appeal to the hearing officer on July 1, 2010. In the complaint, she asserted that the school district did not "take her" to due process within forty-five days of her request for an independent evaluation, that the hearing officer should not have granted the school district's request for an extension, that the hearing officer should have granted her request for a free post-hearing transcript, that the hearing officer should not require her to file a due process complaint to challenge the behavioral intervention plan, and that the school district's due process complaint was frivolous. This was a highly irregular and ineffective way for her to register her disagreement with the hearing officer and the school district. She simply did not understand how to follow the Florida administrative process to object to a behavioral plan and other matters.

After her federal court strategy failed to produce any results, Johnny's mother filed a motion to dismiss the due process complaint on July 12, 2010, on the grounds that the school district had not proceeded in a timely manner. The hearing officer denied that request and began the hearing on July 13, 2010. The hearing was not completed on that day and was continued on July 29, 2010. On July 23, 2010, Johnny's mother requested a continuance for the July 29 hearing because she could not attend the hearing for unspecified reasons. The hearing was then scheduled for August 23, 2010, and, if necessary, August 25, 2010. The hearing ended early on August 23 because Johnny's mother had an appointment to speak with a surgeon treating one of her children. Shortly before the due process hearing was to resume on August 25, the hearing officer was told that Johnny's mother could not attend the hearing because of her own medical emergency. She had been taken to an emergency room, was being "closely monitored" by doctors, and would take "several days to recover."[3] The hearing was continued on September 15, 2010, although Johnny's mother had notified the school district by e-mail on August 30, 2010, that she would no longer be participating in the due process hearing. The hearing resumed on September 15 with no one representing Johnny. The school district, but not Johnny's mother, filed a post-hearing brief. Johnny's mother introduced no exhibits. She also does not appear to have testified or offered testimony from any of her own witnesses.

In light of the fact that Johnny's mother never offered a response to the school district's case and misunderstood that the hearing was limited to the question of the appropriateness of the evaluation, it is not surprising that the hearing officer ruled in the school district's favor. Clearly, Johnny's mother could not adequately handle the complicated nature of the due process hearing along with the stresses of her life. Her real objection—that Johnny was receiving an environmental plan rather than learning positive behavior through applied behavioral therapy—was never addressed. Johnny was only in first grade at the time of this failed process, and his prognosis looked poor. He was certainly not one of the middle-class children whose parents convince a court that the school district must provide them with private instruction at a facility that specializes in applied behavioral intervention. Consider how much better his prognosis might have been if he had had Sandee Winkelman (chapter 8) acting as his parent-advocate. As Johnny's case reflects, it is simply not realistic that a parent can properly represent a child when she is acting as an advocate on her own while trying to deal with other challenging issues in her life.

Johnny's case also reflects the fact that we also cannot rely on school districts to act cooperatively when faced with poor parents who are having trouble navigating the special education system. The school district chose to go to a due process hearing rather than provide an independent evaluation of Johnny. As many cases involving middle-class parents reflect when they pay for their own outside evaluations, the IEP team very much benefits from such outside evaluations. Johnny clearly presented quite significant educational challenges for the school district. Using experts beyond their in-house staff would likely have yielded important, additional information. The IDEA, however, does not require the school district to pay for an independent evaluation if its own evaluation is minimally adequate. The school district had the option of refusing to pay for an outside evaluation and defend its decision by taking Johnny's mother to a due process hearing where it could easily win in light of the difficult issues raised at such a hearing. Johnny's mother misunderstood the scope of the issues before the hearing officer, did not know how to submit exhibits, had no experts who could testify on her son's behalf, and, ultimately, could not even attend the hearing. Having the burden of proof was really not a "burden" for the school district. It is unconscionable that Johnny's education could be determined through such an unbalanced process.

* * *

Derek Hughes was a child with autism and a seizure disorder who attended school within the Collier County School District from September 2001 to January 2006.[4] Derek was also speech-language impaired and used sign language as his primary mode of expression.

Derek's parents participated in an IEP meeting with the school district on December 13, 2005, and January 17, 2006. They also held a section 504 conference with the school district on February 3, 2006. Because Derek had begun to have seizures and was making poor educational progress, his medical and educational experts had made several important recommendations about his education: that he should have a sign language interpreter in class, that a nurse should be available to give him anti-seizure medicine rectally, and that he should have access to his service dog, Bo, who was able to offer him comfort and help him avoid seizures. Without these procedures, his parents believed, he could not safely attend school and benefit from an education.

Following the January 17 IEP meeting, Derek's parents filed a due process complaint with the state. Although a hearing is supposed to take place within forty-five days, the district repeatedly asked for delays. A fourteen-day due process hearing began on May 1, 2006, and ended on June 22, 2006. The transcript of this hearing consisted of fifteen volumes.

Concerned about Derek's safety, his parents took him out of public school on January 17 and did not enroll him in school at all. In the fall, they moved to Chester County, Pennsylvania, where they enrolled their son in a public school that provided him with each of his needed services without recourse to litigation. Because Derek's family had moved, the hearing officer in their previous school district ruled that their Florida complaint was moot.

Derek's parents appealed the hearing officer's decision to federal court. The court ruled that Derek's case was not moot and that the hearing officer did need to rule on the merits because they might be entitled to some reimbursement for expenses. A remanded decision was not rendered until September 15, 2009. The hearing officer ruled against Derek on all issues. With respect to the service animal, he concluded that the school district was allowed to choose a "human severity aide" rather than a service animal because "a choice of methodologies is the exclusive province of the District."[5] Although a child neurologist had testified that Derek's anti-seizure medicine needed to be administered rectally by a registered nurse, the hearing officer concluded that the principal and assistant principal had received sufficient training to administer the medicine. Because the risk of status epilepticus (a life-threatening condition in which the brain is in a state of persistent seizure) if Derek did not receive medication quickly was "very unlikely," this choice was found acceptable. As to the sign language interpreter, because Derek had made "educational progress" without one, the hearing officer found that the school district was not required to provide one. "Decisions concerning methodology and staffing are the exclusive province of [the school district]."[6] Citing the *Rowley* decision, the hearing officer found that the IDEA requires only a "basic floor of opportunity."[7] Hence, it was acceptable for a child not to have access to his primary mode of communication and be in an environment in which seizures were likely (without the service dog) and the appropriate medical personnel were not available in the event of a seizure.

Derek's family would not give up. They appealed (for the second time) the hearing officer's decision to a federal court. In April 2010, the school district finally reached a settlement with the family under which the district agreed to pay them $125,000. Not only had the school district been found to have violated the IDEA (under which families cannot obtain damages), but it had been found to have violated the Americans with Disabilities Act and section 504 of the Rehabilitation Act, under which damages are sometimes available.

Derek was a fortunate boy in that his family was willing to move to a new community in order to attain for him the services he needed for a safe and adequate public education. And we might hope that his parents' persistence will cause the school district to reconsider its position for other children. But the underlying story is a school district and hearing officer that had a very narrow understanding of what is an "adequate" education under the IDEA. The burden of proof for parents, as we will see shortly, is nearly insurmountable in Florida. Parents like Johnny's mother lose through procedural/technical issues; parents like Derek's parents lose through bad substantive decisions.

Hearing Officer Decisions

My goal for each state was to analyze at least one hundred decisions over the past couple of years. Because some states, like Florida, have a low level of due process hearings, I was not always able to attain that goal. In Florida, my research assistants were able to locate only thirty-three decisions decided between January 2, 2009, and June 30, 2011.

Even though the data set was relatively small, the Florida cases do offer some important insights into the due process experience. The rate of success by parents was low—five of thirty-three (15.1 percent). Two of five parents who prevailed proceeded with an attorney and two proceeded with a non-attorney advocate. The only parent who prevailed who did not have an attorney or an advocate was a social worker who seemed to have some expertise in special education matters. Of the thirty-three parents, fourteen had attorneys (42.4 percent) and three had non-attorney advocates (9.1 percent) so, overall, seventeen of thirty-three parents (51.5 percent) had professional assistance. Although the numbers are too small to make statistical analysis meaningful, the rate of success for cases in which parents had non-attorney advocates (two of three) is even better than the rate for cases in which parents had lawyers (two of fourteen). This could be attributable to the high skill level of one non-attorney advocate. Lilliam Rangel-Diaz, a non-attorney advocate, brought forward two of the successful claims. President Bill Clinton appointed her to a seven-year term on the National Council on Disability and Governor Jeb Bush appointed her to the Florida Developmental Disabilities Council and the State of Florida Independent Living Council.

Hence, she would appear to be an exceptional advocate. Her company also prevailed in other cases that preceded the time period of this investigation.

In Florida, like many other states, the range of disabilities reflected in hearing officer decisions is not reflective of the overall pattern of disabilities within the population. Although only 4 percent of children in the state are classified as having autism, that disability classification reflected half of the due process complaints. Nationally, children are more likely to be classified as autistic (rather than as emotionally disturbed) if they are white and middle class. Thus, parents of these children are disproportionately likely to have the financial resources to bring a due process complaint.

Two themes emerge from the Florida cases. First, it is very difficult for parents to attain any relief for what are described as "procedural violations." Second, even when parents do convince hearing officers that a substantive violation has occurred, the remedies that are imposed are often inadequate.

Procedural Violations

A parent can rarely demonstrate that procedural violations resulted in a denial of a FAPE even when those violations were quite significant. A case against the Duval County School Board demonstrates that a hearing officer is unlikely to order relief despite evidence of numerous procedural violations.[8]

The student in this case, whom I will call Charlie, had been on an IEP since third grade, when he suffered a stroke and heart attack during a medical procedure to repair a heart valve. At the time of the hearing, Charlie was in the eighth grade. Despite numerous procedural errors on the part of the school district, the hearing officer concluded that no relief was appropriate.

Charlie was scheduled to have a new IEP on April 7, 2007, but, on that day, his special education teacher was in a motor vehicle accident and missed the rest of the school year. The school had waited until the last minute to write an IEP and had no draft in place that it could implement without the participation of the special education teacher. Without notice, the school decided to hold an IEP meeting on May 25, 2007, and contacted Charlie's parent to attend the meeting that very day. The parent could not get time off work to attend and the meeting took place anyway.

The IEP was procedurally invalid because it had only two signatures (not including that of a special education teacher or a parent) and did not include accommodations set forth in the prior IEP. Charlie's parent was not given a copy of the IEP and did not learn of its existence until August 16, 2007, when a meeting was scheduled to revise the IEP. The IEP was not revised until September 26, 2007. It was revised further on October 17, 2007.

As of September 14, 2007, Charlie had B grades in all subjects except for math, in which he had an F. When the IEP was revised in the fall of 2007, the deleted accommodations were put back in the IEP. Although the hearing officer found procedural errors, she concluded that none of them resulted in a denial of a FAPE despite Charlie's failing grade in math until accommodations were put in place.

The challenge for Charlie's parent under the IDEA is that a hearing officer may not provide relief for a procedural violation unless he or she concludes that the procedural inadequacies (1) impeded the child's right to a free and appropriate education, (2) significantly impeded the parent's opportunity to participate in the decision-making process regarding the provision of a free and appropriate public education to the parent's child, or (3) caused a deprivation of education benefits.[9]

Charlie's parent tried to demonstrate that the first or third provisions had been violated—that the procedural errors caused educational harm to Charlie. The hearing officer, however, imposed an insurmountable burden of proof on Charlie's parent to establish such proof. For example, she said:

> Petitioner's performance at the beginning of the 8th grade year was not as good as it had been at the beginning of the 7th grade year when a valid IEP was in place. It does not necessarily follow, however, that the relatively lower level of performance at the beginning of the 8th grade year was due to the lack of a timely or valid IEP being in place, or from accommodations from 7th grade to 8th grade not been carried over. It could have been that the course work overall was simply more difficult.

Of course, many explanations are *possible*. But how could a parent persuade the hearing officer of a causal relationship between a lack of a valid IEP and poor performance if that kind of evidence was insufficient?

The school district had no evidence that the existing IEP was effective or adequate in light of Charlie's declining school performance. But the hearing officer concluded that Charlie's parent could not *prove* that the lack of a valid IEP caused the declining school performance. The parent was a special education teacher and had lots of relevant expertise. The parent had also hired a lawyer. Nonetheless, vague statements by school officials were allowed to call into question whether the student's poor performance was caused by an invalid IEP. The hearing officer seems to have imposed a criminal law standard (beyond a reasonable doubt) rather than a civil law standard (preponderance of the evidence) in ruling for the school district. Thus, no remedy at all was imposed despite clear evidence of procedural violations and strong evidence that those violations caused educational harm to Charlie.

Ineffective Remedies

One highly problematic aspect of the Florida decisions is that victories by parents on behalf of their children rarely resulted in effective remedies. Two cases illustrate this problem well.

SEAN

A good example of this problem involves a child whom I will call Sean.[10] Although it is not always possible to determine the race and class of children from reading hearing officer decisions, it is fairly clear in this case that Sean was an African American child from a working-class family. His mother worked the night shift at Walmart and his father, who was absent from his life, lived in the Cayman Islands. Sean's story is typical of that of many African American boys in that his problems in school have been attributed entirely to an "emotional disturbance," he was frequently suspended, and he was given virtually no academic support until he had languished in school for about five years. Even though the hearing officer concluded that Sean had not received an appropriate education for many years, no relief was ordered because the school district had finally put in place a program that would provide academic support. But the benefits of that program were clearly too little and too late.

Sean had difficulty in school beginning in first grade. He was on an IEP for speech and language therapy beginning in kindergarten but was not receiving academic or appreciable behavioral support despite evidence of significant problems in these areas. By the end of Sean's first-grade year, the school's planning document noted that he was failing to learn, not following directions, and engaging in disruptive classroom behaviors. Although the student assistance program recommended that he be retained in first grade, he was promoted to second grade. During second grade, he spent an unspecified amount of time at the Mt. Olive Youth Motivation Program to serve an external suspension, but his IEP still did not have a behavioral modification component. It had only speech and language therapy.

Following second grade, Sean's mother took him to a psychiatrist who diagnosed Sean with ADHD and prescribed medication. The school district conducted testing and did not put a new IEP in place until December of Sean's third-grade year. As described by the hearing officer, the "IEP team seemed to pin its hopes on interventions of a medical nature to the exclusion

of interventions of an educational nature." Also, as noted by the hearing officer, this confidence in a successful medication intervention was unfounded
because Sean had already been prescribed medication for several months
with no change in his classroom behavior. Although the team concluded that
Sean would benefit from a "strong behavior management plan," it did not
prepare a behavioral intervention plan at that time. Sean was finally given
behavioral goals on the December IEP; he was not given any academic goals.
Academic goals were finally added to his IEP at the end of third grade. After
he failed the Florida Comprehensive Assessment Test for third grade, he
repeated third grade and passed the test on his second attempt.

In November of Sean's second third-grade year, a behavioral intervention
plan was finally put in place. This plan was apparently unsuccessful because
Sean was transferred to the Pine Ridge Alternative Center in February of
his second third-grade year. Six weeks after Sean transferred to Pine Ridge,
he attempted to commit suicide by hanging himself at home. Although his
mother informed the school of this fact, no planning document ever references it.

During the first quarter of fourth grade, the school district decided to
transfer Sean back to his home school. His mother was hesitant about that
placement but did not formally object to it. Despite Sean's record of behavioral and academic difficulties, the new IEP provided him with only speech
therapy and a twice-weekly consultation for socialization. His IEP continued
to list academic and behavioral goals that he did not meet, even on a partial
basis. In January of his fifth-grade year, the school district eliminated speech
therapy for Sean.

In May of fifth grade, Sean's academic performance was quite poor. He was
performing at the second- or third-grade level on most measures. Although
Sean was suspended for twelve days during fifth grade, the IEP says that he is
"able to interact appropriately with peers and adults" and "there is no impact
of the disability on this [area]." The hearing officer inferred that the school
district concluded that Sean was "able" to interact appropriately but refused
to do so. One week after this IEP was prepared, Sean threatened his mother
with a knife and she called emergency services to transport him to a psychiatric hospital. The school district was informed of this incident, but it was
never reflected in any planning documents.

During sixth grade, the school district prepared an IEP that included some
targeted specialized instruction and behavioral support. Sean was described
in the IEP as a "sweet" child even though he had been suspended for twenty
days that school year. There were no academic goals or objectives because the
planning document stated that Sean was performing at grade level. A school

social worker evaluated Sean in April of sixth grade and described him as having "major behavior problems" such as "temper tantrums, blaming and bullying others, arguing and talking back to teacher, [and] using foul language." Although the social worker recommended that Sean be transferred to another academic setting, the school district decided instead to assess him for a new behavioral intervention plan and kept him in the regular public school.

A new psychological evaluation was conducted by the school district in fall of seventh grade. Sean was described as having both ADHD and Oppositional Defiant Disorder (ODD). He was described as antagonistic, sexually assaultive, and physically threatening at school. With only brief mention of his academic performance, he was described as performing at grade level and requiring no specialized instructional services. The IEP therefore contained no academic goals at all. One day after one October IEP meeting, Sean created a disruption at school, threatened to hurt his mother, and walked out into traffic. Although no school planning document mentioned these incidents, he was soon transferred back to the alternative education setting he had attended during his second attempt at third grade.

When Sean attended the alternative middle school, his mother was working closely with a psychotherapist who also advised the school district on what techniques were effective with Sean. Sean's attendance at the alternative middle school was not a successful experience. When a staff person tried to restrain Sean at the end of the school year, Sean suffered a fractured elbow.

For eighth grade, Sean returned to a regular public school. After years of the school's insisting that Sean was performing at grade level, the school district intervention team prepared a new IEP in the fall of his eighth-grade year. The school psychologist concluded that Sean's reading level was at a third- or fourth-grade level. The IEP contained an academic objective—that he should improve his reading level to eighth grade in one year—but with no specialized instruction. Other school district tests conducted that fall produced similar results with his best performance in math, where he was found to be performing at a fifth-grade level. His written expression essentially stayed the same for five years; in eighth grade, it was measured at the 2.4 level.

Sean attended the regular public school for the fall of eighth grade and his performance deteriorated dramatically by Thanksgiving, even in the classroom of a seemingly gifted history teacher who tried to follow the behavioral intervention plan quite closely. The history teacher's testimony at the hearing demonstrated the severe challenges faced by teachers in Sean's school. Sean's teacher was trying to teach out of the state-mandated U.S. history textbook which was written with the expectation that students would read at an eighth-grade level. Sean and many other students were not reading at an eighth-grade level, so the teacher read many passages of the book aloud. The teacher testified that he did not even try to meet all the state's educational standards because his students' educational levels made that impossible. His testimony reflected that the educational system was not working for most students, not simply those with disabilities, because it was not consistent with their educational level.

Following winter break in eighth grade, the school district reconvened the intervention team to consider Sean's placement in Sunset School, a day school operated by the school district with a prominent therapeutic component. Based on the recommendation of a mental health therapist at Sunset School, the intervention team decided not to recommend Sean for that program because his needs were deemed not sufficiently severe to warrant that placement. On January 30, 2009 (while Sean was in eighth grade), Sean's mother filed a due process request, challenging the 2008 IEP.

In March 2009, the school district prepared a transition interim IEP in which it provided Sean with extended school year services and 100 percent instruction in an alternative education environment. Sunset School became an option for that education. Sean's mother objected to the 2009 IEP because she considered it to be too ambitious. (The IEP included the goal that Sean would go to college.)

A hearing officer finally rendered a decision regarding Sean in September 2009, when he had just begun ninth grade. The hearing officer found that the 2008 IEP was inadequate under the *Rowley* standard because the school district should have known by that point that Sean could not succeed in a regular education setting with no specialized educational services. The hearing officer also found other violations with respect to how the school district handled some suspensions. Nonetheless, the hearing officer concluded that the 2009 IEP was adequate. Because Sean was not suspended at the time of the hearing, the hearing officer also found that the prior procedural violations were moot. Thus, in ninth grade Sean was possibly receiving an appropriate IEP for the first time after years of persistence on the part of his mother and the assistance of legal counsel. But the hearing officer provided no compensatory education, so the decision simply preserved the status quo.

After eight years of advocacy on the part of Sean's mother, the school district finally conceded that Sean needed therapeutic services and significant academic support. But, unfortunately, Sean made virtually no progress in language arts since the time he attended an alternative school in third grade.

The odds of his successfully completing high school and going on to college seem slim. As his academic performance has declined, his career goals have shifted from "lawyer" to "professional football player." It is hard to see that the intervention process provided him with much, if any, educational benefit. And it is astonishing that the school district could describe him as performing at grade level for years when he, in fact, was making virtually no educational progress. The higher standards implemented by the 2004 amendments to the IDEA had no bearing on how the school district evaluated Sean's educational needs.

LARRY

Another successful case with unsatisfactory relief involves a boy whom I will call Larry.[11] The most recent due process hearing concerning Larry is an outgrowth of longstanding issues with the school district. Larry's parent had reached a settlement agreement with the school district seven years earlier, but that settlement agreement was not being followed and was not included in the child's current IEP. The hearing officer found that the school district was not in compliance with the IEP. Larry did not get occupational therapy, inclusion in a regular classroom setting, lesson plans and study materials sent home on a timely basis, progress reports, weekly meetings, accommodations for standardized testing, assistive technology, FM system, study carrels, specialized bus supervision, and speech/language therapy.

As an example of the school district's complete lack of bad faith, it tried to discipline Larry for not following the school dress code when health reasons required him to wear special clothing because of his sensitivity to sunlight. The school district also did not follow the discipline rules for a child with a disability when Larry violated school policies. When Larry refused to attend school as an aspect of his disability, the school district tried to get the state to prosecute his parent for truancy.

Larry was fortunate to have legal assistance from the Children's Legal Services division of the Southern Legal Counsel. The case shows that it is not enough to get the school district to write an appropriate IEP. It takes enormous energy on behalf of the parent to have the IEP implemented. The mother in this case reached a settlement with the school district in 2002 and then filed a due process complaint in 2005. After losing in 2006, she received a due process hearing that began in 2007 and continued in 2009. She finally attained a favorable due process decision in 2011, shortly before Larry's eighteenth birthday. The only relief granted was compensatory education. By then, it was too late to grant effective relief.

Conclusion

There were very few successful hearing officer decisions in Florida for the time period under investigation. Many of the successful cases were brought by public interest organizations. In none of the winning cases did a hearing officer order the school district to prepare a new IEP. Usually, the parent was seeking merely to enforce an existing IEP. In one case, the litigation pressure from the parent may have caused the school district to modify the IEP to make it more effective. Even the successful cases reflect exhaustive efforts on behalf of parents to get school districts to implement and follow IEPs. These parents nearly always had outside assistance. It is hard to imagine how these parents could have attained adequate educational plans on their own.

10

New Jersey

New Jersey is an important state to investigate because it assigns the burden of proof to the school district in IDEA cases unless the parent is seeking "emergent relief."[1] One might expect that parents would fare better in New Jersey than in other states because of the assignment of the burden of proof to the school district. The empirical results suggest otherwise. Before proceeding with the empirical data, it is helpful to examine the story of one child—E.R.—to give a human face to the difficulties of proceeding with any kind of petition in New Jersey.

E.R. was a four-year-old boy who was in the custody of his grandmother L.R.[2] She also had custody of E.R.'s two siblings. The family lived in New Monmouth, New Jersey; L.R. worked in Red Bank, New Jersey, about five miles from New Monmouth. With the assistance of the Department of Family Services, she paid for E.R. to attend a daycare center in New Monmouth.

When E.R. became old enough to attend preschool, the school district scheduled an IEP meeting for July 9, 2009. He was found to be delayed in social and emotional development and considered eligible for speech and language services as well as a behavioral intervention plan to help him to deal with his aggressive behavior toward other students. At this meeting, the team decided to place E.R. in a two-and-a-half-hour special education preschool classroom containing approximately seven children at the New Monmouth School Preschool Program five days per week. The program lasted from noon to 2:30 p.m. The walk to the preschool program was considered "hazardous," so the IEP also provided that E.R. would receive transportation from his residence to the preschool program. L.R. signed and consented to this IEP.

This program may have been appropriate for E.R., but the IEP had an important problem. E.R. spent his day at a childcare program, not at home. He needed transportation to and from the special education program from his childcare program. But the IEP provided transportation from his *residence* only, not from his childcare program. L.R. worked full-time and could not take E.R. to the special education program at noon from his childcare program and pick him up at 2:30. On a temporary basis, she left work around noon and transported him to the special education program, and a friend picked him up afterward. But L.R. could not continue to rely on her friend to provide this transportation and needed to keep her job to support her family. The school district was willing to provide round-trip transportation from L.R.'s home to the special education program but refused to provide roundtrip transportation from the childcare program to the special education program because of a "firm policy of no courtesy busing." Thus, on August 7, 2009, L.R. filed a due process complaint, requesting that the school district be required to provide transportation to and from the childcare program so that E.R. could take advantage of the special education program. She proceeded without the benefit of legal counsel.

In a legalistic decision, the hearing officer cited decisions from Pennsylvania and New Jersey to conclude that school districts should not be required to provide transportation "to accommodate the needs, work schedules or domestic arrangements of parents or guardians." He concluded that school districts needed to provide transportation only when the need was "disability related" (as in the case of a child who cannot walk) but not when it is merely for the "convenience" of the parent. Because the special education program would provide E.R. with a free and appropriate public education, L.R. had no legal basis to insist on a modification of the IEP to add transportation services. The term "convenience" forced L.R. to choose between paid employment and special education services for her grandson.

The problem in this case stems, in part, from the fact that L.R. consented to E.R.'s IEP on July 9, 2009. It is possible that she did not understand, when she gave her consent, that the transportation specified in the IEP could occur only from her home. Had that fact been explained to her, she might not have consented to the IEP. She also might have been able to negotiate for a better preschool schedule even if she could not negotiate for transportation from the daycare center. For example, E.R. could have been sent to a special education program that began early in the morning so that the school district could have, at least, provided transportation to the program. Then, L.R. might have been able to schedule her lunch break so that she could pick him up at the special education program and transport him to the childcare center. That would have been less than ideal but might have been feasible.

Unfortunately, a similar case from New Jersey suggests that L.R. had few viable options for arguing that the school district should transport her grandchild to and from a childcare center rather than to and from her home. In *S.H. and M.H. o/b/o Minor Child, L.H. v. Caldwell-West Caldwell Board of Education*,[3] the parents signed an IEP similar to the one signed by L.R. But, unlike L.R., they testified that they discussed transportation from their child's daycare center to the special education program when they signed the IEP and were told that they could request that the School Board provide that service after they signed the IEP. They sent a letter to the board requesting the transportation, noting that the new location was on the school district's bus route and closer to the preschool than their home. In other words, the new location would be more convenient to the school district. They also agreed to release the board from any liability for this transportation. Nonetheless, the board denied their request and a hearing officer concluded that such denial was legal. He found that the parents had been "misled" about a possible exemption, but the board was allowed to maintain its transportation policy because it was not "arbitrary, capricious, or unreasonable."

In understanding these transportation cases, it is also important to recognize the limited value of placing the burden of proof on the school district to justify an IEP. Because the school district offered the child an education plan that met the *Rowley* standards for an adequate education, there was no issue in any of these transportation cases about the validity of the underlying IEP. These cases focused only on the right of the school district to apply its "no transportation policy to anyplace other than the home" to children with disabilities. The school district was allowed to adhere to this policy because its application was found not to be "arbitrary and capricious." That standard was easily met by the school district because it was consistent in applying the "no courtesy busing" policy to all of its students.

The real problem in these transportation cases is not the burden of proof. The real problem is that the IDEA is not written for families who do not have the transportation options to make it possible for their children to benefit from special education.

Not surprisingly, the transportation cases always involve parents representing themselves on a *pro se* basis. Middle-class parents who can afford lawyers and other kinds of assistance are likely to have other options. For example, when my son was in a special education preschool program, the program was housed in the same building as his childcare program. The special education teacher walked from the second floor to the first floor to retrieve him from his childcare class and then walked him back to his childcare program at the conclusion of his special education program. The "courtesy" transportation issue never arose in my middle-class suburban community, but if it had, I would have had the resources to hire someone to provide transportation.

The case law reflects that middle-class and wealthy parents can sometimes hire lawyers to get tuition reimbursement at expensive private schools; poor parents must represent themselves to seek to get transportation for their children.

* * *

To discern consistent patterns, I analyzed 101 due process decisions in New Jersey from April 2009 to July 2011. Of the 101 decisions, 64 were emergent relief requests. Therefore, the parents or guardians did bear the burden of proof in most of these cases. In order to assess whether the burden of proof affected these decisions, I divided them into two categories depending on the allocation of the burden of proof—regular petitions and emergent relief petitions. "Emergent relief" petitions are emergency petitions wherein the parties seek expedited relief to avoid immediate and serious harm. It is limited to issues concerning placement, interruption of services, discipline, and participation in graduation ceremonies. Interestingly, the assignment of the burden of proof appears to have had little or no effect on the outcome in these cases.

Regular Petitions (Not Emergent Relief)

The school district bears the burden of proof in regular petitions. Nonetheless, parents are rarely successful in these petitions.

Of the thirty-seven cases that were not emergent relief petitions, the parent or guardian prevailed in only two cases (5.4 percent). Five of the thirty-seven cases were hard to categorize, as the parties essentially settled them at the hearing. If those five cases are excluded, then the parent or guardian prevailed in two of thirty-two cases (6.2 percent). One might also categorize seven of the thirty-seven cases (18.9 percent) as ones in which the availability of the due process hearing process facilitated the parents' obtaining the relief they desired. Lawyers represented both of the parents who prevailed in their due process hearings. Overall, fourteen of the thirty-seven (37.8 percent) petitions involved situations in which an attorney represented parents.

Successful Regular Petitions

None of the successful cases involved a critical issue in IDEA cases—the appropriateness of the educational plan proposed by the school district. Of the two outright victories, one case involved a unilateral placement in private school.[4] The parents had unilaterally sent their child to a private school after being unsatisfied with the placement proposed by the school district. The hearing officer concluded that the parents were not entitled to reimbursement for the first year of such schooling. When the parents requested IEPs to determine if they wanted to keep the child in private school in subsequent years, the school district refused to cooperate. The hearing officer therefore concluded that the school district was responsible for private school expenses in subsequent years. This case was essentially decided on procedural grounds—the school district's failure to hold IEP meetings after the parents unilaterally sent their child to private school made the school district responsible for the cost of private schooling. These parents acted with a fair degree of sophistication to obtain reimbursement without ever showing that the school district's IEP was inadequate. Their victory was partial in that they did not obtain relief for the first year of private schooling.

In the other successful case,[5] the hearing officer ruled in favor of the parents with respect to how to implement an IEP for a preschooler whose fragile medical condition necessitated home instruction. Because of the child's severe disabilities as a result of a stroke at birth, there was no question that he was entitled to significant services. The parents and school district essentially agreed on the child's need for speech and language services, but the child's inability to attend a public preschool made implementation of the IEP as written impossible. The question then became how to implement home instruction to best replicate the proposed IEP. The hearing officer relied heavily on the parents' expert, agreeing with the evaluation tools she used and her recommendation for how the child could receive effective speech and language therapy. The hearing officer also agreed with this expert's conclusion that a speech and language pathologist, rather than someone working under her supervision, should deliver services. Of all the cases in the New Jersey database, this is one in which the burden of proof seemed to matter. Nonetheless, the parents had to retain a lawyer and a speech and language pathologist in order to prevail.

Five cases also settled at the hearing. The first case involved a behavioral plan that the school district began to implement after the due process request was filed. A lawyer did not represent the parents. A second case involved the school district's desire to keep a child in an in-district placement. The district was able to persuade the parents at the hearing of the appropriateness of that placement. Those parents were also not represented by a lawyer. In a third case, the parent brought a due process hearing to get an independent eye exam for her child because she never had received the results of the school district exam. She ended that request when she received the desired information at the hearing. She was also not represented by a lawyer. In the fourth case, the parties agreed to attend mediation and dropped the due process request. The parents in this case had a lawyer. In the final case, the parent brought a due process hearing to clarify that the school district had already agreed to pay for a private placement. The case was made moot when the district agreed that it would pay for the placement. Those parents also had a lawyer.

Of the seven cases in which parents seemed to obtain some relief by using due process, two cases involved reimbursement for private schooling (with the assistance of a lawyer), one case ended with an agreement to mediate so there is no way to know the ultimate outcome, one case (with the assistance of a lawyer) resulted in a trained professional's delivering the services at home, one case involved the implementation of a behavioral plan, one case involved a parent's learning the results of a medical exam, and one case involved a parent's acquiescing to the school district's proposed placement. The parents who used a lawyer got the most extensive relief—private schooling and home services by trained professionals. In the cases in which parents won without a lawyer, they received a plan or information that was already available to the school district except for the one case in which the parents obtained a new behavioral plan. The most extreme example of modest relief for an unrepresented parent was that of the parent's finally learning the results of an eye exam conducted by the school district when she filed for due process.

Unsuccessful Regular Petitions

The non–emergent relief (regular) petitions were rarely successful despite some claims that went to the heart of a student's ability to obtain a free and appropriate public education. For example, several petitions involved critical issues relating to transportation. As discussed above, E.R's grandmother lost her transportation case involving the need for the child to be transported to and from a preschool program that ran from noon to 2:30 p.m. each day.[6]

This case reflects the difficulties that parents have in attaining successful outcomes under the IDEA. E.R.'s grandmother proceeded without counsel and must have had to miss work in order to pursue the due process hearing. On balance, she must have decided it was worth missing work in order to make it possible for E.R. to attend the special education program on a regular basis. But the kind of relief she sought was not possible under the IDEA even though it was critical to E.R.'s being able to attend a special education program. If the grandmother had not worked outside the home, the school district would have been willing to provide door-to-door service between home and the special education program. But because the grandmother had a job—and therefore had to use childcare—her grandson could not receive needed special education services. That makes no sense as a matter of policy but is typical of the class bias under the IDEA.

Although more likely to prevail than low-income parents, middle-class parents often did not fare well in what appeared to be strong cases in which they were represented by legal counsel. For example, E.S.'s parents sought reimbursement for their unilateral placement of their daughter in an out-of-district program.[7] They experienced enormous frustration with the school district's resistance over a period of several years. In kindergarten, E.S. threatened to kill another child and, in first grade, she was diagnosed with bipolar disorder. During the summer between third and fourth grade, she threatened to jump out of a moving car and asked her mother to kill her because she couldn't "take it" anymore. She had enormous trouble in school, and her parents reported that it would take her as long as four hours to complete homework on a given night. The documents from the case demonstrate that the school district kept disorganized records on E.S. and failed to diagnose her learning needs adequately. The district had classified her as having mental health problems but not a learning disability, even though she had a large number of extremely low test scores. The hearing officer also did not seem to understand how to analyze the records to obtain a complete picture of this child's academic performance.

E.S.'s parents had gone to great lengths to demonstrate that the school district program was inappropriate after years in which E.S. struggled in school. They hired an expert in childhood and adolescent psychiatry as well as a clinical psychologist. The experts concluded that E.S. suffered from bipolar disorder, ADHD, and a learning disorder. They also concluded that E.S. was regressing in school because she was not meeting state standards. Both experts testified that E.S. needed to attend a private school because exposure to typical peers exacerbated her bipolar disorder, and this, in turn, impeded her ability to process information.

By contrast, the district recommended for fifth grade a program that was quite similar to E.S.'s program in fourth grade. She was to have both math and reading in the resource room and have science in the general education classroom with two teachers. She would also be in the regular classroom for physical education and the special classes, such as art and music. Although the school district had the burden of proof to demonstrate that the IEP was appropriate, it is hard to see from the record how it met this burden. Because the fifth- and fourth-grade IEPs were similar, there should have been some measures to demonstrate that E.S. was making appropriate progress. Instead, the record includes some scattered scores without attention to benchmarks to see if progress was adequate. For example, the record reveals that she scored forty-one of seventy-two on one of the reading tests but was making "good progress" on her fourth-grade goals. It is hard to imagine that forty-one of seventy-two is grade-level work. The record also states elsewhere that E.S. was scoring in the second-grade level on reading in fourth grade. That is usually considered an indication of a learning disability, yet the school district did not classify her as having a learning disability.

The hearing officer's decision is long and disorganized. It is not clear that he understood how to consider the various test scores in the record. His lack of understanding of the IDEA and this case is reflected in the following sentence: "Taken together [the experts'] arguments, largely clinical in nature, appear to seek to force a conclusion that the nature of E.S.'s bipolar disorder is such that no public school placement could possibly provide E.S. (or potentially any student with bipolar disorder) with a FAPE, without undermining the record produced by the district which demonstrates E.S.'s progress during third and fourth grade." That sentence—about "any student with bipolar disorder"—entirely misses the point that an IEP is supposed to be *individualized*. E.S. was not "any" child with bipolar disorder; she had quite severe bipolar disorder with suicidal tendencies as early as kindergarten. And the conclusion that she was progressing during third and fourth grade was based on anecdotal reports from the teachers rather than on standardized testing (the standardized testing suggested a quite different picture). One of the plaintiff's experts did visit E.S.'s classroom, so it also was not the case that the conclusions were entirely clinical in nature. It is hard to see what more the plaintiffs could have done to demonstrate that the school district's IEP was inadequate for their child, especially in a system in which the school district supposedly had the burden of proof.

Emergent Relief Petitions

The parent usually has the burden of proof in emergent relief petitions.

New Jersey law is quite strict with respect to emergent relief petitions. The following four factors control these cases:

1. The petitioner will suffer irreparable harm if the relief is not granted;
2. The legal right underlying the petitioner's claim is settled;
3. The petitioner has a likelihood of prevailing on the merits of the underlying claim; and
4. When the equities and interests of the parties are balanced, the petitioner will suffer greater harm than the respondent will suffer if the requested relief is not granted.[8]

In addition, there are procedural requirements for filing an emergent relief petition. The applicant must set forth the specific relief sought and the specific circumstances that the applicant contends justify the relief sought. The application must be supported by an affidavit prepared by an affiant with personal knowledge of the facts contained in the petition. Parents who were not represented by lawyers often made procedural mistakes that precluded them from prevailing, such as failing to state the relief they sought or seeking relief, such as compensatory education, that is not possible in an emergent relief application.

Of the sixty-four cases involving emergent relief petitions, the parent or guardian prevailed in eleven of them (17.2 percent), but two cases were settled favorably at the hearing so it is more accurate to say that the parent or guardian prevailed in eleven of sixty-two cases (17.7 percent). Seven of eleven of those parents were represented by an attorney (63.7 percent). Of the thirty cases in which parents were not represented by lawyers in an emergent relief petition, they won four cases (13.3 percent), but one of those cases was settled so it would be more accurate to say that parents won four of twenty-nine cases in which they were not represented by a lawyer (13.7 percent). Of the thirty-four parents who were represented by a lawyer in an emergent relief petition, the parent won seven of the cases (20.6 percent), but one of those cases was settled so it would be more accurate to say that parents won seven of thirty-three cases (21.2 percent). Thus, emergent relief petitions were more successful than non–emergent relief petitions even though the parent typically had the burden of proof in those cases. (If the district sought an emergent relief petition then it had the burden of proof; the district was the petitioner in seven of the emergent relief cases; the district won six of those cases so, again, the assignment of the burden of proof seemed to have little impact on the outcome.) Parents did somewhat better with the assistance of legal counsel, but the biggest factor influencing their likelihood of success was if they filed petitions for emergent relief.

Successful Emergent Relief Petitions

Of the eleven cases in which petitioners successfully obtained emergent relief, all but one involved the parent's wanting the child to stay in his or her current program pending a due process hearing. These programs were private or public or involved home schooling. One case involved whether a program was a free and appropriate public education.

P.B.'s case typifies a successful petition.[9] P.B.'s parents used a lawyer to help them obtain high-quality private education for their child, who has Asperger's Syndrome. P.B. was initially enrolled in the Washington Township School District, where his IEP placed him in a private, out-of-district placement: Yale Academy. He began enrollment at Yale Academy in 2007; his parents moved to the Winslow school district in 2010 and sought a new IEP for their child. The school district recommended an in-district placement in a self-contained classroom and the parents rejected that placement, wanting to keep their son at Yale Academy. Under New Jersey law, P.B. was entitled to a program in his new school that was "comparable" to the program he had at his old school. The school district's program appeared to be of high quality. It had fifteen students, one certified special education teacher, and one teaching assistant. P.B. would have an aide and many hours of instruction each day in rather long segments of time. At the Yale program, there would be eight students, three certified regular education teachers, and one special education teacher, with a teacher-to-student ratio of 2:1. Classes were quite short in recognition of the short attention span of the students. Ordinarily, one could imagine the hearing officer's concluding the in-district program was "adequate," but P.B.'s lawyer was aware that the boy was entitled to a "comparable" program when moving to a new school district under an existing IEP. Under that standard, it was possible to argue that the two programs were quite different. Thus, P.B.'s parents prevailed on their son's behalf by using a technical legal argument.

P.B. was represented by Disability Rights New Jersey, a nonprofit organization that serves as New Jersey's federally funded protection and advocacy organization for people with disabilities. Each state has one of these federally funded programs to serve the needs of individuals with developmental disabilities, mental illness, and traumatic brain injury.[10] In theory, these organizations can act as an advocate for children who need special education assistance. In practice, few of the cases in my database were litigated by these organizations. Because they also advocate for individuals who live in institutional settings, they may not be able to devote a lot of resources to litigating IDEA claims. As we saw in P.B.'s case, though, when they do litigate, they can have access to sophisticated legal arguments.

Unsuccessful Emergent Relief Petitions

Of the cases in which petitioners were unsuccessful, they involved the following kinds of issues: continuation of services rather than high school graduation, transportation, placement, modification of stay put in light of serious discipline issues, participation in graduation exercises despite discipline rules, and extended school year services. Although parents have a better chance of prevailing on emergent relief petitions than on other kinds of matters, such numbers are misleading. In reality, parents virtually win *only* when they seek to have the stay-put rules enforced. They are not able to use emergent relief to prevail on any other kinds of issues.

Less successful petitioners are like the mother of K.S.[11] K.S. attended Hackensack Middle School. He repeated seventh grade after failing language arts, science, and math. He then failed all of his academic subjects a second time. At that point, the school district referred him for special education identification and concluded that he had ADHD and should receive services under the "other health-impaired" category. Although he was classified as disabled in July 2010, the IEP meeting was not held until October 13, 2010. K.S. began the school year with home instruction. At the October meeting, the school district recommended that K.S. be educated in a pull-out resource room. His mother requested that he be placed in an out-of-district program at the Community High School in nearby Teaneck, a private school. Alternatively, she argued that his home instruction should continue pending the due process hearing on the merits. In support of her argument that K.S. should not attend the Hackensack Middle School program, she offered evidence that she had filed a complaint against a teacher who had allegedly physically harmed her son, causing him to fear attending that school.

The hearing officer ruled that there was no evidence that failing to send K.S. to the out-of-district school would cause irreparable harm. It was not enough for K.S. to show a "risk" of irreparable injury; there had to be a "clear showing of immediate irreparable injury." The school district sought to have K.S. return to the middle school in a regular education class (as his stay-put placement) pending a due process hearing on the merits. Fortunately for K.S., the hearing officer found that the "stay put" placement was home instruction, because that was his placement at the beginning of the school year. On the basis of that technicality, he was not returned to the regular education class in the school. This case represented one of the few "victories" in my database for parents who proceeded without an attorney, but it seems unlikely that K.S. will enroll in the private school. Because his mother could not afford the services of a lawyer for the due process hearing, she is unlikely to be able to afford to pursue unilateral placement in the private school pending resolution of the due process hearing. Instead, her son will likely receive minimal home instruction while the due process hearing schedule unfolds. The emergent relief petition was not decided until December 1, 2010, so K.S. has likely spent two-and-a-half years receiving little or no educational benefit without an IEP even in place. Because he has not yet enrolled in the school district's program, his mother is unlikely to be able to demonstrate that that program is not adequate.

K.S.'s mother proceeded without an attorney or any expert witnesses. A lawyer would likely have argued that K.S. was entitled to compensatory education for the two years in which he was failing his courses, yet the school district did not seek to determine if he was disabled. Although K.S. might have ADHD, it is also possible that the school district's identification was wrong. A learning disability might explain his poor educational performance and call for a different type of educational program. The Community High School in Teaneck specializes in teaching children with learning disabilities, so it might have been more appropriate than the pull-out program recommended by the school district. Without expert witnesses, K.S.'s mother could not possibly pursue those arguments. Although the record does not indicate K.S.'s race or class, his treatment is typical of that of poor and minority children in that it is not clear that he has been correctly classified and he is receiving minimal services to improve his educational performance.

Conclusion

With the burden of proof on the school district in regular petitions, one might expect to see many parents obtain significant relief through due process. In practice, few parents received meaningful relief for their children. The parents who did prevail retained lawyers and often had the financial resources to afford private placements for their children. The parents or guardians who were clearly indigent had great difficulty using due process to obtain effective relief. Experts played a big role in many of the successful cases, and the hearing officers also did not demonstrate the ability to understand the significance of the experts' testimony. Except for one case involving a medically fragile preschooler who was receiving home instruction, the placement of the burden of proof on the school districts made no difference in these cases.

Emergent relief petitions are equally troubling. Parents rarely prevailed on behalf of their children, except for cases involving the appropriate stay-put placement during the resolution of a dispute. Successful emergent relief petitions required sophisticated legal arguments that could be made only by highly competent counsel. New Jersey does have several nonprofit organizations that represent parents and their children in special education cases. These organizations, rather than the burden of proof, seem to be the most important factor in predicting whether parents prevail in New Jersey on behalf of their children.

11

California

California is an important state to investigate for many reasons. First, it probably has the most sophisticated system of hearing officer decisions in the United States. The decisions are word-searchable in a database. The hearing officers clearly receive significant training in writing opinions because all of the opinions follow a similar structure and contain the same boilerplate language about the legal rules that apply to IDEA matters. Second, California has a comparatively high rate of litigation so it is a rich source of hearing officer decisions.[1] Third, California has a lot of students for whom English is the second language. The hearing officer decisions sometimes delineate these cases by noting that a foreign language interpreter was present at the hearing. Thus, these cases can provide a lens into how the special education system deals with students whose primary language is not English. Finally, California has a relatively high rate of cases brought by school districts, often when they contest the parents' right to an independent educational evaluation. Because the district bears the burden of proof when it brings cases, these cases can lend insight into the impact of the burden of proof on outcome. A survey of the California decisions reflects a hearing officer structure that is heavily biased in favor of school districts, even when the district bears the burden of proof. Children whose parents require an interpreter to participate in these cases have a particularly difficult time prevailing.

An example of a case reflecting the difficulty of children receiving adequate special education services when their parent or guardian does not speak English is reflected in a case against the Los Angeles Unified School District.[2] Pedro was an eight-year-old boy who resided with his mother, baby sister, and grandparents. His mother was cognitively impaired; his grandmother had legal guardianship of him; his grandmother's primary language was Spanish. Pedro's mother lived in the household and struggled to play an active role in his life. The school district successfully contested Pedro's grandmother's request that the school district provide transportation from their house to his special educational program, which was not given at Pedro's neighborhood school. A close reading of the case makes one wonder if Pedro was receiving an adequate education in the segregated educational environment selected for him by the school district, but his grandmother challenged only the lack of adequate transportation services.

Pedro had been receiving special education services since he was three years old. As a preschooler, he was classified as developmentally delayed. When he turned five, and that classification was no longer available, he was classified as having a specific learning disability and a speech and language impairment. When he became school-age in 2009, his placement for services was in an early education special day class, where he would also receive speech and language services. Because his nearby grade school did not have such a classroom, he was assigned to another grade school. His IEP for the 2009–10 school year mandated that the school district provide Pedro with home-to-school and school-to-home transportation.

When the IEP team met in November 2010 to write an IEP for the 2010–11 school year, the school district insisted that Pedro no longer receive home-to-school transportation. His family would be responsible for transporting him to his nearby elementary school, and the district would then transport him from his local elementary school to the elementary school where he would receive services. His mother and grandmother refused to consent to that transportation plan but did not otherwise challenge his IEP.

At the due process hearing, Pedro's grandmother, but not his mother, attended. Patricia Valdivia, who was employed by Buena Vista Learning Services to provide life skills training for his mother, accompanied Pedro's grandmother. Maria Aherm, who was described as a volunteer advocate and the parent of a special education child, also accompanied Pedro's grandmother. The record does not disclose the educational qualifications of either of these individuals except to note that Aherm had eighteen hours of advocacy training but that the hearing officer did not consider her to be a special education "expert." Pedro's grandmother did not receive the assistance of an attorney. Paula Geary provided interpreter services for Pedro's grandmother and for several of Pedro's witnesses.

Pedro's witnesses documented the difficulty involved in transporting Pedro to the local school to take the bus to the other grade school. His mother had attempted to provide him with transportation by walking with Pedro and her eighteen-month-old daughter to the local school. Pedro's grandmother, as well as Valdivia and Pedro's maternal aunt, testified how difficult it was for Pedro to walk that distance safely. They testified that he sought to run away during the walk, that he got very upset about going to school, and that his mother could not control him because she, too, got "out of control" when Pedro got out of control.[3] Because the family did not have a car, the grandmother had to transport Pedro to school by public Metro bus when he missed the school bus. The picture portrayed by Pedro's witnesses was that he had severe behavioral problems, had tried to jump out of a moving car, and had threatened to kill people.

None of the school district witnesses testified that they had seen Pedro being transported to the local grade school by a family member. They testified only about his behavior once he was in school. They reported no significant behavioral issues. Further, they reported that Pedro had no physical disabilities that would impair his ability to walk to school.

The hearing officer ruled for the school district in an opinion that was typical of a California case. The hearing officer quoted *Rowley*[4] to reach the conclusion that a school district needs to provide only a "basic floor of opportunity" in a way that supplies a student with "meaningful access to education" and that a school district need not "guarantee successful results."[5] Because the IDEA does not explicitly define transportation as door-to-door services, the hearing officer concluded that transportation decisions are within the discretion of the IEP team. The school district was entitled to exercise that discretion by not providing home-to-school transportation services.

The hearing officer concluded that Pedro's grandmother had not demonstrated that the district had denied Pedro a free and appropriate public education by denying him home-to-school transportation services. While the hearing officer agreed that Pedro's "behavior at home and in the presence of his family is far more challenging than his behavior at school," that factor alone did not entitle him to transportation services because his grandmother was unable to demonstrate that "his behavior at home has any connection to his behavior at school."[6] The fact that Pedro's mother's "cognitive impairment and other small children in the home impact the family's ability to manage [Pedro's] behavior" had no bearing on the legal outcome of the services that the school district needed to provide Pedro. The school district successfully argued that the primary rationale for the transportation request was to assist Pedro's mother, rather than Pedro himself.[7] Under the IDEA, the school district has no responsibility to address Pedro's home environment.

It is impossible to know how this case would have been resolved if Pedro's grandmother had had qualified legal counsel, but many other results certainly seem possible. First, no one challenged the underlying educational plan or Pedro's disability classification. The school district reported no test scores to determine Pedro's academic aptitude or his record of achievement. His cognitive aptitude was considered to be in the average range on the basis of highly subjective testimony, and he was also found not to have any behavioral difficulties at school that negatively affected his educational progress. An Independent Educational Evaluation might have determined that Pedro's disability was misclassified and that the educational plan was not consistent with his educational needs. The hearing officer opinion offers no explanation as to why he was classified as having a specific learning disability (or even in what area he was supposedly learning disabled). The diagnosis was made on the basis of a report by Danie Melendez, who was described as having a B.A. in psychology and a M.A. in education and counseling, based on direct observation, interviews of various people, and review of school records and test scores. There is no indication that Melendez could converse with Pedro in Spanish, or that Melendez had proper training to make a clinical assessment of Pedro's disability.

Second, no one challenged why Pedro, with a seemingly average cognitive aptitude and no behavioral issues, was being educated in an early education special day class—a segregated educational environment—away from his home school. The school district insisted that Pedro was so disabled that he needed to be educated in that restrictive environment yet also claimed he was sufficiently capable of walking to and from school by himself. Those claims seem inconsistent yet were not challenged. The school district also asserted that walking to his neighborhood school to catch the bus was a component of Pedro's being in the "least restrictive environment."[8] But it is hard to see how walking to one's local school and then being transported from it to a segregated environment lessens the "restrictiveness" of one's educational experience. It would have been more appropriate to consider why Pedro could not be educated at his local school—why his basic educational plan was in such a restrictive environment.

Third, it is hard to see how the IEP meets Pedro's "unique needs."[9] It seems improbable that Pedro could safely walk six or seven blocks to and from school by himself at the age of eight. The only way Pedro could be transported to school with assistance was if he walked with his mother and baby sister. Although it may be the case that a typical mother could have walked with Pedro to school, that was not Pedro's situation. The hearing officer found that school-to-school transportation was not needed to "assist [Pedro] to benefit from special education."[10] In what sense was it not "necessary"? How was Pedro supposed to get to school? The hearing officer rendered the decision as if Pedro lived in a middle-class family and had a nondisabled mother to walk with him to school. Despite the individualized nature of educational plans, the hearing officer was able to render a decision that ignored the actual resources available to Pedro.

Finally, Pedro's grandmother did not press the argument that a change in an IEP must be made in a way that is likely to provide a successful transition. This was not the first IEP the school district had prepared for Pedro. He had had home-to-school transportation for four or five previous years. The school district was implementing a major change in Pedro's services without providing for a transition plan. The need for a transition plan is an argument that has often been made successfully in other cases in other states in which the parent had the benefit of legal counsel.[11] The school district, however, does not appear to have offered any assistance whatsoever to make this transition successful. And Pedro's grandmother did not have the legal sophistication to make that argument.

In sum, one must wonder why the school district used its resources to challenge the transportation issue rather than continue providing Pedro with transportation. One would think that its concern for Pedro's well-being would cause it to volunteer and offer transportation even if it is not technically required. Transportation was certainly an option, and the school district was already providing a bus for Pedro from the local school. If his home was only six blocks away, why not offer to have the school bus, rather than Pedro's mother, travel those six blocks? This case, like the New Jersey transportation cases,[12] suggests that the school district has little interest in making sure children even have access to special education services, let alone providing them with services that will allow them to make educational progress. It is easy to predict a record of truancy for Pedro as he improves his ability to defy his mother and not get to the local school in time to catch the bus. If he is not in the classroom, it is also easy to predict that his family will not be able to offer supplementary educational services. The school district's intransigence has become another risk factor in Pedro's life.

Hearing Officer Decisions

I reviewed 101 decisions that were decided between May 3, 2010, and June 20, 2011. Parents or guardians prevailed in 35 of 101 cases (34.6 percent). There were 7 cases for which the disability classification could not be determined and 14 cases in which the student had more than one disability. The most frequent disabilities were autism (30 students), emotional disturbance (19 students), speech and language impairments (17 students), Other Health Impairment (OHI) (15 students), learning disabilities (13 students), and mental retardation/cognitive impairment (9 students). These statistics are typical of what was found in other states—parents of children with autism seem the most likely to pursue a due process hearing. Most of these cases involve requests for reimbursement for private school tuition so the parents have a lot at stake financially, making a due process hearing a viable option. Because reimbursement is possible only when the parent has already paid the tuition, these are likely to be middle-class or even high-income parents.

Of the 101 cases I reviewed, the hearing officer noted in 7 cases that a foreign language interpreter was provided. The student prevailed in only 1 of 7 (14 percent) of those cases. The winning case was one in which the parents had requested an independent educational evaluation on behalf of their son, Cesar.[13] Cesar was a 7-year-old boy who attended a dual language immersion program commencing with kindergarten. He qualified for an IEP under the category of speech and language disorder.

Cesar was having a lot of trouble in first grade because he would refuse to take spelling tests and crumple up his work paper in frustration. He also seemed to have few friends and was often quite withdrawn in class. Although he had qualified for special education in kindergarten under the category of speech and language impairment, his parents wanted an independent educational evaluation (IEE) to determine if he was autistic. Because the school district opposed their request for an IEE, the school filed a due process complaint to support their refusal. The parents succeeded in convincing the hearing officer that they were entitled to an IEE to assess for the possibility of ADHD and to properly measure their son's cognitive aptitude but, ironically, did *not* convince the hearing officer to allow more testing for autism. And, as a further irony, they were able to prevail on those issues only because of excellent expert witness testimony by Robert Goode Patterson, whom the hearing officer described as "an extraordinarily well-qualified expert whose multiple degrees include a PsyD. in psychology and family therapy, a master's degree in developmental psychology, and a master's degree in education."[14] Cesar's parents were also represented by legal counsel. Thus, with the use of a lawyer and a highly qualified expert, they were able to obtain a partial victory that did not address their chief concern.

In the other six cases, the parents typically made very modest requests but still did not prevail. Two other parents requested IEEs, but the school district successfully challenged those requests. One case (Pedro's) involved transportation (and had no lawyer), one involved a student who had been deemed ineligible for special education (and had no lawyer), one involved a student with autism whose parents sought additional services (but not a private placement), and one involved a student whose parents unsuccessfully challenged the IEP (and had the assistance of the Disability Rights Legal Center).

Of course, it would be simplistic to say that these parents lost their due process claims because they needed an interpreter at the due process hearing. Many factors likely led to the failure of their claims. But these statistics (admittedly from a small sample) do suggest that we should consider whether parents who do not speak English are able to attain a fair hearing.

Parents who were not represented by legal counsel stood very little chance of prevailing in California, even if they had an educational advocate. Of the twenty cases in which a lawyer did not represent parents, the student prevailed in only one case. And, in that case, the remedy was an IEE for a fourteen-year-old boy with cerebral palsy.[15] In four cases, no one appeared for the student at the hearing; in one case, a parent attended only one day of the hearings. In each of the cases in which no one appeared for the student, the school district was the petitioner bringing the case because the parent had refused to sign the IEP. The district therefore went to a hearing officer to have the IEP approved.

The five cases in which the parents did not meaningfully participate at the due process hearing reflect some of the challenges we face in providing children with appropriate educations. The IDEA presumes an active level of participation on the part of parents, but not all children live in households to which that assumption applies.

Substantive Analysis in California

It is always hard to tell if cases are "wrongly" decided by reading a hearing officer opinion because the hearing officer will tell the story in a way that is persuasive to him or her. The following five cases brought by one lawyer, Jennifer Guze Campbell, however, show the reluctance of hearing officers to order relief even when violations of the statute have occurred. Further, the burden of proof on the parent in California seems insurmountable. The school district easily prevailed even when it had the burden of proof and weak evidence in support of its position. California hearing officers seem to bend over backward to rule in favor of school districts.

Reluctance to Order Relief

The first case involved Amanda, a nine-year-old girl who appeared to be quite bright but struggled tremendously with spelling.[16] The school district agreed to perform a scotopic sensory sensitivity evaluation in 2009 but failed to do so. When it still had not performed the evaluation in 2010, her parents filed a due process complaint. Even though there was no question that the school district had violated the IDEA by failing to perform the agreed-upon evaluation, the hearing officer ordered no remedy.

The hearing officer cited *Rowley* in support of her position, but *Rowley* should not have been the relevant legal standard. The issue in this case was whether the district had properly assessed the potential scope of the student's disabilities. The fact that her educational performance—with accommodations—was at or above grade level was irrelevant to the question of whether she had been assessed in all areas of suspected disability. The regulations state that a student must be "assessed in all areas related to the suspected disability."[17] The assessment requirement is independent of the rules governing educational programs. In *Rowley*, the student's disability—hearing impairment—was never at issue. The only issue was whether her educational program was appropriate. In this case, the district was arguably not developing an educational plan in response to the student's disability because it had an incomplete picture of her disability. This hearing officer's inclination to cite *Rowley* seems typical of California cases—hearing officers cite *Rowley* for nearly any issue rather than merely for the issue of whether the educational program is appropriate.

The second case involved Tricia, a ten-and-a-half-year-old girl who was born prematurely and had a number of significant health impairments.[18] Tricia's mother asked the school district to assess her daughter for dyslexia in 2009 because she felt the girl was not making adequate educational progress in light of her cognitive aptitude. The district did not conduct that assessment. It scheduled an assessment in 2010 only after Tricia's lawyer sent a nine-page letter to the district on her behalf. Rather than credit the lawyer with causing the district to follow the law, the hearing officer described the filing of a due process request as "gamesmanship" because the hearing request was filed a day after the district received the attorney's letter. Because the mother's requests were made orally, and not in writing, the hearing officer concluded that she had not made a sufficiently specific request to trigger the district's assessment obligation. There is no requirement in the IDEA that a request to be evaluated must be in writing. In fact, the "child find" obligation is the school district's, not the parent's. Given the record of Tricia's significant educational challenges over the years, and the mother's repeated assertion that her daughter might have dyslexia, the district's obligation to assess for dyslexia should have been triggered before the lawyer, Jennifer Guze Campbell, sent the nine-page letter to the district documenting the need for an assessment.

The third case involved Sandy, a 6-year-old girl.[19] Her parents wanted the school district to conduct a more thorough assessment and, in particular, to assess her in the areas of auditory processing, motor skills, and vision. The district agreed to conduct an assessment but did not do so on a timely basis, causing a delay in an increase in Sandy's speech therapy from 120 minutes per month to 240 minutes per month. Even though the hearing officer concluded that the student missed 4 hours of speech and language therapy as a result of this delay, no remedy was ordered. As with Amanda, the hearing officer refused to conclude that a procedural violation caused substantive harm although, in both cases, it delayed services.

The fourth case involved a nine-year-old girl, Jessie, who had been found ineligible for special education services.[20] She was struggling in math and her mother wanted her assessed for ADHD. Although an assessment should occur merely on the basis of the *possibility* that a child has a disability, the school district took the position (which the hearing officer accepted) that it should not have to assess Jessie for ADHD unless the mother could present evidence that her daughter had ADHD. That turns the "child find" obligation on its head by requiring evidence of a diagnosis before an assessment is made. The hearing officer also cited *Rowley* in support of his position that an assessment was not required but, as discussed above, *Rowley* has nothing to do with assessments; it has to do with the adequacy of the educational plan.

The fifth case involved a seven-year-old boy, Antonio, with autism, who lived in a home in which Spanish was the primary language.[21] Antonio's parents were not satisfied with the school district's evaluations and sought an IEE. Although the IDEA specifies that the school district must respond to such a request within thirty days, it filed its complaint objecting to the IEE fifty-three days after the parents' advocate made their request. Because the school was on winter break for twenty-four of those days, the hearing officer concluded that the delay did not constitute a substantive IDEA violation. The district had the burden of proof in this case to demonstrate that its evaluation was adequate, so the parents were not entitled to their own independent evaluation at public expense. Even though an audiologist testified that she was not able to obtain results through traditional hearing instruments, the hearing officer concluded that the assessment was adequate. The fact that the district's own witness testified that she "was unable to rule out whether

Student has a hearing loss" was not a sufficient basis to conclude that an independent assessment was warranted. Thus, neither the delayed reply nor the incomplete assessment was considered a ground for relief.

In California, hearing officer opinions end with a statement as to whether the student or the school district prevailed on each issue. That statement is used as a basis for a determination of whether attorney fees are warranted to the students' lawyers. In each of these five cases, despite the fact that technical violations were found to have occurred in two of the cases, the hearing officer concluded that the district prevailed on all issues. That meant that the district had no responsibility to reimburse the parents for their attorney fee expenses.

Hearing Officer Reversed

The five cases that I discussed above are ones in which the hearing officer's decision had not been challenged on appeal by the time this book was written in July 2012. Two cases in which the hearing officer was reversed on appeal reflect the problematic nature of some of the California decisions. In both of these cases, the hearing officer's opinion made it very difficult for the parents to have sufficient "firepower" as contemplated by the U.S. Supreme Court in *Schaffer v. Weast*[22] (as discussed in chapter 6) to obtain an appropriate IEP for their child.

RIGHT TO AN INDEPENDENT EDUCATIONAL EVALUATION

One important principle under the IDEA is that a parent has the right to request an IEE if the parent considers the school district's evaluation to be inadequate. This right is so important that the Supreme Court has held that the *school district* rather than the parent has the burden of demonstrating that its evaluation was adequate if it wants to challenge the parent's request for an IEE. Nonetheless, school districts in California routinely prevail when they challenge parents' requests for an IEE. The following case reflects a miscarriage of justice at the hearing officer level that was corrected on appeal to the district court.

In the case, *In the Matter of Los Angeles Unified School District v. Parent on behalf of Student*,[23] the school district filed a due process complaint on October 19, 2010, against John Nagel and Michelle Short-Nagel on behalf of their eight-year-old daughter, K. Short-Nagel, whom I will call Kathleen, in order to challenge the parents' right to an IEE.

Kathleen was first identified as struggling in school in first grade, during the 2008–9 school year. At the end of the school year, on June 3, 2009, the school district convened a Student Success Team (SST) to discuss her diffi-culties and challenges. The team recommended modifications and an action plan, including one-on-one assistance.[24] The hearing officer opinion then states that the action plan was implemented during the 2010–11 school year. But the plan should have been implemented during the 2009–10 school year. The reference to the 2010–11 school year was an apparent mistake, which makes it difficult to follow the factual record.

Because of continued difficulties in school, the SST referred Kathleen for an initial special education assessment on February 17, 2010. At the time of the assessment, Kathleen was receiving in-school pull-out intervention classes for reading and writing; twice weekly private tutoring funded by her parents; small-group, individual, and modified instruction and expectations; extended time for testing and assignments; preferential seating; repetition of directions; and the breaking of assignments into smaller components.[25]

A school district has sixty days in which to conduct an educational assess-ment and make an eligibility determination.[26] The opinion does not state the precise date on which the parent consented to the assessment, but it appears that the school district squeaked under the wire by holding a combined eligi-bility/IEP meeting in late April. Barbara Zafran, a special education teacher, administered various tests of academic achievement on March 19, 23, and 24, 2010. School district psychologist Karen Menzie prepared a report, dated March 23, 2010, which was written before Zafran completed her evaluations. Menzie administered various other tests as part of her report process. Men-zie concluded that Kathleen qualified as a student with a specific learning disability.[27] That report should have been shared with an eligibility team, including Kathleen's parents, in order for the district to make an eligibility determination.[28] Based on conversations with the parents' lawyer, it appears that the parents first saw the eligibility report at the IEP meeting.

An IEP meeting was held on April 29, 2010. The topic of the IEP meeting was both the eligibility decision and the IEP for Kathleen because Menzie's report includes recommendations concerning whether Kathleen was dis-abled and what program should be put in place for her. The IEP team consid-ered two possible areas of suspected disability (attention deficit disorder and specific learning disability) at the April 29 meeting[29] with the IEP team deter-mining that Kathleen was "eligible for special education as a pupil with a spe-cific learning disability due to deficits in oral and visual processing."[30] The hearing officer says nothing about the content of the IEP that was approved by the IEP team at that meeting (or if one was approved at all).

Kathleen's mother did not disagree with the adequacy of the school dis-trict's assessment at the April meeting. Nonetheless, she had increasing concerns that the district did not fully understand the nature of her daughter's visual processing disorder and sought further information from the district. After the district made the odd suggestion that she see an eye doctor to learn more about her daughter's visual processing deficit (which was neurological in nature), she consulted with a lawyer about her next appropriate step. Her lawyer suggested she request an IEP meeting and seek a school-funded IEE. On September 27, 2010, Kathleen's mother requested an IEP meeting to register her disagreement with the assessment report and, immediately thereafter, provided a written request for an IEE, at district expense.[31]

Rather than comply with this request, the district filed a due process hearing request on October 19, 2010, in which it argued that Menzie's assessment was appropriate and that, therefore, the district did not need to pay for Kathleen's parents to obtain an assessment from their own experts. After a failed, expedited mediation attempt, a due process hearing was held. The hearing officer's decision in the case was not rendered until February 3, 2011, because a continuance was granted on November 4, 2010, at the request of the parties. Although Congress specifies that these cases be decided quickly, that is an unrealistic aspiration. Kathleen's parents could not participate in the due process hearing until they had retained an expert and reviewed the school district's evaluation closely.

The district had the burden of proof at the due process hearing to demonstrate that its assessment was adequate. As the U.S. Supreme Court explained in *Schaffer*, the expectation is that the district will pay for the parents' educational evaluation of their child when the parents seek to contest the eligibility classification or the adequacy of the IEP, because the parents, who would have the burden of proof in such challenges, need to have the same "fire power" as the parent.

In this case, like many cases in which the district is not able to demonstrate that its evaluation was adequate, the parent retained an expert as well as a lawyer. (The child's mother also appears to be licensed to practice law in California.) In fact, in every case I read in which the hearing officer or the federal judge found the district's evaluation to be inadequate, the parents hired both an expert and a lawyer. That is unfortunate because it turns the IEE process on its head—parents can succeed in forcing a district to pay for an IEE, when the district objects, only if the parents pay for the expenses of an expert.

In order to maintain any semblance of fairness, the parents should not be expected to hire an expert who would conduct a full psychoeducational evaluation. The parents' expert should merely assist the parent in arguing that the district's evaluation is not adequate, in a context in which the district, not the parents, has the burden of proof. The hearing officer in this case claimed to place the burden of proof on the district but, in reality, placed a very heavy burden of proof on the parents. For example, the hearing officer considered in evaluating the credibility of the parents' expert whether the expert had met Kathleen.[32] But whether the parents' expert had met Kathleen is not relevant to the issue of whether the *district* had conducted an appropriate evaluation. Rather than place the burden of proof on the district to show that its evaluation was appropriate, these cases often sound as if the hearing officer is comparing the parents' evaluation with the district's evaluation and deciding which is more complete or thorough. For example, the hearing officer in this case says:

> [The school psychologist's] report was not perfect. However, [her] testimony was honest and she capably explained the foundation for her opinion. When weighed against Student's criticisms, [the school psychologist's] were given more weight [than the Student's expert] due to her direct observation of Student, her reliance upon extensive school records, and her demonstrated ability to apply her experience and make a reasoned judgment as to the source of Student's deficits.[33]

Nowhere in that paragraph does the hearing officer use the correct legal standard. The parents' expert—without ever meeting the child—was highly qualified to say why the school psychologist's report was not "appropriate" and, as discussed below, did not come close to meeting many of the statutory requirements. Their reports should not be weighed against each other, as if it is a balancing test. The district must *demonstrate* that its report met the statutory requirements. The parents should not even have to use an expert to make that showing.

The hearing officer loses sight of the bigger picture—if the parents prevail, then the district will have to pay the parents' expert to conduct a full and appropriate IEE. The parents should not have to pay to conduct a full evaluation in order for the hearing officer to conclude that the district had not conducted an appropriate evaluation. The hearing officer's opinion was overturned, in part, by the district court, but the district court did not fully acknowledge the full extent to which the hearing officer had misallocated the burden of proof and the full extent to which the district's evaluation was inappropriate.

The district's evaluation had a tremendous number of problems that, cumulatively, made it impossible to know what was the correct eligibility classification or what kind of program should be put in place to assist

Kathleen. I'll next discuss some of the problems with how the district conducted its evaluation through reference to the requirements found in the statute and accompanying regulations.

1. The school district must provide a copy of the evaluation report and the documentation of determination of eligibility at no cost to the parent.[34] The district's educational records were missing much of the raw data that formed the foundation for the school psychologist's report, making it impossible for the district to demonstrate that it had administered and scored the tests correctly. Their existing records also included some errors. The school's inability to produce complete and accurate test results should have been a factor in determining whether its testing was adequate.

2. Assessments are supposed to be used for the purposes for which the assessments or measures are valid and reliable.[35] The school psychologist administered the TVPS-3 for the purpose of determining whether Kathleen had a visual processing deficit, relying heavily on one subscore from that test. The parents' expert testified that the TVPS-3 is not considered to be a reliable assessment tool by the *Buros Mental Measurement Yearbook*, a reference book used by clinical psychologists to confirm the validity and reliability of assessment instruments. The *Yearbook* stated that "the use of this instrument beyond research purposes cannot be recommended, because of the absence of useful reliability and validity information."[36] Further, it stated that "[i]nterpretation of individual subtest scores or index scores also cannot be recommended, as these scores have not been demonstrated to be psychometrically differentiable."[37] Thus, the test is overall not considered valid or reliable, and, more specifically, it is not valid or reliable to use one subscore to draw this type of conclusion, yet the hearing officer accepted the school district's interpretation of the TVPS-3 test results.[38]

3. Assessments are supposed to be administered in accordance with any instructions provided by the producer of the assessments.[39] The school psychologist administered the basic battery of the Cognitive Assessment System (CAS). This test was supposed to measure Kathleen's utilization of the mental process to focus thinking on particular stimuli, while ignoring other stimuli.[40] It was the only test the district administered that supposedly would have provided some data on whether she had ADHD, so the test results were quite important. The hearing officer overlooked evidence that the school psychologist did not follow the test instructions when administering this important test.

4. Similarly, the school psychologist failed to follow instructions for administering the Behavior Assessment System for Children (BASC-2)—a test of social skills. The test is a set of rating scales and forms that are completed by those who are familiar with the child. The school psychologist read the questions on the forms aloud to Kathleen's mother over a telephone while she was shopping at a mall and recordered her answer by hand; she did not even try to have Kathleen's father or grandmother, who were important caregivers, complete the forms. That test administration was contrary to the instruction manual's suggestion that the forms be completed in a "controlled setting."[41]

5. A child is also supposed to be assessed "in all areas related to the suspected disability."[42] In this case, there were repeated suggestions that Kathleen might have ADHD, yet the school psychologist stubbornly ignored all the evidence in the record of ADHD to avoid administering an appropriate test to measure for ADHD. The school psychologist put the cart before the horse in insisting on clinical evidence of ADHD before agreeing to administer a proper clinical test to determine the existence of ADHD.[43] Because the evidence suggested that ADHD was a *possibility*,[44] it should have been validly assessed.

Notwithstanding these and other problems with the school psychologist's report, the hearing officer found that the difference of opinion between the school psychologist and the parents' expert was based on "differences in their respective professional judgment as to the conclusions reached from test data, record, and classroom observations. Despite her apparent competence and candor, [parents'] expert testimony was not persuasive."[45]

Kathleen's parents appealed the hearing officer's decision to a federal district court. The judge ruled in their favor on March 20, 2012, more than a year later.[46] She found that the IEE should commence within thirty days of the order so that the results of the assessment could be used to formulate an IEP for the 2012–13 school year, when Kathleen would be in the fifth grade.

Although the hearing officer's decision was overturned on appeal, the district court did not find that each of the problems I discuss above constituted evidence that the school district's evaluation was inappropriate. One reason the district court judge likely did not issue a broader decision is the limited scope of review available to the district court judge. Although the district court judge is supposed to conduct a "*de novo* review," under which he or she reviews all the factual findings, the judge is also supposed to give "due weight" to the decision of the hearing officer.[47]

The district court judge agreed with my assessment of the first problem, finding "that the missing files weigh in favor of the District funding an Independent Educational Evaluation."[48] The district judge also agreed with part of my assessment of the fifth problem, finding that the "insufficient classroom observation weighs in favor of the District funding an Independent Educational Evaluation."[49] In addition, the district judge agreed with my discussion of the fourth problem, finding that "the uncontrolled and distracted nature of the BASC-2 interview with Mother . . . weigh[s] in favor of the District funding an Independent Educational Examination."[50] With respect to the third problem, the district court judge found that the "irregularities are not as problematic."[51]

The district court judge did not agree with my discussion of the fifth problem, concluding that "while it appears that the District did evaluate Student in all possible areas, there are areas in which the District spent an insufficient amount of resources."[52] The district court judge never explained how one could conclude that the district evaluated Kathleen in the area of ADHD *at all* because of the faulty administration of the only tests intended to evaluate in that area. And the district court judge never even discussed most of the second problem—how the district chose inappropriate testing instruments that were not accepted in the professional literature for the purposes for which they were used—because the parents' lawyer decided not to press this issue as a result of page limitations. Following this decision, the school district may consider it still appropriate to administer the TVPS-3 for children thought to have visual processing deficits.

More troubling, though, was that the district court judge refused to conclude that the hearing officer inappropriately allocated the burden of proof with her language about "weighing" the testimony of each of the experts.[53] Instead, the district court judge interpreted that language to mean that the hearing officer was merely making a "credibility determination" regarding the witnesses.[54] But that is an implausible interpretation of the hearing officer's decision. This was not a case in which plaintiff and defendant's experts had witnessed a traffic accident and the court was trying to figure out whom to believe. The hearing officer talked about "weighing" the experts' testimony in the same sentence in which she also criticized the parents' expert for not having met Kathleen. The parents' expert was not suggesting that she had met Kathleen and had an independent basis for offering an evaluation based on personally conducted assessments. The use of the word "weighing" by the hearing officer suggests that she expected to hear that kind of direct testimony from the parents' expert rather than confine the case to whether the school district had met *its* obligation to test Kathleen appropriately.

Although the hearing officer's decision was overturned on appeal, it is important to understand the impossible burden this hearing officer placed on the parents in order for them to obtain an educational evaluation at public expense. The mother, who was a lawyer, hired an attorney to represent them at the due process hearing. The family also hired an expert who conducted an extremely thorough review of the school psychologist's report. When they were unable to prevail before the hearing officer, they appealed the decision to a federal district court judge and won a year later. Meanwhile, their daughter, who was in second grade at the beginning of this process, will be in fifth grade by the time an IEP based on an appropriate evaluation will be in place. It is hard to see how the IEE requirement gives parents equal "fire power," as required by *Schaffer v. Weast*, to sue school districts if it takes three years merely to get the school district to pay for the IEE. And by refusing to find that the hearing officer had misallocated the burden of proof, the district court did a poor job of preventing this kind of problem in the future.

It is impossible to understate how important a proper evaluation is in an IEP case. Kathleen's parents' health insurance plan would not cover a complete psychoeducational evaluation, and her parents did not have the $5,000 (or so) that it would cost to hire a private consultant to conduct one. Because of the strength of their case, they could find a lawyer to take it. But what about the other children whose parents are not able to secure a lawyer and an expert to challenge the denial of an IEE? It is hard to see how they will have equal "firepower" if they seek to challenge an IEP as not providing a fair and appropriate public education. Without clear instructions from the California courts about the appropriate burden of proof in an IEE case, we can expect California school districts to continue to resist IEE requests.

CHILD FIND VIOLATION

Another important requirement under the IDEA is the school district's Child Find obligation. This rule requires a school district to assess any child who it "suspects" may be disabled; the child is supposed to be evaluated in all areas of suspected disability. Like the IEE rules, this rule is crucial to the overall operation of the IDEA process and particularly important to early identification of children with disabilities when intervention can be most fruitful. Unfortunately, California school districts do not always meet their Child Find obligations, and hearing officers can be reluctant to find in favor of parents and their children when such violations occur. A 2009 case involving a child I'll call William suing the Clovis Unified School District provides a good example of a hearing officer's applying an overly narrow interpretation of the relevant law and being overturned by a district court.[55]

Because of William's academic and behavioral problems in school, the school district held eligibility meetings regarding him in February 2005, June 2006, and December 2006. At each meeting, the district concluded that William was ineligible for special education services.[56] Meanwhile, William repeated first grade, a section 504 plan was put in place for him under which he was expected to complete only 50 percent of class work, and a behavioral plan was established. Even with these rules in place, William completed about half of the required work (or 25 percent of the work altogether). In particular, he very much disliked writing and completed few writing assignments.

William's parents thought he had ADHD and a writing impairment and that these impairments were having an adverse effect on his educational performance. They filed a due process complaint on June 20, 2007, at the end of William's third-grade year. The hearing officer ruled that the school district had met its Child Find obligations and that, even if William had a specific learning disability or other health impairment, he did not need special education and related services.[57] William's parents appealed that determination, and a district court judge reversed the hearing officer, in part, in a decision on June 8, 2009, at the end of William's fifth-grade year. The district court judge ruled that the "District failed to assess Student properly in the area of writing, and failed to provide Student a FAPE based [on] its failure to identify [him] as eligible for special education under the category of OHI."[58] The procedural ground for relief was the deprivation of an education benefit (IEP) caused by a failure to identify William as disabled. Unlike the case involving Kathleen, the school district was not following an existing IEP; the procedural violations caused William to not have an IEP at all.

A close examination of the record shows how difficult it is for parents to have the necessary "firepower" to win this kind of case even though the U.S. Supreme Court presumed equal "firepower" when it assigned the burden of proof to parents in *Schaffer v. Weast.*[59]

William was identified in 2003 as having ADHD, prior to beginning first grade at a public elementary school within his school district.[60] He repeated first grade, so he attended first grade in both 2003–4 and in 2004–5. The school district first assessed William in January and February of 2005 and held an eligibility meeting on February 22, 2005. The team determined that William was not eligible for special education and related services because it concluded that he was making adequate progress in the regular classroom, but it also convened a section 504 meeting (with the same group of people) and created an accommodation plan for him (suggesting that they did not really believe he was making adequate progress).[61]

The February 2005 evaluation indicated that William received a standard score of 79 on the visual-motor integration evaluation, placing him in the sixth percentile.[62] Although that score could have been the basis for the conclusion that he had a learning disability in writing, the school psychologist concluded that his writing problems were "behaviorally based" because he simply refused to write.[63] The February 2005 evaluation also indicated that William had a standard score of 83, which is in the thirteenth percentile, on a test of working memory.[64] Although a low working memory score can be an indication that a student's ADHD is having an adverse educational effect, the school district did not consider that score sufficient to qualify William as disabled under IDEA. The February 2005 evaluation also included an assessment in the area of social/emotional functioning. These scores reportedly placed William in the "at risk" range with respect to adaptive skills, depression, and hyperactivity.[65] William's parents' expert testified at the due process hearing that there were numerous scoring errors with this instrument and the hearing officer observed: "Overall, [school psychologist] did not know what the differences in Student's BASC scores would be in the absence of the errors."[66] Despite these low scores, significant behavioral problems in the classroom, and errors in reporting test results, the hearing officer concluded that the school district had no obligation to evaluate William for a behavioral disability prior to April 2006.[67]

The hearing officer opinion does not describe William's section 504 plan, but the district court opinion states that, under the section 504 plan, William was required to complete only 50 percent of the schoolwork assigned during the 2005–6 school year (second grade).[68] Despite this accommodation, he completed only 50 percent of his accommodated work—in other words, he was completing about 25 percent of the work assigned to the second-grade class. Because William was struggling with writing, the section 504 team met in October 2005 to discuss whether William had a written-language disorder. Rather than suggest testing to determine if William had a language disorder, the team relied on his second-grade teacher's report that he was "probably at grade level" based on the few writing projects that William would complete.[69]

Meanwhile, William began having behavioral problems. He was behaving aggressively toward other children, having tantrums in class, and not completing class work. The school district put in place a behavioral support plan in February 2006; the support plan stated that his behaviors were interfering with his learning.[70] The school district began to suggest to William's parents that William might qualify as eligible for special education under the category of "emotional disturbance."[71]

The school district agreed to assess William for special education eligibility in April 2006, but its assessment plan was quite incomplete, based on the assumption that his problems in school were due primarily to an emotional disturbance. Thus, the school district did not assess William for a deficit in visual-motor integration despite the low score from the 2005 assessment in that area. Nonetheless, a private psychologist had administered a visual-motor integration test to William in November 2005 and he had attained a standard score of 85, within the average range.[72] Based on these test results, the hearing officer concluded (and the district court affirmed) that the "District had no reason to suspect that Student had a disability in the area of visual-motor integration." Unfortunately, this conclusion confuses the issue of whether there is any reason to "suspect" a disability with the substantive result after such an evaluation is completed. The change in William's standard score from 79 to 85 is likely within the error of measurement of the testing instrument. An 85 is exactly one standard deviation below the mean (100) and is barely within what can be called the "average" range. Later tests may have concluded that William did not have a visual-motor disability, but the legal question should have been whether there was any reason to *suspect* that William had a visual-motor deficit in April 2006 when the school district agreed to conduct additional testing. And such evidence did exist from both the scores of 79 and 85 within the previous six months.

The April 2006 evaluation did include an attempt to evaluate William's writing. One reason for not conducting this assessment until that time was that he was receiving A and B grades in his classes; but that observation ignored that he was completing only about 25 percent of the class work. In fact, William was producing very little writing in class. The scope of his writing problems should have triggered an evaluation before April 2006.

The writing evaluation that was conducted as part of the April 2006 assessment was woefully incomplete. The school district's resource specialist tried to get William to produce a writing sample in May 2006 but was unable to do so. The school district based its evaluation of William's writing abilities on his average score of 104 from the Woodcock-Johnson assessment, but that assessment did not require William to produce any sustained writing; it required him only to fill in the blanks and write simple sentences.[73] The school district also had *one* piece of writing that William had produced at school on a favorite topic and with tremendous assistance from the school psychologist[74]—a three-paragraph, nine-sentence writing sample describing his favorite Pokémon character.[75] Although William's parents challenged the adequacy of the April 2006 assessment of his writing, the hearing officer does not explain why the April 2006 writing assessment could be considered adequate.

Nonetheless, the hearing officer does explain why she believed it was appropriate for the school district not to conduct a thorough writing assessment in the fall of 2006 and spring of 2007. The hearing officer placed weight on William's proficient score on the spring 2007 California Standardized Testing and Reporting (STAR) exam[76] even though that exam was exclusively a fill-in-the-bubble examination and did not require students to write[77] and was taken under conditions of accommodation. She also placed much weight on the Pokémon writing sample, which she described as having been written "without any help,"[78] ignoring the extensive assistance offered by the school psychologist to get him to complete that piece of writing.[79] Finally, she ignored the evidence that William's writing had deteriorated even further in third grade because he "rarely produced written work in the classroom."[80] Despite the absence of much evidence that William could produce grade-level writing, the hearing officer credited testimony from the school psychologist that William was "capable" of doing grade-level work and that his failure to complete work was "his choice."[81]

The district court judge was quite critical of the hearing officer's determination that William's difficulties in writing were simply a result of his "choice." That conclusion ignored evidence that William would "freeze up" or "shut down" when he tried to write and that he often could not even write on a topic that he enjoyed greatly. Similarly, it ignored his mother's testimony that he could not write even if he wanted to do so. The district court judge concluded: "At best, Student's ability to write was inconsistent and based partly on his behavior. For these reasons, writing expression was an area of suspected disability for Student, and District's [C]hild [F]ind obligation was triggered at the beginning of the relevant time period and continued throughout."[82]

One reason the hearing officer and the district court judge reached different conclusions about the adequacy of the writing evaluation is that they gave different weight to William's expert's testimony. William's expert, a Dr. Patterson, testified that William was unable to sustain writing effort. The hearing officer discredited Patterson's testimony because he was unaware of the Pokémon writing sample and had not spoken with William's teachers or observed William in the classroom. These are the same kinds of errors the Los Angeles School District raised in the case involving Kathleen—they criticized Kathleen's expert for not having personally tested her in a case involving the adequacy of the school district's evaluation. But in a case involving the *adequacy* of the school district's evaluation—wherein the parents are seeking an independent educational evaluation or a violation of the district's Child Find obligations—the parent's expert need *not* have evaluated the child at all. The parent's expert can merely review the testing done by the school district. In William's case, the expert *did* conduct an extensive evaluation of William and concluded he had ADHD and a disorder of written expression.[83] But William's parents should have been able to prevail merely by attacking the district's sloppy evaluation rather than by conducting an evaluation of their own.

Hence, the District Court concluded:

> The testimony of every witness supported Dr. Patterson's expert opinion that Student is unable to sustain writing effort. Thus, Student's single writing sample does not negate Dr. Patterson's professional opinion, even if he was unaware of it. In evaluating Student's written expression, District ignored the undisputed evidence that Student rarely produced written work in the classroom. The overwhelming and consistent testimony from all witnesses is that Student is impaired in written expression, sustained writing, and the initiation of writing.[84]

The district court judge was correct to conclude that the district had sufficient evidence of William's writing difficulties to justify a full writing assessment. But William's witnesses need not have proved that William was *actually impaired* in written expression to justify an assessment. The district court judge's discussion confuses the question of whether an assessment should occur with the issue of whether the child is actually disabled.

Although William's parents eventually prevailed on this issue in the district court, it is important to emphasize how difficult it was for them to do so. They filed the due process complaint on June 20, 2007, after more than two years of pressing the school district to identify their child as having a disorder in written expression. Their original due process hearing was scheduled for August 28, 2007, but they had to ask for a continuance because they could not get Dr. Patterson to evaluate William until August 25, 2007. The due process hearing was rescheduled for September 13, 2007, but William's parents were not able to use Dr. Patterson as an expert at that time with respect to William because they had not yet shared his report with the district. They had to ask for another continuance until October 15, 2007, so they could share his report. Similarly, Kathleen's parents also had to seek a continuance because their expert could not meet the expedited time frame of IEP matters.

The hearing officer issued a decision in favor of the school district on December 17, 2007, about six months after William's parents filed their due process complaint. That decision was not overturned until June 8, 2009, when he would have completed fifth grade. And the district court judge merely remanded the case back to the hearing officer. It is quite possible that William did not receive special education services in the area of writing for third, fourth, and fifth grades based on the hearing officer's decision from 2007.

Conclusion

California appears to be an extraordinarily difficult state in which one might work as a special education lawyer in the hope of earning a living by collecting attorney fees from school districts when one is able to prevail on behalf of a client. The hearing officers are inclined to cite *Rowley* to help resolve nearly any issue that might arise. Even when violations are found to exist, they are considered to be nonsubstantive, and no relief (or attorney fees) is ordered. California has one of the highest rates of litigation in the United States, which likely reflects that school districts are not concerned about losing if they take a case to a due process hearing.

This is not to say that parents are always right in California. Many parents refused to sign proposed educational plans and then did not even show up at the hearings when the districts filed due process complaints to receive permission to implement the proposed plan. Many parents also sought independent educational evaluations but did not bother to defend those requests at due process hearings when the district opposed their requests.

Nonetheless, the odds really seem stacked against parents and their children in California. I did have the opportunity to share some of my findings and conclusions with California hearing officers at a training session in April 2012. I hope my work can help persuade them to apply both the burden of proof and the educational adequacy standards more fairly so that parents will have a more realistic chance of prevailing at due process hearings.

District of Columbia

The District of Columbia is the home of the litigation that demonstrated the relationship between race, poverty, and inadequate services for students with disabilities in the 1960s and 1970s. Yet its educational system, including its assistance for students with disabilities, remains a complete mess.

In 1967, Judge Skelly Wright found that the District of Columbia school system unconstitutionally used "ability" tracking as a way to relegate African American and poor students to inferior schools and classrooms.[1] The "special academic" track was for students who had "emotionally disturbed behavior, an IQ of 75 or below, and substandard performance on achievement tests."[2] Those in the "special academic" track were disproportionately poor and African American[3] and received an inferior education. Judge Wright's hundred-page opinion was a ringing indictment of the special education system in the District as disserving poor and minority children.

In 1972, Judge Cornelius Waddy ruled in the *Mills* case that the District of Columbia violated the U.S. Constitution by excluding various children with disabilities from the educational system.[4] Once again, the plaintiffs were African American, but the court's ruling was not dependent on that fact. Instead, the court concluded that denying an education to children with disabilities while offering it to typically developing children was a denial of equal protection. The District of Columbia case coupled with the *PARC* case from Pennsylvania[5] helped draw national attention to the millions of children who were being denied an education altogether because of their disability status.

Although the D.C. litigation helped inspire the enactment of the EAHCA, the District of Columbia has a terrible record of being out of compliance with the IDEA on both procedural and substantive grounds. In 1999, in *Blackman v. District of Columbia*, a federal district court judge appointed a special master to oversee what he described as the extraordinary circumstances of the District's lack of compliance with the special education laws in ways that caused the potential for immediate harm to children.[6] For example, after one mother had successfully obtained a ruling from a hearing officer that the school district must administer medication and catheterization to her child in order to avoid serious medical harm, her child returned home from school with her medication and catheterization kit untouched.

The judge also found that D.C. was starkly out of compliance with the timelines required by the special education laws. Of the 655 hearing requests that had been filed by parents or guardians on behalf of their children, a final decision had not been issued within the applicable timeline in 482 cases. Children had waited as long as 177 days to receive their due process hearings rather than the mandated 45 days. Lawyers complained that, in some cases, they could not even get the school district to respond to their phone calls as they pursued a complaint. The district court found: "[A]s the District fails to provide services, fails to return phone calls and fails to meet the Court's deadlines, time continues to pass, aggravating the threat of injury to children."[7]

The D.C. litigation lasted more than a decade. On January 28, 2011, the D.C. Circuit affirmed the district court's order of $1.4 million in attorney fees. Circuit Judge Janice Rogers Brown concurred in that decision and also detailed the extensive failures of the D.C. educational system. Despite spending an average of $20,596 per pupil, D.C. has the highest per capita rate of hearing officer requests in the country. In 2002, it received 3,044 hearing officer requests for a student population of less than 50,000. California received 2,670 requests for a population of 670,000. Yet, D.C. also has the twelfth-lowest high school graduation rate in the country—68.8 percent.

From this set of circumstances, Judge Brown concluded:

The District of Columbia Public Schools' biggest problem should be having more pro bono services offered than it can use. Instead, in the bizarre world inhabited by the District, the more its student population shrinks, the bigger its legal bills grow. If there is an answer to this problem, it will likely come from concerned parents, committed teachers, and conscientious volunteers. One thing is clear. It will not come from adjusting the spigot directing the flow of public funds to lawyers.[8]

It is easy to understand why Judge Brown would be critical of the high volume of litigation against the D.C. schools as a waste of valuable resources. But a close examination of the due process decisions rendered in D.C. suggests that these cases were sorely needed because many of these children received little or no extra help until high school, even though they were performing at an extraordinarily low level throughout their educational experience. Because of the delay in providing services and the weak education available in the public schools, many of these hearing officers had to order private placements for these children. The volume of those private placements helps explain the high level of expenditure for the District on a per-pupil basis. It would be interesting to know how much money is being used to fund classroom education for the students not in special, private schools. Because of the small student population, private schooling at public expense could be adding significantly to the per-pupil educational expense without providing an adequate education for the public school population. It also is not clear whether the per-pupil educational figure includes the District's litigation expenses.

Before turning to a survey of the hearing officer decisions in D.C., it is helpful to read about one case that reflects the inability of the District to provide appropriate services without a private school placement. The case also reflects the positive role of case managers and educational advocates for some of the low-income children in the D.C. public school system. As mentioned earlier, parents cannot get reimbursed for their expenses in hiring an educational advocate even though those advocates can perform work that is critical to a child's receiving an appropriate education.

Amanda[9] was diagnosed with autism in 2005 and found eligible for special education on February 13, 2008, before entering a D.C. public school kindergarten. Her full-scale IQ was 53, which was below the first percentile. Her verbal comprehension, working memory, and processing speed were also below the first percentile. Her performance in talking, listening, reading, and writing were in the first percentile. She had very weak daily living and socialization skills. She did not engage in communication with others and showed no recognition that another person was present. She also had the benefit of an educational advocate.

In D.C., the school week in grade school consists of 27.5 hours of instruction. In second grade, the educational advocate recommended that Amanda receive 27.5 hours of specialized instruction and related services in a private school. Amanda had been receiving 17.5 hours of specialized instruction and related services outside the general education curriculum during first grade. Because of the discrepancy between what she needed and had been receiving, the educational advocate also requested 120 hours of tutoring as compensatory education.

The school district proposed that Amanda spend two hours per day in a general education classroom with twenty-four students and one teacher. However, the record indicated that Amanda had not been able to receive any educational benefit in that kind of setting in first grade, even when the teacher worked one-on-one with her (while neglecting the other students). The school district proposed that for the remainder of the day she be in a special classroom with one teacher and six students; she had made some academic progress in such a setting in first grade.

The educational advocate recommended that Amanda attend a private school where each classroom had a maximum of ten students, one teacher, and one teaching assistant. The private school also had several special programs for children like Amanda who had autism to help their social functioning and academic skills. The public school offered none of those programs. When the school district refused to adopt the program recommended by Amanda's educational advocate, her parents filed for due process with assistance from the advocate.

Although the school district refused to place Amanda in the private school, it did not offer a vigorous defense of its proposed educational program at the due process hearing. None of the school district's witnesses contradicted the witnesses on behalf of Amanda who testified that she needed a full day of special education programming with some attention to social functioning as well as academic skills. Further, the school district's occupational therapist and speech and language pathologist corroborated Amanda's witnesses with respect to services she needed that were not being provided at the public school.

While recognizing that the burden of proof was on Amanda's advocate, the hearing officer found in Amanda's favor. The hearing officer did not describe the burden as starkly as it had been described in the Florida decisions discussed in chapter 9. He said that the preponderance of the evidence standard "allows both parties to share the risk of error in roughly equal fashion, except that when the evidence is evenly balanced, the party with the burden of persuasion must lose."[10]

The uncontradicted evidence and realistic burden of proof made this an easy case for the hearing officer to rule in Amanda's favor. He found that the school district's own psychological evaluation "unequivocally supported full-time, specialized instruction outside the general education environment for the Student."[11] Thus, he ruled that the school district must revise Amanda's IEP to provide for education at the private school on or before March 21, 2011 (during second grade). Thus, three years after she was found eligible for special education, Amanda was assigned to a placement that might help her make appropriate educational progress. Nonetheless, the hearing officer denied the request for compensatory relief, such as supplementary tutoring or extended school year services, because Amanda had made some progress under the prior IEP.

This case makes little sense. Why would a school district pursue a case to a due process hearing without any evidence supporting its position? How could it have expected Amanda to benefit from two hours of instruction per day in a regular classroom? The toll on the regular education teacher as well as on Amanda must have been enormous because Amanda did not have the social skills to be in that classroom.

It is possible that the school district could not obtain the funds to educate Amanda unless it lost at the due process hearing. The waste of resources for everyone involved, though, seems ridiculous. With that kind of meager defense, it is no surprise that families often prevail in due process cases filed in D.C. That success, however, was possible only because of the support from pro bono legal counsel and an educational advocate. The school district was not otherwise willing to provide an appropriate educational plan.

Hearing Officer Decisions

My team of research assistants read one hundred decisions that were decided between November 1, 2010, and March 31, 2011. Plaintiffs prevailed in fifty-seven of one hundred cases. Unlike in other jurisdictions (states), legal counsel nearly always represented the plaintiffs. And unlike in other jurisdictions, few plaintiffs had autism. The most frequent disabilities were learning disabilities (34 percent), emotional disturbance (34 percent), and other health impairments (27 percent). The D.C. public schools are 76 percent African American, 13 percent Latino, and 9 percent white.[12] Mirroring the national statistics on the basis of race by disability classification, the category of "emotional disturbance" was overrepresented among this client population and "autism" was underrepresented.

Parents were also often successful when they appealed adverse administrative decisions to federal court. Reviewing the cases in which opinions were issued between June 2009 and June 2011 in the district court for the District of Columbia, we found that parents prevailed in seven of twenty-three (30.4

percent) of those appeals. Hence, it is likely that the 57 percent figure from the administrative process understates the ultimate victories for parents in special education cases in D.C.

These cases reflect strong evidence of how lawyers can strengthen the educational programs for students. The lawyers often tried to get school districts to recognize the educational needs of students who were labeled emotionally disturbed. For example, the University of the District of Columbia Clinic brought a case on behalf of Shannon, a fifteen-year-old female student, who was receiving educational services for emotional disturbance.[13] Shannon's IEP was providing her with ten hours per week of specialized instruction in the general education setting and eight hours a week outside the general education setting, along with one-and-a-half hours of behavioral support services. Her lawyers convinced the hearing officer that Shannon should also receive services as learning disabled and other health impaired. The legal team was successful, and Shannon's case was remanded to the IEP team to include education for specific learning disability, math deficits, other identified symptoms, and a behavioral intervention plan with more specific goals.

Similarly, the firm of James E. Brown & Associates (which handles many special education cases) brought a case on behalf of Sally, a sixteen-year-old female student who had been held back twice, was truant and failing, and was regressing.[14] The hearing officer rejected the school district's proposed placement because it served only students who were emotionally disturbed. Sally needed a program that also served students with learning disabilities.

Finally, in another case brought by the firm of James E. Brown & Associates, the hearing officer rejected the school district's proposed neighborhood school placement for Billy, a high school student with a wide range of disabilities, including emotional disturbance.[15] The hearing officer approved the parent's unilateral placement at a private full-time therapeutic school with small settings and full-time counselors, where Billy progressed.

Although the parents and their children prevailed in these and similar cases, it is important to note that many of these children were already in high school, and sometimes in serious legal trouble, before these cases were brought. I examined half the cases in the database to get a better sense of the age distribution of cases in D.C. Of these fifty cases, it was possible to determine the child's approximate age in forty-five cases. Only ten of these cases involved children in elementary school, and rarely were children in the early years of their elementary education. By contrast, twenty-two cases involved students who were already in high school, typically at least seventeen years old. Because of the entirely inadequate education they had received (often leaving them six to ten years below grade level), the relief sought was often a private school and compensatory education. It is hard to imagine, however, that this delayed relief could adequately remedy the damage done during the many years that they were receiving inadequate educational services.

Many of the lawyers who brought these cases clearly did a fine job, but it is also disturbing to see that Brown & Associates, a firm with a questionable ethical reputation, is representing some of these children. In February 2002, the *Washington Post* published a story detailing how Brown & Associates also ran a private school and served as an educational diagnostic service provider.[16] In the fiscal year preceding the article, D.C. Public Schools paid its various businesses $9.6 million. After the story was published, the firm sold its stakes in those companies and reached a fee reduction with the school district.[17] But their legal problems continued as several disciplinary actions were filed against members of their firm for failing to supervise an attorney and allowing an attorney to practice law in a jurisdiction in which he was not licensed.[18] Thus, it seems that the low quality of education in the District of Columbia has allowed a questionable law firm to bring many cases on behalf of children and make inappropriate profits through a conflict of interest. If the District voluntarily offered these children an appropriate education, there would be little incentive for a firm to prey on the misfortune of families with children with disabilities.

Conclusion

One theme that stands out in this study of hearing officer decisions in the three states and the District of Columbia is that parents need lawyers if they are to prevail at due process hearings. Even when school districts bore the burden of proof in New Jersey on regular petitions, parents could not obtain significant relief unless they had the assistance of legal counsel. And even when parents were represented by legal counsel, it appears that the New Jersey hearing officers are quite lenient on school districts. In fact, it is hard to see that the change in the burden of proof has any meaningful impact on the results. Parents fared better in emergent relief petitions, where they had the burden of proof, than in regular petitions, where they did not. Nearly all these successful emergent relief petitions involved stay-put requests. In New Jersey, as elsewhere, parents almost never succeed in demonstrating that an IEP is inadequate under the *Rowley* standard.

The hearing officer decisions from these jurisdictions show that school districts will sometimes take fairly minor issues to due process, suggesting that they have little fear of losing, especially when the parent is not represented by a lawyer. For example, one New Jersey parent had to go all the way to due process merely to get the results of an eye exam conducted by the school district. In Ohio, school districts aggressively challenged complaints as not being "sufficient" when parents made clerical errors like omitting a name or address. In California, the school districts routinely contested requests for IEEs.

These cases also reflect that a school district will often defend a case at due process because it is "legally correct," even though it is obvious that the remedy sought by the parent or guardian is very important to a child's potential to obtain an adequate education. It is hard to understand why a New Jersey school district could not find a way to provide transportation to and from a daycare center to a special education program so that the child's grandmother (who had custody of four children) could work to support her family rather than miss work to provide transportation. Similarly, it is difficult to understand why a California school district would refuse to provide home-to-school transportation for an eight-year-old boy whose mother was cognitively impaired and trying to help raise two children with the assistance of his grandmother. It is also hard to understand why the Parma School District in Ohio would fight the Winkelmans for years over the issue of their child's attending a private school when it would have been very expensive and difficult for them to educate him in the public schools with a full-time aide. Further, the school district could obtain some scholarship assistance to assist with the private school education.

The most disturbing set of cases was from the District of Columbia. These cases reflected the national data about special education's doing a poor job of meeting the needs of minority children. These children were often in high school by the time a due process hearing was held. They were usually classified as emotionally disturbed even though evidence of learning disabilities was also often present in the records. They did usually have the assistance of counsel and even prevailed in the majority of cases. But even their successful lawyers did not always raise all the claims possible in their cases, sometimes overlooking the need for compensatory education. Poor representation on the part of their lawyers sometimes caused criticisms from the hearing officers or judges even as they ruled in favor of the children with disabilities. Lawyers with questionable legal ethics sometimes victimized them.

After reviewing these records, it is hard to feel optimistic about the hearing officer process. Clearly, children need lawyers and qualified experts in order to prevail. But they especially need ethical lawyers who will seek all the available relief rather than simply enough relief to put them in the category of "prevailing party" for the purpose of collecting attorney fees.

The toll on families is the untold story in these hearing officer opinions. Parents who were struggling at low-wage jobs to support their families had to attend many meetings and hearings over the years in order for their children to obtain an adequate education. Few parents have the time to pursue such claims. Being the parent of a child with a disability under the IDEA who pursues litigation is a full-time job. That is wrong.

The District of Columbia reflects how difficult it is to correct problems in special education when faced with a recalcitrant school district. The *Mills* case forced the District to educate all of its children, including African American children who were incorrectly labeled mentally retarded or emotionally disturbed. These children are now in the school district but often receiving highly inadequate services in a situation in which their disabilities are not classified appropriately. The problems these children face—improper and late disability classifications with insufficient services—are typical of the problems faced by racial minorities throughout the country. How can Congress overlook this massive problem in its own back yard, especially given that it has special legal and financial responsibilities for the District? Would it make a difference if the members of Congress were sending their own children to these schools?

13

The Learning Disability Mess

When Congress adopted the Education for All Handicapped Children Act[1] (EAHCA) in 1975, mandating the education of all children with disabilities, a key supporter of the bill noted that "[n]o one really knows what a learning disability is."[2] Because of this lack of understanding of the term "learning disability," Congress used a provisional definition of the term and instructed the Commissioner of Education to further study the term and devise a more refined definition as well as a diagnosis.[3] Almost forty years later, that definition[4] remains in federal special education law under the Individuals with Disabilities Education Act (IDEA)[5]—the modern version of the EAHCA.[6]

In order for a child to receive special education and related services under the IDEA, he or she must qualify as a child with a "disability."[7] The IDEA lists ten impairments that qualify as a disability,[8] including "specific learning disabilities."[9] Congress expressed concern in 1975 that the inclusion of "specific learning disabilities" would overwhelm special education resources and placed a temporary cap on that category to avoid this possibility. Nonetheless, the category of "specific learning disabilities"[10] has become the most common disability classification for children under the IDEA. As of August 3, 2009, nearly 6 million children were classified as disabled under that statute; about 2.5 million (42.8 percent) were considered to have "specific learning disabilities," more than twice the figure for the next most common disability—speech or language impairments.[11]

Although Congress has retained the 1975 definition of specific learning disabilities, it enacted new guidelines for diagnosing the impairment with the 2004 amendments to the IDEA.[12] But that amendment only added to the confusion in the field. Rather than take a clear position on how states should diagnose learning disabilities, Congress gave states the choice of using a "response to intervention model"[13] or a "discrepancy model"[14] while also seemingly disfavoring the discrepancy approach by stating that that approach could no longer be required.[15] The states have complied with the 2004 amendments with a wide range of approaches for diagnosing learning disabilities, creating highly disparate results. For example, in 2008, 15.4 percent of all disabled children met that definition in Kentucky while 60.2 percent met that definition in Iowa.[16] Unfortunately, neither the 2004 amendments nor states' attempts at implementation bear much relationship to the understanding of learning disabilities within the field of educational psychology. Instead, these efforts reflect an attempt to align the IDEA with No Child Left Behind[17] so that children who fall behind grade level can get extra assistance.[18] Although extra help is a good idea, it need not come at the cost of a learning disability label.

Meanwhile, the field of educational psychology has floundered to develop a coherent definition of learning disabilities. The American Psychiatric Association (APA) endorsed the discrepancy approach for diagnosing learning disabilities in the fourth edition of its *Diagnostic and Statistical Manual of Mental Disorders* in 2000 but has proposed new learning disability guidelines in the forthcoming fifth edition[19] that would align its professional standards with the 2004 amendments to the IDEA. Educational psychologists have criticized the APA for caving to Congress rather than following professional norms in their field.[20] Although it is too early to know how this controversy will be resolved, it is disappointing to see politics rather than science seemingly govern the initial recommendations of the APA.

* * *

In the first part of this chapter, I review the legal and psychological literature on what constitutes a learning disability and how such a disability should be diagnosed. This part also examines the disagreement that continues to exist on whether there must be evidence of a psychological or neurological impairment, and whether the discrepancy model should be part of the diagnostic model. In the second part of the chapter, I survey the wide range of definitions of learning disability used by the various states despite the fact that the IDEA is a national statute. In the third part, I discuss the implications of the learning disability classification for college admissions testing. The national testing organizations continue to use the "discrepancy model" for determining whether students are learning disabled even though Congress has given states the choice no longer to use that model under the IDEA. In the fourth part of the chapter, I suggest that we should solve the learning disability mess by giving less weight to the importance of the classification and providing all students with adequate time to complete tests and other assessments.

Learning Disabilities

The term "learning disabilities" has been in use since the 1960s under a wide variety of definitions. It describes individuals who have great difficulty in reading, writing, or math but do not seem to have a cognitive impairment that would explain such difficulties. The definitional areas of dispute are whether a diagnosis of a psychological or neurological dysfunction is required for a child to be deemed to have a learning disability and whether the discrepancy model is an appropriate tool for diagnosing the existence of a learning disability.

Samuel Alexander Kirk suggested the first definition of learning disability in 1962:[21]

A learning disability refers to a retardation, disorder, or delayed development in one or more of the processes of speech, language, reading, spelling, writing, or arithmetic resulting from a possible cerebral dysfunction and/or emotional or behavioral disturbances and not from mental retardation, sensory deprivation, or cultural and instructional factors.[22]

This 1962 definition has many features that are part of the various ways this term is used even today.[23] This definition seeks to distinguish between academic deficits that are a result of a psychological handicap rather than mental retardation or a lack of instruction. The 1962 definition describes the symptoms of the condition but does not suggest how to diagnose its existence.

Barbara Bateman developed the concept of the discrepancy model to diagnose the existence of a learning disability in her 1965 definition:

[C]hildren who have learning disorders are those who manifest an educationally significant discrepancy between their estimated intellectual potential and actual level of performance related to basic disorders in the learning process, which may or may not be accompanied by demonstrable central nervous system dysfunction, and which are not secondary to generalized mental retardation, educational or cultural deprivation, severe emotional disturbance, or sensory loss.[24]

Bateman's definition was similar to Kirk's in that she referenced psychological disorders and excluded other factors, but she added the concept of a discrepancy between intellectual potential and actual performance as a diagnostic tool.[25] She also cast into doubt whether a finding of a "central nervous system dysfunction" was a necessary part of the definition.[26] Kirk had posited that a learning disability was caused by "a possible cerebral dysfunction."[27] Bateman placed less emphasis on that requirement. Bateman's emphasis on the existence of a discrepancy between "intellectual potential" (or what we might call "aptitude") and "actual level of performance" (or what we might call "achievement") is the basis for the discrepancy model that has historically been the primary mode for diagnosing the existence of a learning disability.[28]

Under the discrepancy approach, one would assess a child's aptitude, typically through an IQ test. Then, one would administer various achievement tests. Normally, one would expect the child's achievement to be consistent with the child's IQ. Hence, if a child scored in the fiftieth percentile for IQ (100) then one would expect the child's achievement to be around the fiftieth percentile. If the child's achievement is significantly below what is expected, and that result cannot be explained by other factors, then, under the discrepancy model, the child would be considered to be "learning disabled."

In 1968, the National Advisory Committee on Handicapped Children (NACHC), under Kirk's leadership, offered a definition of learning disability quite similar to Kirk's 1962 definition. The key difference was the addition of the word "specific" to the term so that it became "specific learning disability."[29] The purpose of the addition of the adjective "specific" was to emphasize that "the learning failure was not a generalized problem like [mental retardation] but rather one predicated on the possession of only a discrete number of deficits."[30] The NACHC definition also provided a list of conditions that could cause this disorder: "perceptual handicaps, brain injury, minimal brain dysfunction, dyslexia, developmental aphasia, etc."[31] It provided these examples instead of referring to "central nervous system dysfunction." As Kenneth Kavale, a critic of this approach, observed, "[I]n other words, the simile becomes the metaphor."[32] The issue that existed in 1968, and remains today: determining whether "learning disability" is a general term to describe many specific conditions or a precise etiology that includes the existence of a neurological impairment.

The addition of the term "specific" was supposed to add some refinement to the example provided above for use of the discrepancy model. Students with learning disabilities typically do not have low achievement in every academic subject. Instead, they may have low achievement in one area, such as reading. As the above definition suggests, the child has only a "discrete" number of deficits (maybe reading and writing but not math). If the problem is more generalized, then other hypotheses such as mental retardation are considered.

The NACHC 1968 definition was incorporated into the Education for All Handicapped Children Act in 1975:

> The term "children with specific learning disabilities" means those children who have a disorder in one or more of the basic psychological processes involved in understanding or in using language, spoken or written, which disorder may manifest itself in imperfect ability to listen, think, speak, read, write, spell, or do mathematical calculations. Such disorders include such conditions as perceptual handicaps, brain injury, minimal brain dysfunction, dyslexia, and developmental aphasia. Such term does not include children who have learning problems which are primarily the result of visual, hearing, or motor handicaps, of mental retardation, of emotional disturbance, or environmental, cultural, or economic disadvantage.[33]

The 1975 definition included a requirement of a "disorder in one or more of the basic psychological processes." It is not clear whether that term means the same thing as a "central nervous system dysfunction." Like the NACHC definition, it listed qualifying disorders as well as excluded conditions. It did not indicate how one would diagnose the existence of a specific learning disability.

When Congress adopted the NACHC definition in 1975, there was concern that too many children would receive the "learning disability" classification, detracting from the resources devoted to other disabilities covered by the EAHCA. To address this problem, the bill's supporters agreed to require that the Commissioner of Education provide a more specific definition and specify "diagnostic procedures that will be used in determining whether a particular child has a disorder or condition which places that child in the category of children with specific learning disabilities."[34]

Congress also agreed to a temporary cap so that the learning disability numbers in any given state could not be more than one-sixth of all the children classified as disabled within a state.[35] Representative Bill Lehman of Florida spoke in favor of capping the number of children classified under the learning disability category until the diagnosis and definition become clearer because "no one really knows what a learning disability is."[36] Today, with no cap in place, nearly half of all children served under the special education statutes receive the learning disability classification.[37]

Following the passage of the EAHCA, professional organizations continued to discuss how to best define that term from a diagnostic perspective. The emerging view, as reflected by an institute funded by the U.S. Office of Education, endorsed the need to use the discrepancy model to diagnose the existence of a learning disability.[38] This view posited that "significant deficits are defined in terms of accepted diagnostic procedures in education and psychology."[39] But it did not define how large the deficit would have to be in order to constitute a "significant" deficit. It also added that a learning disability is not the result of "a lack of opportunity to learn,"[40] which was part of the tendency to exclude other explanations for the academic deficit as part of the learning disability definition.

The American Psychiatric Association (APA) began to recognize specific learning disabilities in the third edition of its *Diagnostic and Statistical Manual of Mental Disorders*, published in 1980.[41] It termed them "specific developmental disorders" and recognized that the "inclusion of these disorders in a classification of 'mental disorders' is controversial" but concluded that they should nonetheless be incorporated because they are a type of mental disorder.[42] The third edition used a discrepancy model to define the existence of this disorder. For example, it provided the following description of the diagnostic criteria for a "developmental reading disorder": "[P]erformance on standardized, individually administered tests of reading skill is significantly below the expected level, given the individual's schooling, chronological age, and mental age (as determined by an individually administered IQ test). In addition, the child's performance on tasks requiring reading skills is significantly below his or her intellectual capability."[43] It did not define how much discrepancy is necessary for it to be "significant," but it did approve of the discrepancy model.

The APA refined this definition in 1986, still relying on a discrepancy model for diagnostic purposes. For example, its diagnostic criteria for "developmental reading disorder" included:

A. Reading achievement, as measured by standardized, individually administered test, is markedly below the expected level, given the person's schooling and intellectual capacity (as determined by an individually administered IQ test).

B. The disturbance in A significantly interferes with academic achievement or activities of daily living requiring reading skills.

C. Not due to a defect in visual or hearing acuity or a neurologic disorder.[44]

It connected the specific learning disability in reading with difficulties in school and excluded other explanations for this disorder. On its list of exclusions was "neurologic disorder," which is apparently different from "central nervous system dysfunction," a term that other authors have used to describe a learning disability.

Meanwhile, professional organizations began to emerge in the field. The National Joint Committee on Learning Disabilities (NJCLD) tried to take the lead in reconciling the views of these various organizations.[45] After developing various approaches, the NJCLD endorsed the following definition in 1994:

[L]earning disabilities is a general term that refers to a heterogeneous group of disorders manifested by significant difficulties in the acquisition and use of listening, speaking, reading, writing, reasoning, or mathematical abilities. These disorders are intrinsic to the individual, presumed to be due to central nervous system dysfunction, and may occur across the life span. Problems in self-regulatory behavior, social perception, and social interactions may exist with learning disabilities but do not by themselves constitute a learning disability. Although learning disabilities may occur concomitantly with other handicapping conditions (for example, sensory impairment, mental retardation, serious emotional disturbance) or with extrinsic influences (such as cultural differences, insufficient or inappropriate instruction), they are not the result of those conditions or influences.[46]

This definition took the position that a learning disability was "presumed to be due to central nervous system dysfunction." The NJCLD's current web page continues to take that position. In its section labeled "What is a learning disability," it says in the opening sentence that a "learning disability is a neurological disorder."[47] Its definition also deleted reference to the word "specific" that had been added by the 1968 NACHC definition and incorporated into the federal definition. It took the position that a learning disability was a lifelong condition based on central nervous system dysfunction, but it took no position on whether the discrepancy model was the best way to diagnose the existence of this condition.

The APA published the fourth edition of *Diagnostic and Statistical Manual of Mental Disorders* in 1994.[48] It continued to endorse the discrepancy model for diagnosing a learning disability (now termed a "learning disorder") and defined with more precision how much of a discrepancy was necessary in order to be a "significant" discrepancy:

> Learning [disorders] are diagnosed when the individual's achievement on individually administered, standardized tests in reading, mathematics, or written expression is substantially below that expected for age, schooling and level of intelligence. The learning problems significantly interfere with academic achievement or activities of daily living that require reading, mathematical, or writing skills. A variety of statistical approaches can be used to establish that a discrepancy is significant. Substantially below is usually defined as a discrepancy of more than 2 standard deviations between achievement and IQ. A smaller discrepancy between achievement and IQ (i.e., between 1 and 2 standard deviations) is sometimes used, especially in cases where an individual's performance on an IQ test may have been compromised by an associated disorder in cognitive processing, a comorbid mental disorder or general medical condition, or the individual's ethnic or cultural background.[49]

This definition was much more specific in stating how much discrepancy was needed for a learning disability to be considered significant. It also deleted the exclusion for neurological disorders.

The next big development in the definition of learning disability came as a result of action by Congress as a result of complaints about the discrepancy model. The state of Connecticut explains this development in its recent guidelines for identifying students with learning disabilities:

> Another critical problem with the IQ-achievement discrepancy is that research does not support excluding students from services based on their failure to meet IQ-achievement discrepancy criteria. Struggling readers with an IQ-achievement discrepancy and those without a discrepancy tend to have similar remedial needs and benefit from similar types of interventions (Gunderson and Siegel, 2001), yet nondiscrepant low achievers may be erroneously viewed as intellectually limited and incapable of improvement. The IQ-achievement discrepancy also appears to contribute to biased identification practices. For example, several studies have found that the use of a discrepancy model in reading favored identification of Caucasian students and middle- and upper-income students[,] whereas students of color and

students from lower socioeconomic backgrounds were more likely to be identified as having an intellectual disability (Fletcher et al., 2007; Speece, Case, and Molloy, 2003). Since students from nonmainstream cultural groups often possess cognitive styles that differ from those typically promoted by the schools, the inappropriate use of standardized tests that are not normed or validated for a specific population often perpetuates cultural misunderstandings, which in turn contributes to poor instructional decision-making (McIntyre, 1996). Aaron, Joshi, Gooden and Bentum (2008) and Vaughn, Levy, Coleman, and Bos (2002) argued that testing for an IQ-achievement discrepancy often does not provide instructionally useful information and may contribute to inadequate remedial efforts.[50]

Researchers therefore argued that the definition of learning disability should be expanded to encompass a wider variety of children who might benefit from educational intervention, not only those who would fit within the discrepancy model.

In response to complaints about exclusive reliance on the discrepancy model, Congress amended the IDEA in 2004 to indicate that states could no longer require school districts to use the discrepancy model to determine whether students have learning disabilities but, instead, could develop another approach, called the "response to intervention" (RTI) approach.

The new language reads:

(6) Specific learning disabilities.
  (A) In general.
  Notwithstanding section 607(b), when determining whether a child has a specific learning disability as defined in section 602, a local educational agency shall not be required to take into consideration whether a child has a severe discrepancy between achievement and intellectual ability in oral expression, listening comprehension, written expression, basic reading skill, reading comprehension, mathematical calculation, or mathematical reasoning.
  (B) Additional authority.
   In determining whether a child has a specific learning disability, a local educational agency may use a process that determines if the child responds to scientific, research-based intervention as a part of the evaluation procedures described in paragraphs (2) and (3).[51]

Despite creating those new rules for diagnosing a learning disability, Congress retained the longstanding definition of "specific learning disability" earlier in the statute.[52] In other words, Congress created new rules to diagnose a learning disability but did not modify the underlying definition of what is a learning disability. As in 1975, a specific learning disability means "a disorder in one or more of the basic psychological processes involved in understanding or in using language, spoken or written, which disorder may manifest itself in the imperfect ability to listen, think, speak, read, write, spell, or do mathematical calculations."[53] Congress maintained the longstanding requirement that a disorder exists in "one or more of the basic psychological processes," suggesting that a learning disability is a lifetime, neurological deficit.

The ambiguous language used by Congress under the 2004 amendments makes it difficult to understand what it meant by the RTI model. But this is what it likely means. When a student falls behind his or her peers, a school district is supposed to employ scientifically based interventions to see if the student can meet peer-level expectations without receiving special education and related services. This intervention is "tiered" with schools' trying increasingly more intensive intervention before concluding that intervention is unsuccessful. A student is classified as learning disabled only if he or she performs below his or her peers even after scientifically based intervention is attempted through this tiered process. Depending on the school district, this process can take between six months and several years. A student's IQ is not supposed to be a factor in determining the effectiveness of intervention.[54]

Congress allowed use of the RTI model in 2004 because of concerns about the exclusive use of the discrepancy model. In addition to concerns that the discrepancy model favored children with high IQ scores, the federal government concluded that the discrepancy model reflects a "wait to fail" model under which children do not receive services "until the student's achievement is sufficiently low so that the discrepancy is achieved."[55] The federal government believed that a move to an RTI model would save districts money because the discrepancy model "consumes significant resources, with the average cost of an eligibility evaluation running several thousand dollars."[56]

One problem with the federal government's perspective is that it underestimates the expenses associated with the RTI model. Under RTI, a school district must find the resources over an extended period of time to offer a child extra assistance to see if the child attains grade-level standards with that extra assistance. These resources are supposed to be allocated *before* the student is classified as learning disabled, so that possibly extra special education resources might become available if RTI is unsuccessful.

The RTI model, like much of the special education statute, is based on assumptions about the resources of school districts. Even suburban school districts with small class sizes can find it difficult and expensive to develop a tiered intervention model before a child is classified as disabled and eligible for special education resources. But how is RTI supposed to work in cash-strapped urban school districts with thirty-person classes and many students who might qualify for RTI resources? RTI, as we will see, has worked well in Iowa, which has a relatively monolithic and nonurban school population. But Congress has now allowed use of the RTI model on a nationwide basis without thinking about how it might operate within the classroom.

Although RTI was supposed to solve the "wait to fail" problem with the discrepancy model, many parents and advocates have criticized RTI as causing massive delays in identification for all children, as the tiered intervention process can take months or even years. In response, the federal Department of Education issued guidance on January 21, 2011, stating that RTI should not be used as a means of delaying appropriate intervention.[57] There is no evidence, however, that school districts have changed their policies in light of the Department of Education guidance.

The RTI model was not developed on the basis of science; it was developed to align the IDEA with No Child Left Behind (NCLB),[58] by identifying children who have fallen below grade-level expectations and need help beyond what is available in the regular classroom so that they can meet the NCLB requirement of being proficient in reading and math by 2014.[59] Thus, the IDEA cross-references the NCLB when it mentions the RTI model.[60] The NCLB, however, is also a tremendously underfunded and unrealistic federal mandate. Aligning IDEA with the NCLB is not a positive development for the IDEA.

Educational psychologists did not develop the RTI model as a tool to identify the existence of neuropsychological factors that may explain a child's academic deficits.[61] This diagnostic model is not consistent with the IDEA's requirement that a learning disability be the result of a "psychological impairment."[62] As we will see, states have responded to this approach inconsistently, with some, but not all, requiring independent evidence of a neurological impairment for students diagnosed under the RTI approach.[63] States are uncertain whether Congress still requires them to demonstrate evidence of an *impairment* before classifying a child as learning disabled when the child has failed to make sufficient progress under RTI.

Although no professional groups within the field of educational psychology endorsed the RTI approach when Congress adopted it in 2004, the APA has taken steps to endorse it. The proposed fifth edition of the *Diagnostic*

Manual (*DSM-5*) seeks to change the professional standards for diagnosing a learning disability to align them with the legal standards embodied in the 2004 version of the IDEA. The proposed revision states that "a specific learning disorder" can be made "by a clinical synthesis of the individual's history . . . psycho-educational reports of test scores and observations, and response to intervention."[64]

This language reflects, in part, an attempt to be consistent with the 2004 amendments to the IDEA by referring to "response to intervention." The proposed *DSM-5* also removes reference to IQ test results as part of the learning disability diagnosis; it refers only to deficits in academic achievement. In the rationale section, the authors of these proposed rules stated:

> However, the diagnostic criteria do not depend upon comparisons with overall IQ and are consistent with the change in the USA's reauthorized IDEA regulations (2004) which state that "the criteria adopted by the State must not require the use of a severe discrepancy between intellectual ability and achievement for determining whether a child has a specific learning disability, as defined in 34 C.F.R. 300.8(c)(10)."[65]

The proposed *DSM-5* emphasizes the importance of standardized achievement tests but moves away from overreliance on "overall IQ" tests. This approach, if adopted, would not necessarily result in the cost savings mentioned in the language accompanying the IDEA regulations[66] because the battery of achievement tests would need to be psychometrically sound.

School psychologists have been critical of the proposed *DSM-5* as well as the RTI-only move by the 2004 amendments to the IDEA. In 2004, the American Academy of School Psychology took the position that an RTI-only approach is not professionally appropriate because it is important to have a

> "comprehensive evaluation" that includes "multiple sources of information, including standardized, norm-referenced tests; interviews; observations; curriculum-based assessments; and informed clinical judgment." A student's response to scientific, research-based interventions can be a part of a comprehensive evaluation, but a response-to-intervention process should not be viewed as a sole criterion for diagnosing LD.[67]

In 2009, as states began to implement the RTI model aggressively, Cecil Reynolds and Sally Shaywitz published an article quite critical of this approach.[68] They argue that Congress rushed to endorse RTI with a "very weak experimental base."[69] They also argue that the RTI approach is likely be ineffective because cognitive testing—which is not permitted under the RTI approach—is an essential component of developing effective instruction for a student who has been identified as disabled after he or she fails to respond to intervention. Understanding a student's cognitive profile is an essential part of developing instruction that is more effective than what the student has already experienced. Further, they argue that the absence of IQ testing under RTI could cause "bright struggling readers" to fail to be identified.[70] "It would be no fairer to leave out these bright struggling readers than it would be to leave out their lower functioning classmates."[71]

Hence, it is not surprising that the number of students identified as having a learning disability has declined since Congress gave states the latitude to use the RTI-only method for learning disability identification, with the declines being the largest for young children who have newly entered the school system.[72] Although it would be nice to think that this decline is a result of effective early intervention that has caused a reduction in the need for special education services, that is a highly unlikely hypothesis, especially when we understand the unscientific nature of the RTI process as well as the inexplicable state-by-state variation in learning disability identification, as discussed below.

In 2012 we are still therefore left with a basic question: How do we know that a child has a learning disability? The movement to the RTI-only model has not assisted students in being properly identified as having a learning disability.

IDEA Implementation by the States

Because of the discretion provided to the states by the 2004 amendments, dozens of approaches exist. Some states have a rigid discrepancy approach whereas others have banned the discrepancy approach. Within the RTI approach, there is also enormous variation, with some states requiring evidence of a neurological impairment, some states requiring evidence of a discrepancy between aptitude and achievement, and some states merely requiring substandard academic achievement. Because states are always amending their regulations, this summary is known to be valid only through 2011. It gives a good snapshot of states' initial inclinations to respond to Congress's invitation to eliminate the discrepancy approach.

Under the discrepancy model, seven states specify that there must be at least a 1.5 standard deviation variation between achievement and aptitude: California,[73] Missouri,[74] Mississippi,[75] South Dakota,[76] Tennessee,[77] Vermont,[78] and Wyoming.[79] New Mexico uses the 1.5 standard deviation rule for children in grades seven through twelve.[80] The state of Washington uses a 1.55 standard deviation discrepancy test.[81] Minnesota and Wisconsin insist on a 1.75 standard deviation discrepancy.[82] North Carolina requires at least a 15-point discrepancy, which would be only 1 standard deviation.[83] Similarly, Alabama requires only a 1 standard deviation discrepancy.[84] Florida requires only 1 standard deviation discrepancy for students aged seven to ten but requires 1.5 standard deviations for students aged eleven and above.[85]

Other states follow various unique approaches under the discrepancy model. Montana's rule states that a "severe discrepancy is defined as a 50 percent or higher probability of a two standard deviation discrepancy between cognitive ability and achievement in one or more of the areas identified [in the regulations] when adjusted for regression to the population mean."[86] It is not clear what that standard even means because educational psychologists would not normally report a score merely within a 50 percent confidence band.

In Utah, under the discrepancy model, the team must "produce a report that states that the team can be 93 percent confident there is a severe discrepancy between the student's expected achievement score and the obtained achievement score, based on the Utah Estimator software" or "produce a report that shows a significant discrepancy, based on a commercial software program that employs a clearly specified regression formula that considers the relationship between the intelligence and achievement tests as well as the tests' reliability."[87] It is not clear what standard of significance is employed with this approach—1 S.D., 1.5 S.D., or 2 S.D.

In practical terms, these differences matter. In Alabama, for example, a child with an IQ in the eighty-fifth percentile (115) and achievement in the fiftieth percentile (100) on a reading test would be considered to have a specific learning disability in reading.[88] If that child moved to California,[89] Missouri,[90] Mississippi,[91] South Dakota,[92] Tennessee,[93] Vermont,[94] or Wyoming,[95] that amount of discrepancy would be insufficient for a learning disability diagnosis. The child's IQ would have to be as high as 122 or the child's achievement would have to be as low as 92 to meet the 1.5 standard deviation requirement for those states.

There is even more variation in how states have implemented the RTI approach. Some states, such as Connecticut, Illinois, Iowa, and North Dakota, consider only a student's achievement (and not aptitude) in determining if he or she should be classified as learning disabled. Connecticut focuses on how a student compares to his or her peers with respect to both his or her knowledge and his or her rate of acquisition of knowledge. The student's aptitude is not a factor to be considered as part of this inquiry.

Connecticut has also abandoned the requirement that there be evidence of a specific processing disorder before a diagnosis of a specific learning disability is made.[96] Similarly, in Illinois, children with low achievement are to be classified as having a specific learning disability unless "appropriate curriculum choice and the delivery of effective instruction cannot be demonstrated."[97]

North Dakota offers the following as an example of an appropriate RTI approach:

1. Organize the lowest 20 % of students in the group (class, grade level, or school) to receive interventions.
2. Students in group interventions are monitored regularly.
3. Change interventions when 4 consecutive data points do not meet the student's goal line.
4. Move students to an individual intervention after two unsuccessful group interventions.
5. Students in individual interventions are monitored at least 1 time weekly.
6. Refer a student for special education after one unsuccessful individual intervention.[98]

This approach requires no documentation of a psychological processing disorder. A child who falls behind academically and does not respond well to group-based intervention becomes eligible for special education services. And a bright child who should be expected to be reading well above grade level but is merely in the twenty-first percentile because of a learning disability would not be identified as potentially needing special education assistance.

One of the most permissive states in defining learning disabilities is Iowa. It appears that many school districts in Iowa use the RTI approach to improve instruction for all children, not as a means of limiting the number of students classified as learning disabled. For example, one elementary school screens students early in the year using the Dynamic Indicators of Basic Early Literacy Skills (DIBELS) along with other diagnostic tests that pinpoint problems and guide interventions. In the first year of this program, 30 percent of the school's students began to receive intervention during an intensive data collection exercise. "The principal, reading-support teachers, and classroom teachers meet once a month to discuss the data they are collecting on students. Three times a year, the school has 'data days' to take a deeper look at the overall curriculum and student performance based on other tests."[99] Although Iowa has been a national leader in the use of the RTI approach, it does not see that approach as principally about special education identification. "Special education identification 'is just the toenail on the ele-phant,' said Mr. Tilly, the Heartland official. 'That's not what it was created for, and that's not what its best purpose is.'"[100] One teacher concludes that the Iowa approach allows them to catch "more 'on the edge kids.'"[101] One Iowa elementary school reported that the RTI process improved their passing rate on the DIBELS benchmark in one year from 48 percent to 81 percent.[102] Such improvement is commendable if it reflects genuine improvement in reading fluency, but we should not think of that improvement as having anything to do with the issue of disability. And, as in North Dakota, this approach is likely to miss the bright child who is performing well below his or her ability because of a learning disability but has not fallen below the thirtieth percentile.

In contrast to Iowa are states which require evidence that a child satis-fies criteria under both the RTI and discrepancy models in order to be clas-sified as learning disabled. Georgia requires evidence of a "primary deficit in basic psychological processes and secondary underachievement in one or more of the eight areas along with documentation of the lack of response to instructional intervention as supported by on-going progress monitoring."[103] In other words, Georgia requires evidence of a psychological processing impairment, underachievement (which is presumably a discrepancy model approach), and a lack of response to intervention. Although the RTI method was supposed to broaden the category of children eligible for special educa-tion by eliminating the "wait to fail" model and removing some of the cul-tural bias of an IQ-focused approach, Georgia appears to be using these rules to heighten the eligibility requirements.

The state with the most restrictive application of the learning disability standards is Kentucky. Kentucky's overall disability statistics (2.06 percent of school-age population) are consistent with national norms, but their rate of learning disability classification is quite low (15.36 percent).[104] Nation-ally, learning disabilities are the most common disability classification. In Kentucky, the numbers for learning disability (13,587) are lower than the numbers for mental retardation (16,462), speech or language impairments (20,250), and other health impairments (15,484).[105] Thus, it seems clear that a child who moves from Iowa with its 60.26 percent learning disability classi-fication rate to Kentucky with its 13.5 percent learning disability classification rate faces a significant chance of moving out of the learning disability clas-sification system.[106]

This kind of national variation is part of the learning disability mess. Children can go in and out of the learning disability category as they move from state to state. The happenstance of geography can also materially affect whether students get extra help at school. As we will see below, this variation becomes especially problematic as students begin to apply to colleges and universities because students with learning disabilities are often eligible for extended time on standardized exams. With no national standard, students are disadvantaged as they seek accommodations in college if they were raised in a state like Kentucky with very low rates of learning disability identification.

Aside from the state-to-state variation, there are no accepted metrics for deciding what is a "response" to intervention and what kind of response is sufficiently positive to suggest that a student is not disabled. Reynolds and Shaywitz point out many ambiguities in the states' guidelines, such as (1) Should achievement be measured in comparison to age peers or grade peers or same-gender peers? (2) Should the peer achievement group be students in the same classroom, same building, same district, same state or nationally? and (3) How should changes over time be measured?[107] They argue that existing studies provide many different answers to these questions, resulting in much confusion. Just as state-by-state variation in the definition of RTI will lead to regional differences, the lack of consensus on the answers to those important questions will "inevitably cause clinicians in different locales to identify very different groups of kids as in need of or eligible for special education and will also fail to identify different groups of students who are struggling readers."[108] Because these disability classifications can have enormous implications, as will be discussed below, on the availability of accommodations in higher education, these clinical inconsistencies are very problematic.

University Admissions Testing

Students with learning disabilities often seek accommodations, such as extra time, from testing agencies when they take standardized tests for university admission. The educational psychology literature consistently establishes that students with learning disabilities[109] in reading "perform as well as their normally achieving peers when given extra time, and [that] normally achieving students did not perform significantly better when given extra time."[110] Studies document that it is difficult for students with learning disabilities to demonstrate their knowledge under speeded circumstances because they may simply not have enough time to demonstrate their understanding. Hence, students with dyslexia who demonstrate poor reading fluency are often provided extra time as an accommodation for their disability.[111] The extra time allows them to demonstrate their *abilities* rather than their *disabilities.* Because learning disabilities are neurologically based, students who have been properly identified as dyslexic in reading while in primary and secondary school will face the challenges of being learning disabled for the rest of their lives.

Based on the scientific evidence that learning disabilities are lifelong, neurological impairments, DOJ promulgated regulations requiring testing agencies to give considerable weight to disability determinations made during the primary and secondary education years under the IDEA in deciding whether to grant requests for accommodations:

> When considering requests for modifications, accommodations, or auxiliary aids or services, the entity gives considerable weight to documentation of past modifications, accommodations, or auxiliary aids or services received in similar testing situations, as well as such modifications, accommodations or related aids and services provided in response to an Individualized Education Program (IEP) provided under the Individuals with Disabilities Education Act or a plan describing services provided pursuant to section 504 of the Rehabilitation Act of 1973, as amended (often referred to as a Section 504 Plan).[112]

This regulation was promulgated in response to complaints that some testing agencies were requiring too much additional documentation as part of requests for accommodations such as extra time and not deferring to earlier diagnoses.

In practice, the Law School Admissions Council (LSAC), the College Board, and the ACT are not following these regulations. They require extensive testing and do not defer to earlier disability classification results under the IDEA.

The LSAC guidelines require students to submit test scores from someone who works with adult populations, and their test scores must include an aptitude and achievement battery. These scores must include "a timed reading comprehension measure, which has been normed on adults and which allows for both extended and regular administration."[113] The summary score sheet at the end of their instructions states that the testing professional must "identify an information-processing deficit; and identify an aptitude-achievement discrepancy that meets the appropriate diagnostic criteria."[114] In other words, the results must meet the discrepancy definition of learning disability and be based on the results of an IQ test. Further, all testing must be done under adult norms. These guidelines reflect the misconception that students "outgrow" their learning disability instead of the fact that a learning disability is lifelong and neurologically based. These guidelines also pass the cost of IQ testing on to the student if the student is in an RTI-only state that did not do IQ testing as part of its learning disability identification process.

The College Board makes no mention of RTI as a way to demonstrate the existence of a learning disability.[115] It also fails to reference a child's classification under the IDEA as relevant to the College Board's disability determination.[116] Its emphasis on scaled achievement and aptitude test scores suggests exclusive use of the discrepancy model. Similarly, the ACT uses the discrepancy model in its explanation of the documentation needed to get extra time on the ACT; it makes no reference to an IDEA diagnosis as being relevant to accommodations under the ACT.[117] Therefore, a student who was classified as learning disabled in an RTI-only state would have to undergo expensive testing to meet LSAC's, the College Board's, or ACT's testing accommodation requirements.

A further difficulty faced by the administrators of these entrance examinations is how to report the scores of students who take the exams under conditions of extra time. It is impossible to know precisely how much extra time is appropriate as an accommodation if an exam has a speeded element, because, by definition, the speeded nature of an exam is a factor that influences the scores of all students who take an exam, although it disparately affects the scores of students with various disabilities.[118] Ideally, a student with a learning disability would be given exactly enough extra time to make exam conditions feel identical to those of nondisabled students, who take the exam under normal conditions. The LSAC takes the position that it cannot provide accommodations with such precision even though it requires extensive documentation of learning disabilities. Hence, the LSAC refuses to give students who take the exam under extra time conditions an "index score" or percentile score to compare them to other candidates. They merely get a raw score.[119]

The LSAC guidelines state:

Candidates who seek additional test time on scored sections of the test should pay particular attention to the following:
- If you receive additional test time as an accommodation for your condition, LSAC will send a statement with your Credential Assembly Service (CAS) or LSAT Law School Reports advising that your score(s) should be interpreted with great sensitivity and flexibility.
- Scores earned with additional test time are reported individually and will not be averaged with standard-time scores or other nonstandard-time scores.

- Percentile ranks of nonstandard-time scores are not available and will not be reported.[120]

In other words, because the LSAC cannot figure out exactly how much extra time to provide a candidate, the candidate is unable to receive a score that is identical to that of other test takers. By contrast, the College Board and ACT do not flag scores taken under conditions of extra time for different treatment although they, presumably, experience the same difficulty as the LSAC in determining exactly how much extra time is appropriate for each test taker who receives accommodations. Under the pressure of litigation, however, the College Board and ACT have had to recognize that they could not defend treating the scores of students with disabilities different from the scores of other students. Of course, this whole mess is caused by the overemphasis on timed exams for all students as part of the admissions process.

Conclusion

As the previous discussion reflects, we have made little progress legislatively since a member of Congress declared in 1975 that "[N]o one really knows what a learning disability is."[121] Rather than define the term with precision, Congress has punted the problem to the states and given them the option of choosing between two methods of diagnosing a learning disability. The states have responded with a wide range of approaches, most of which have little in common with the emerging professional guidelines in the field of educational psychology. And even when allowed to impose its own stringent definition of learning disability, the LSAC cannot figure out how exactly to allocate the right amount of extra time to a student with a learning disability.

The learning disability mess is, in part, a by-product of our fixation on high-stakes testing. Young children have to worry about meeting state proficiency standards as reflected by standardized test scores in order to advance to the next grade. High school students need to score as high as possible on timed, standardized exams in order to be admitted to elite colleges. And law students typically take time-pressured three or hour in-class exams for their entire grade in large classes. "Plodders"—who sometimes have learning disabilities—struggle with all of these examination instruments as we emphasize speed and performance under stressful conditions over competency and knowledge.

The way out of the learning disability mess is not to develop better diagnostic instruments for evaluating the existence of learning disabilities. The way out is to ask why we have such an overemphasis on whether students meet a definition of "learning disability." Iowa's approach to K–12 education seems like a sound one that has produced some solid improvement in basic reading skills. All children in the country should have access to such reading resources, but these children should not have to be classified as "learning disabled" under the IDEA in order to get those resources. We should also alter the norms for test taking at the college entrance exam stage. All students should be allowed to take exams under conditions that we now define as "extra time." Rather than make the individual student justify why he or she should get extra time, test designers should have to justify why tests must be given under timed conditions. Perhaps a test for air traffic controllers would meet such a necessity standard. However, it is hard to see why it matters if a student takes forty-five minutes rather than thirty minutes to read a passage with good comprehension and whether this should even be a measure of whether he or she should be admitted to a top college.

I realize it is unlikely that the College Board or other testing agencies will decide on their own to abandon time-pressured exams. After all, it is less expensive to give a shorter exam. But what if universities started demanding that applicants be given more time to take entrance exams? What if universities started demanding admission of the most thoughtful students rather than the fastest, and needed different kinds of standardized exams to identify such students? Could Plodder University become the next Harvard, with students scrambling to be admitted under admissions criteria that give no weight to the speed under which students can complete exams?

14

A New Beginning

It has been very difficult to use legal sources to tell the story of poor and minority children within the special education system because their experiences are, with rare exceptions, invisible. This book's accounts of cases that reached the U.S. Supreme Court were typically stories of white middle-class children who also languished while their cases were winding their way through the judicial system. The experiences of poor and minority children were hidden in the pages of hearing officer opinions that did not explicitly state their race or class background and identified the children with anonymous labels like "E.R." or "Student" that made it even harder to recognize their humanity. Congress tried to make these stories more visible in 1997 when it required school districts to collect special education data on racial lines. But that data collection does not seep into the hearing officer opinions themselves because the decisions make no reference to race. Nonetheless, these data help reveal the tremendous inequities in the special education system along racial lines through disparities in discipline, disability classification, and services.

The tables prevously shown in chapters 1 (page 7) and 5 (page 106) demonstrate patterns of classification and suspension that reflect systematic discrimination.[1]

Table 1 reflects the racialized nature of the disability classification system. In 2010, for example, when African Americans constituted 14.8 percent of the school-age population,[2] they constituted about 21 percent of all students who were classified as disabled. Those overall statistics might be attributed to high rates of poverty in the African American community but cannot explain why African Americans constitute 32.5 percent of those classified as mentally retarded, 28.5 percent of those classified as emotionally disturbed, but only 14.0 percent of those classified as autistic. The characteristics of autism—marked delay in cognitive development and abnormal social and emotional development[3]—are similar to those of mental retardation and emotional disturbance. Yet, these statistics suggest that when an African American child and a white child exhibit similar symptoms, the white child is likely to be classified as autistic and the African American child is likely to be classified as mentally retarded or emotionally disturbed. Although whites constituted 54.8 percent of the school-age population in 2010,[4] they constituted nearly 70 percent of the students classified as autistic.

Similarly, the suspension data found in Table 2 reflect that school districts are much more likely to seek to suspend an African American child who is disabled than a white child who is disabled. The discrepancy between African American and white children has become especially stark since 2004, when Congress relaxed the rules for school districts that sought to suspend children with disabilities. In 2010, the suspension rate for African American children was four times that of white children.

These data suggest that we have not come very far since Judge Skelly Wright held in 1975 in *Hobsen v. Hansen*[5] that the District of Columbia used the special education system as a way to relegate African American students to inferior schools and classrooms. Tracking promoted racial segregation because the students in the "special academic" track were disproportionately "the poor and the Negroes."[6] As the data indicate, African Americans are still disproportionately tracked in the "mental retardation" and "emotional disturbance" categories while also subject to much higher rates of suspension from school. Meanwhile, the high-quality private schools for children with autism are more likely to be filled with white children whose parents have been able to take advantage of IDEA funding.

The IDEA was initially inspired by a desire to create structural reform and end the days of warehousing children with disabilities in substandard environments. Since the enactment of the EAHCA in 1975, 90 percent fewer children with developmental disabilities are living in institutions.[7] In 1975, more than 1 million children with disabilities were excluded from public school; today, virtually no child with a disability is excluded from public school.

Today, however, the IDEA is insufficiently connected to needed structural reform for those who are the most disadvantaged in society. As stated in its name, the IDEA is about the "individual" with disabilities. It is about the individual, not the system. Individual children who benefit from the law are those likely to have parents who have the resources of time, expertise, and money to attain the benefits offered by the statute.

The stories of successful cases discussed in this book sometimes do *not* involve children whose parents sought an adequate public education for them in the public schools. Instead, they sometimes involve middle-class parents trying to get the public school system to fund their children's private education. Michael Panico's parents eventually were able to persuade the school district to allow him to attend the private Carroll School. Brian Schaffer's parents sought to require the school district to pay for him to attend the private McLean School; they transferred Brian back to the public schools only when the private educational option was unsuccessful. Joseph Murphy's parents were able to get the school district to pay for him to attend the private Kildonan School. Jacob Winkelman's parents received public funding for him to attend the private Monarch School.

Nonetheless, the parents of Derek Hughes, Amy Rowley, and E.R. sought remedies that would permit the children in their care to stay in the public school system. A recalcitrant school district, however, forced Derek's and Amy's families to move in order to obtain an adequate education within the public schools. The toll on all these families was enormous as they changed schools, moved, and pursued expensive litigation to help their children obtain an adequate education.

The stories of poor children, however, reflected even more stark struggles. Except for the cases from the District of Columbia, where families typically received assistance from pro bono lawyers and educational advocates, the parents of poor children typically lost their cases even though their requests were often quite modest. In Ohio, Marilyn, who was a single mother and had myriad health problems of her own, left voicemail messages for the hearing officer rather than participate in the hearing process. She gave up even trying to attend the multiple-day hearing to help her grade-school-age son avoid suspension from school. In Florida, Johnny's mother could not figure out how to use the administrative process effectively to have the school district pay for an independent evaluation and put an effective behavior plan in place for her young child. She was so confused by the process that she filed a complaint in federal court rather than respond to the school district's claims before the hearing officer. In New Jersey, E.R.'s grandmother could not persuade the school district to pay for her grandson to be transported to preschool. She had to choose between losing her job and sending her grandson to a preschool special education program. These parents or guardians lost their cases, and the patterns of injustice they sought to challenge remain unabated.

What would it take for the IDEA to become a more effective tool for children and their families? How could the IDEA be a tool to transform the public schools into a site of excellent education for children with disabilities rather than a mechanism that diverts resources from public schools to private schools? And could such changes be made without losing bipartisan support for special education in Congress?

Systemic problems require structural solutions. We cannot solve these problems one child at a time through a cadre of well-meaning volunteers. There are not enough volunteers to make that possible, and there is a systemic unfairness to children's welfare's being dependent on the happenstance of volunteers being available. So, we need to fight for structural reform even in a time when Democrats and Republicans are trapped in legislative gridlock. This final chapter discusses the kinds of reforms needed so that all children can receive a free and appropriate public education irrespective of their disability status.

Needed Reforms

The Individualized Family Service Plan (IFSP) process, provided from birth to age three, is where special education begins for many children. This process appears to work better than the IEP process because it is family-based and coordinated with the needs of the child within the family unit. The key challenge within the IFSP process is making sure that services are delivered in a way that is respectful of families. Studies suggest that professionals providing educational and social welfare support need to be sensitive to linguistic and cultural differences. It seems to help if the service coordinator and the intervention specialist are the same person, because then it is easier for the family to provide direct feedback on the kinds of services that would be useful.

When the IFSP process ends, then the challenges of preschool begin under the IDEA framework. A key issue is determining which children are eligible for assistance under the IDEA's definition of disability. Everyone knows that early intervention is vital, but it is easy to miss children who are not yet school-age because we do not have a system of compulsory preschool through which educators become aware that a child at an early age needs assistance. Many children in low-income families do not even have a health care provider.[8] The larger health care issues are beyond the scope of this book, but they obviously affect our ability to identify children who need extra help at a young age. As part of a system of national health insurance, all children should receive periodic screenings to help determine if they are making appropriate progress toward developmental milestones. That information is critical for early intervention to take place on a timely basis.

One advantage to the preschool identification process is that children merely need to be classified as "developmentally delayed" under the IDEA in order to get extra help. They do not need to be classified into one of the ten school-age IDEA disability categories. That flexibility is a very positive attribute that allows us to provide assistance to many children without dealing with problems of misclassification. The children can simply receive assistance with all academic skills because they are performing below grade level.

One impediment to getting assistance in preschool, though, for many poor children is transportation. Special education preschool programs are typically a few hours a day with staff teaching one morning session and one afternoon session. Many preschool-age children attend child care for eight to ten hours per day because their parents work (or attend school) during the day. Most states refuse to transport children from child care to special education programs even though they will transport children from home to special education programs. A simple transportation problem precludes many children from attending early intervention programs, and this problem should be resolved. This impediment to services should be removed.

When children enter grade school, these difficulties often deepen. At this point, children need to be classified into one of the ten disability categories in order to get special education assistance. Two major problems arise at this point. First, many parents do not have the resources to get an independent professional evaluation to help with the classification process. If they do request that the school district pay for an independent evaluation, school officials can file a due process complaint and seek a finding that their evaluation was adequate. A parent who does not even have the resources to challenge the school district's evaluation is not likely to be able to successfully defend this due process complaint. School districts should not have the option of using due process to resist a parent's request. All parents should be entitled to an independent professional evaluation at public expense.

Another problem with the classification/evaluation system that has been discussed by others is the discretion given to classroom teachers to make special education referrals.[9] That referral process is a part of the racial bias with white teachers more likely to refer black children to special education. Congress tried to reform the classification referral process by encouraging more members of minority groups to become special education teachers. That may be a good idea, but it is not likely to have an impact on the classification problem because special education teachers do not have a significant role in the classification process. We need more highly qualified minority teachers in the regular classroom to help solve the referral process problem.

Second, there is a serious problem in how children are classified within the disability categories. Rather than solve the problem by improving classification, the classification system itself needs to be abandoned. Congress should adopt the broad definition of disability recommended by Professors Maynard Reynolds and Bruce Balow in 1974 that would avoid the need to place a child in a discrete disability category in order to receive extra assistance. Their proposed definition was: "Handicapped children includes the mentally and physically handicapped and those who, *for any other reason*, are severely handicapped in their ability to proceed with their school [*sic*] under ordinary arrangements."[10] Their suggestion was the polar opposite of the existing definition of "specific learning disability" under which children are *not* covered if their "learning problems are primarily the result of . . . environmental, cultural, or economic disadvantage."[11] Rather than exclude children from federal funding because their educational challenges are due to income, environmental, or cultural factors, they would include children, who for *any* reason, were having difficulty in school. In other words, a child's difficulties with school would become his or her "handicap." Even their definition, however, might not be sufficiently broad if it did not recognize bright children who perform well below their potential because of a disability even if they are technically "proceeding in school."

It is not enough, however, for children to qualify for special education services because the classification itself can become an excuse to create unnecessary and harmful segregation. Once children become eligible for special education, they need to receive *appropriate* services. Children need advocates who are qualified to help make such decisions. Even children in middle-class families with highly educated parents need outside advocates to obtain successful results in the school system. All children who are classified as disabled (under the liberal definition mentioned above) should be eligible to receive the services of an independent educational advocate who is not an employee of the school district. This advocate should attend all meetings, review all documents and, if the parent decides to file a due process complaint, should participate in the hearing process. If a parent files a due process complaint, the school district should have to pay for the costs of the educational advocate.

Under current law, the courts have ruled that parents are not entitled to be reimbursed for their expenses in hiring an educational advocate to assist them during the IEP process or a due process complaint. Although Congress should correct that problem, reimbursement is not a sufficient solution. It is difficult for most parents to advance the costs of an educational advocate in the hope of recovering their expenses. It is crucial for parents to be provided with the free services of an educational advocate as soon as there is reason to believe that their child may qualify for special education services. Conceptualizing the issue as one of *reimbursement* provides relief for only high-income households.

Another huge problem is the high suspension rate for African American children in the special education system. These problems began to become more significant following the 2004 amendments to the IDEA. School districts should not be allowed to use the special education system as a way to maintain or impose racial segregation. A disproportionate suspension rate for a racial minority group within a state should trigger a joint, automatic investigation by the U.S. Department of Education and the Civil Rights Division of the U.S. Department of Justice. We need to stop the school-to-prison pipeline at its earliest manifestations—school suspensions.

As for the educational services provided to children with disabilities, all children within a state should receive the same amount of special education expenditures on a per-pupil basis without regard to race or class or even whether they are incarcerated. Expenditures must be proportional to the state's school-age population. Quite simply, children in middle-class school districts should not be receiving more expensive special education services than children in poor school districts. Our system of funding public schools through property taxes must end in order to create more education equity.

This point about funding cannot be overstated. Teams of educational advocates and pro bono lawyers cannot transform the special education system unless schools have the financial resources to provide the services that children need to obtain a free and appropriate public education. The IDEA will always be a statute only about the "individual" so long as the *system* is insufficiently resourced.

This list is only a small beginning. Others have documented the need to have culturally sensitive teachers in classrooms to help avoid the cycle of low expectations for many children.[12] And our health care crisis exacerbates the challenges faced by children with disabilities. My training is in law, not education or health care, so I have largely confined my list to changes that can be made by legislators and courts within the law of special education. I leave to others the task of suggesting how we can transform the classroom and the health care system to better serve all members of our society.

A Model for Hope

All children, especially those with disabilities, need an educational advocate, comparable to what is provided through the IFSP process wherein a social worker coordinates services within a family environment. A model program that should be instituted on a national basis is Dedril (Dee) Moore's Targeting Our People's Priorities with Service (TOPPS) program in Jefferson County, Arkansas, a community in which one out of every four people lives in poverty.[13] TOPPS staff offers a full range of services for children of all ages in tutoring, physical fitness, public speaking, cooking, computer training, art, travel, and mentoring. Volunteers serve a hot, nutritious meal to 280 children daily after school and more than 500 children throughout the summer months when they do not receive a meal at school. Moore has successfully reached teenage boys and girls who already had trouble with the juvenile justice system and, with her support, managed to graduate from high school and even go on to college. Her belief is that all children are entitled to someone who demonstrates that he or she really cares about their well-being. To succeed in school, a child needs a broad collection of services, not just good teachers. She tries to provide the support services necessary for success to be possible.

But Moore is just one person working from a shoestring budget with a collection of low-paid staff and volunteers. Her work is consistent with the literature on "resiliency" that children who grow up in poverty can break the cycle of poverty with assistance from strong mentors in their lives.[14] Ideally, those mentors are their parents, but those mentors can be others as well. Moore fills that gap for many children when their families cannot offer that kind of assistance.

The IDEA presumes that all children have such a mentor in their lives who can act as an educational advocate. The IDEA also presumes that schools will have the financial resources to be responsive to the needs of each child. Both of those presumptions are inaccurate for most children in our society. When each child, and his or her family, can work constructively with an educational advocate within a sufficiently resourced public school environment, then we may start becoming a society in which all children, irrespective of disability status, have access to a free and appropriate public education.

Notes

CHAPTER 1

1. Lloyd M. Dunn, *Special Education for the Mildly Retarded—Is Much of It Justifiable?*, Exceptional Children 20 (September 1968).
2. For further discussion, see chapter 2.
3. Racial Inequality and Special Education (eds. Daniel J. Losen & Gary Orfield 2002).
4. Beth Harry & Janette Klingner, Why Are So Many Minority Students in Special Education? Understanding Race & Disability in Schools (2006).
5. Losen & Orfield, *supra* note 3, at xv.
6. Harry & Klingner, *supra* note 4, at 9.
7. I use the term "mentally retarded" in this book because that is the term found in the special education laws. Some states have begun to use the term "intellectual disability" in their laws, and a bill has been introduced in Congress to do likewise. At this time, however, the term "mental retardation" is an accurate description of a disability classification found in the federal special education laws.
8. See Parent O/B/O Student v. Upper Arlington School District, No. 2269–2009 (August 21, 2009) (Marcie M. Scholl, Impartial Hearing Officer).
9. For further discussion of CAPD, see Lois Kam Heymann, The Sound of Hope: Recognizing, Coping with, and Treating Your Child's Auditory Processing Disorder (2010).
10. This story is based on Parent O/B/O Student, No. 2125–2007E (September 8, 2008) (Linda R. Warner, Impartial Hearing Officer). The record is quite incomplete and has been embellished in this narrative. The child's race is not indicated in the record. The individuals' names are not included in the hearing officer decision, so I have provided pseudonyms to humanize the stories.
11. See http://www2.ed.gov/about/offices/list/ocr/docs/impact.html.

12. These data were generated from the following website: https://www.ideadata.org/DACAnalyticTool/Values_2.asp?STUDY=Part%20B%20Child. I thank Katherine Hall for helping me generate these data.

13. See U.S. Census Bureau, Sex by Age Universe: Total Population 2010 Census Summary File 1; Sex by Age (Black or African American Alone) Universe: People Who Are Black or African American Alone 2010 Census Summary File 1, available at http://www.census.gov/population/www/socdemo/age/c2kguide.html. See also Data Across States, http://datacenter.kidscount.org/data/acrossstates/Rankings.aspx?ind=103 (The Annie E. Casey Foundation).

14. See U.S. Census Bureau, Sex by Age (Hispanic or Latino) Universe: People Who Are Hispanic or Latino 2010 Census Summary File 1, available at http://www.census.gov/population/www/socdemo/age/c2kguide.html.

15. See U.S. Census Bureau, Sex by Age (White Alone, Not Hispanic or Latino) Universe: People Who Are White Alone, not Hispanic or Latino 2010 Census Summary File 1, available at http://www.census.gov/population/www/socdemo/age/c2kguide.html.

16. Tom Parrish, Disparities in the Identification, Funding, and Provision of Special Education, submitted to the Harvard Civil Rights Project for the Conference on Minority Issues in Special Education in Public Schools 25–26 (November 6, 2000).

17. *Id.* at 16.

18. *Id.* at 13 (Table 3).

19. *Id.* at 22–23.

20. For that reason, I have made in another book the (controversial) argument that segregation is not inherently bad under the special education laws. It has often been used for the benefit of whites. But, for racial minorities under the special education laws, segregation is often accompanied by substandard programs. See Ruth Colker, When Is Separate Unequal? A Disability Perspective (2009).

21. See generally Harry & Klingner, *supra* note 4.

22. *Id.* at 172.

23. *See* chapter 2.

24. Harry & Klingner, *supra* note 4, at 18.

25. *See generally* Tracy Gershwin Mueller and Francisco Carranza, *An Examination of Special Education Due Process Hearings*, 22 J. of Disability Studies 131 (2011).

26. Eloise Pasachoff, *Special Education, Poverty, and the Limits of Private Enforcement*, 86 Notre Dame L. Rev. 1413, 1417 (2011).

27. *Id.* at 1427.

28. *See* Mark Kelman & Gillian Lester, Jumping the Queue: An Inquiry into the Legal Treatment of Students with Learning Disabilities (1997).

29. Passachoff, *supra* note 26, at 1482.

30. Bernice Johnson Reagon, *Ella's Song* (1983) (Sweet Honey in the Rock) ("We who believe in freedom cannot rest, We who believe in freedom cannot rest until it comes, Until the killing of Black men, Black mothers' sons is as important as the killing of white men, white mothers' sons . . .").

CHAPTER 2

1. Watson v. City of Cambridge, 157 Mass. 561, 32 N.E. 864 (Mass. 1893).

2. *Id.*

3. State v. Board of Education of City of Antigo, 169 Wis. 231, 172 N.W. 153 (Wis. 1919).

4. *Id.* at 153.

5. *Id.*

6. *Id.*

7. *Id.* at 155.

8. See Robert L. Osgood, The History of Inclusion in the United States (2005).

9. John G. Richardson & Tara L. Parker, *The Institutional Genesis of Special Education: The American Case*, 101 American Journal of Education 363, 373–74 (August 1993).

10. Osgood, *supra* note 8, at 22.

11. Scott B. Sigmon, Radical Analysis of Special Education 22 (1987).

12. Osgood, *supra* note 10, at 67.

13. Sigmon, *supra* note 11, at 20.

14. *Id.* at 21.

15. *Id.* at 32–33.

16. Paula S. Fass, Outside In: Minorities and the Transformation of American Education 55–56 (1989).

17. David B. Tyack, The One Best System: A History of American Urban Education 205 (1974).

18. See Fass, *supra* note 16, at 53.

19. Richardson & Parker, *supra* note 9, at 359.

20. *Id.* at 374.

21. *Id.* at 378.

22. Hobson v. Hansen, 269 F. Supp. 401 (D.D.C. 1967).

23. *Id.* at 448.

24. *Id.* at 512 ("those who are being consigned to the lower tracks are the poor and the Negroes").

25. *Id.* at 473.

26. Lloyd M. Dunn, *Special Education for the Mildly Retarded—Is Much of It Justifiable?*, Exceptional Children 5 (September 1968).

27. *Id.* at 6.

28. *Id.*

29. *Id.* at 5.

30. *Id.* at 7.

31. Larry P. v. Riles, 343 F. Supp. 1306 (N.D. Cal. 1972), *aff'd*, 502 F.2d 963 (9th Cir. 1974).

32. Larry P., 793 F.2d at 980.

33. Mills v. Board of Education, 348 F. Supp. 866 (D.D.C. 1972).

34. See Pennsylvania Association for Retarded Children v. Pennsylvania, 334 F. Supp. 1257 (E.D. Pa. 1971).

35. Edward W. Martin, *Breakthrough for the Handicapped: Legislative History*, Exceptional Children 493, 494 (March 1968).

36. See Pub. L. 85–905, 87–715, 89–258 (supporting instructional media for the deaf); Pub. L. 85–926 (training of teachers for the mentally retarded); Pub. L. 87–276 (funding teachers of the deaf).

37. Martin, *supra* note 35, at 496.

38. Pub. L. 89–10.

39. Report of the House Committee on Education and Labor, No. 94–332 (94th Cong. 1st Sess. June 26, 1975), at 2.

40. *Id.* at 2.

41. Pub. L. 89–750.
42. *Id.*
43. See Forest Grove School District v. T.A., 200 U.S. 321 (2009).
44. See Pub. L. 89–313.
45. See Martin, *supra* note 35, at 499.
46. H.R. 16847.
47. See Martin, *supra* note 35, at 500.
48. See Pub. L. 89–313, 90–170, 90–247.
49. See http://www.ldanatl.org/about/history.asp.
50. Pub. L. 91–230, Sec. 601–662 (1970–71).
51. Pub. L. 91–230, Sec. 613(a)(1), 84 Stat. 179.
52. Martin, *supra* note 35, at 27.
53. Pub. L. 91–230, at Sec. 601(1), 84 Stat. 175.
54. Pub. L. 91–230, at Sec. 661, 84 Stat. 187.
55. *Id.* at Sec. 602(15), 84 Stat. 177.
56. 20 U.S.C. § 1401(30)(C) (emphasis added).
57. Martin, *supra* note 35, at 29.
58. Pub. L. 93–380, 88 Stat. 582 (1974–1975).
59. *Id.* at 582.
60. *Id.* at 583.
61. Hearings were held on March 20, 21, and 23, 1973; April 9, 1973; May 7 and 14, 1973; October 19, 1973; March 18, 1974; June 17 and 24, 1974; and April 8, 9, and 15, 1975.
62. Hearings were held on March 6, 7, 18, and 22, 1974; August 5, 1974; April 9 and 10, 1975; May 21, 1975; June 9, 1975; and July 22, 1975.
63. Debate occurred on January 15, 1975 (S. 6); House and Senate on March 20, 1975 (S. 1256 and H.R. 7217); Senate on June 11, 12, 17, and 18, 1975 (S. 6); House on July 18, 21, and 29, 1975 (H.R. 7217); and Senate on July 31, 1975 (Senate disagrees with House Amendments).
64. *Id.* at 651.
65. Congressional Quarterly Almanac 651 (1975).
66. *Id.* at 656.
67. Public Law 94–142, Sec. 8, 89 Stat. 796.
68. Congressional Quarterly Almanac, *supra* note 68, at 527 (Dr. Gerald M. Senf, Leadership Training Institute in Learning Disabilities, Department of Special Education, College of Education, University of Arizona, Tucson).
69. *Id.* at 536.
70. *Id.* at 527.
71. *Id.* at 287 (March 21, 1973) (Dr. Charles Banov).
72. U.S. Senate, Subcommittee on the Handicapped of the Committee on Labor and Public Welfare 44 (April 9, 1973) (Carolyn Heft, New York Legal Services).
73. *Id.* at 44.
74. *Id.* at 84–85 (Dr. Laura Wilbur, New York Speech Hearing Association).
75. U.S. Senate, Subcommittee on the Handicapped of the Committee on Labor and Public Welfare 579 (May 7, 1973) (Report on Special Education in Connecticut).
76. *Id.* at 579.
77. U.S. Senate, Subcommittee on the Handicapped of the Committee on Labor and Public Welfare 155 (March 20, 1973).

78. U.S. Senate, Subcommittee on the Handicapped of the Committee on Labor and Public Welfare 672–74 (May 14, 1973).

79. *Id.* at 684.

80. *Id.* at 659.

81. *Id.* at 670.

82. *Id.* at 709 (Project on Classification of Exceptional Children: Public School System Task Force: The Intellectually and Behaviorally Handicapped).

83. *Id.* at 757.

84. U.S. Senate, Subcommittee on the Handicapped of the Committee on Labor and Public Welfare 36 (April 9, 1973) (Mrs. Stuart Brown, PARC).

85. *Id.* at 315 (April 9, 1973) (Dr. Philip A. Bellefleur, Headmaster of the Pennsylvania School for the Deaf).

86. *Id.* at 1207 (October 19, 1973) (John C. Groos, Director of Special Education, Minnesota Department of Education) (hearings held in St. Paul, Minnesota).

87. *Id.* at 111 (April 9, 1973) (PARC).

88. *Id.* at 111.

89. *Id.* at 78 (April 9, 1973) (Patricia Koechlin, New Jersey Association for Retarded Children).

90. *Id.* at 8 (April 9, 1973) (Phillip Bellefleur, Headmaster of the Pennsylvania School for the Deaf).

91. *Id.* at 388 (May 7, 1973).

92. *Id.* at 402 (May 7, 1973).

93. *Id.* at 446 (March 21, 1973) (Stephen Kurzman).

94. *Id.* at 1439 (March 18, 1974) (Senator Richard Schweiker).

95. *Id.* at 1461 (March 18, 1974).

96. *Id.*

97. *Id.* at 1465.

98. *Id.*

99. *Id.* at 1511.

100. *Id.* at 1287 (October 19, 1973) (Maynard Reynolds).

101. *Id.*

102. *Id.* at 1287–89.

103. U.S. House, Hearings before the Select Subcommittee on Education of the Committee on Education and Labor 15 (March 6, 1974).

104. *Id.* at 36.

105. *Id.* at 41.

106. *Id.* at 226.

107. *Id.* at 231.

108. *Id.* at 190 (Patricia Wald, Attorney, Mental Health Law Project, Washington, D.C.).

109. *Id.* at 195.

110. *Id.* at 207.

111. *Id.* at 338–353.

112. *Id.* at 339.

113. *Id.* at 342 (emphasis added).

114. *Id.* at 344.

115. *Id.*

116. *Id.* at 345–46.

117. *Id.* at 346.
118. *Id.* at 347.
119. *Id.*
120. *Id.* at 364.
121. *Id.*
122. U.S. Senate, Committee on Labor and Public Welfare 6 (S. Rpt. 94–168) (June 2, 1975).
123. *Id.* at 6.
124. *Id.*
125. *Id.* at 27.
126. *Id.* at 28.
127. *Id.*
128. *Id.*
129. *Id.* at 9.
130. *Id.* at 26.
131. *Id.* at 25.
132. *Id.* at 26.
133. *Id.*
134. *Id.* at 10.
135. Senate Report, *supra* note 125, at 11.
136. *Id.* at 11.
137. *Id.* at 12.
138. *Id.*
139. *Id.* at 22.
140. *Id.*
141. *Id.*
142. *Id.* at 23.
143. U.S. House, Committee on Education and Labor (H. Rpt. 94–332) (June 26, 1975).
144. *Id.* at 8.
145. *Id.*
146. *Id.* at 63–65.
147. *Id.* at 63.
148. *Congressional Record* (November 14, 1975) p. H11223.
149. *Id.* at H11226.
150. *Id.* at H11227.
151. Public Law 94–142, Sec. 3(c) (89 Stat. 775) (statement of findings and purpose).
152. *Id.* at Sec. 611(a)(1)(B) (89 Stat. 776-77). But states did not get to account for every handicapped child through some complicated ceilings and exceptions. See Sec. 611(5)(A) (89 Stat. 777).
153. *See* Martin, *supra* note 35, at 30.
154. Martin, *supra* note 35, at 30.
155. Public Law 94–142, Sec. 4(18) (89 Stat. 775).
156. *Id.* at 4(19) (89 Stat. 776).
157. *Id.* at Sec. 612(5) (89 Stat. 781).
158. Public Law 94–142, Sec. 615(b)(1)(C) (89 Stat. 788).
159. Public Law 94–142, sec. 615 (89 Stat. 788–89).
160. *Id.* at 789.
161. *Id.*

162. Public Law 94–142, Sec. 4(19) (89 Stat. 776).

163. Public Law 94–142, Sec. 615(3)(3) (89 Stat. 789).

164. Congressional Quarterly Almanac 651 (1975).

165. *Id.* at 655.

166. Beth Harry & Janette Klingner, Why Are So Many Minority Students in Special Education? Understanding Race & Disability in Schools 12 (2006).

CHAPTER 3

1. Board of Education v. Rowley, 458 U.S. 175 (1982).

2. *Id.* at 210.

3. These facts are taken from Amy Rowley, *25 Years Later: Board of Education v. Rowley: A Look at the Past and Looking Towards the Future*, Proceedings of the PEPNet 2008 Conference 41–52 (2008). I also received the entire court file from the archives of the U.S. courts. These archives are thousands of pages in length and provide valuable information not reported elsewhere. The Ohio State University has created a digital copy of these archives. See http://ada.osu.edu/rowley.html. Throughout this chapter, I refer to those archives as "district court archives."

4. Appendix, at E-4 16 in Board of Education v. Rowley, No. 80–1002, filed on December 15, 1980. The references to the appendix throughout this chapter refer to the appendix prepared in the U.S. Supreme Court in Board of Education v. Rowley, No. 80–1002, and can be found on Westlaw or Lexis.

5. Regulations of the Commissioner of Education, Section 200.4 (as quoted by Hearing Officer, Albert P. Roberts, in his decision rendered on January 12, 1979) (available at Appendix F-17 in Board of Education v. Rowley, No. 80–1002, filed on December 15, 1980).

6. *Id.* at F-16.

7. *Id.* at F-8. See also Memo from J. Zavarella to Dr. Jenkins, dated June 20, 1977, available in district court archives.

8. Memo from J. Zavarella to Dr. Jenkins, dated June 20, 1977, available in district court archives.

9. This complaint is mentioned in a letter from Joseph A. Zavarella to Mr. & Mrs. Rowley (October 4, 1977), available in district court archives. It is also mentioned in the school district's brief, dated July 3, 1979, available in district court archives.

10. Letter from Joseph A. Zavarella to Mr. & Mrs. Clifford Rowley (September 23, 1977), available in district court archives.

11. Letter from Joseph A. Zavarella to Mr. & Mrs. Rowley (October 4, 1977), available in district court archives.

12. Untitled document dated January 18, 1978, signed by Mr. and Mrs. Rowley and Joseph A. Zavarella, Principal, available in district court archives.

13. Rowley, *supra* note 3, at 44.

14. Evaluation by Jack Janik, Interpreter for weeks of February 27 to March 3, March 6 to March 10, available in district court archives. *See also* Appendix, *supra* note 4, at E-3.

15. Appendix, *supra* note 4, at F-9.

16. Letter from William R. Valentine to Mr. & Mrs. Rowley (May 12, 1978), available in district court archives. Letter from William R. Valentine to Superintendent Charles V. Eible (May 12, 1978), available in district court archives.

17. Furnace Woods Elementary School Parent's Response Form for Handicapped Pupil Placement, dated June 14, 1978, available in district court archives.

18. Letter from Adelaide G. Waldron to Mr. and Mrs. Rowley, dated October 10, 1978, available in district court archives.

19. District Committee on Handicapped Notes, dated October 3, 1978, available in district court archives.

20. District Committee on Handicapped Notes, dated October 3, 1978, available in district court archives.

21. Appendix, *supra* note 4, at F-17 to F-18.

22. Rowley, *supra* note 3, at 45.

23. Rowley v. Board of Education, 483 F. Supp. 528, 532 (S.D. N.Y. 1980).

24. Rowley, *supra* note 3, at 45.

25. Appendix, *supra* note 4, at F-19.

26. *Id.* at F-23 to F-24.

27. Affidavit of Nancy Rowley (February 24, 1979), available in district court archives.

28. Affidavit of S. Jack Janik Jr. (February 25, 1979), available in district court archives.

29. Appendix, *supra* note 4, at E-5.

30. Rowley v. Board of Education, 483 F. Supp. 536, 538 (S.D. N.Y. 1980).

31. *Id.* at 538.

32. *Id.* at 529.

33. *Id.*

34. *Id.* at 532.

35. *Id.* at 532 n.6.

36. *Id.* at 532 n. 7.

37. *Id.* at 534.

38. *Id.*

39. *Id.* at 533.

40. *Id.* at 534. This standard was borrowed from a law review note, The Education for All Handicapped Children Act of 1975, 92 Harv. L. Rev. 1103, 1125–26 (1979).

41. *Id.* at 534.

42. *Id.*

43. *Id.* at 535.

44. *Id.* at 536.

45. *Id.*

46. Rowley, *supra* note 3, at 46.

47. *Id.* at 46.

48. Rowley v. Board of Education, 632 F.2d 945, 948 (2nd Cir. 1980).

49. *Id.* at 952 (Mansfield, C.J. dissenting).

50. *Id.* at 952.

51. Rowley, *supra* note 3, at 47.

52. *Id.* at 47–48.

53. *Id.* at 49.

54. Rowley v. Board of Education, No. 79 Civ. 2139 (VLB), order issued on September 23, 1980, by District Court Judge Vincent L. Broderick, available in district court archives.

55. Rowley v. Board of Education, No. 79 Civ 2139 (VLB), transcript of hearing conducted on September 22, 1980, available in district court archives.
56. See Affidavit of Michael A. Chatoff (January 15, 1981), available in district court archives.
57. Notarized Letter from Frances A. Miller to Michael A. Chatoff (December 15, 1980), available in district court archives.
58. Letter from Frances Miller to Warren A. Button, President of the Board of Education (December 7, 1980), available in district court archives.
59. Letter from Raymond Kuntz to Judge Broderick, dated January 21, 1981, available in district court archives.
60. See Affidavit of Michael A. Chatoff (January 15, 1981), available in district court archives.
61. Affidavit of Louise McQuade (January 15, 1981), available in district court archives.
62. See Bangor Daily News, March 24, 1982, available at http://news.google.com/new spapers?nid=2457&dat=19820324&id=kcszAAAAIBAJ&sjid=TCMIAAAAIBAJ &pg=3837,2659968.
63. See http://www.gallaudet.edu/Documents/PublicRelations/GT1989.pdf (describing computer technology used by Chatoff during oral argument).
64. Id.
65. Board of Education v. Rowley, 458 U.S. 175 (1982).
66. Id. at 199.
67. Id. at 201.
68. Id. at 203 n. 25.
69. Id. at 203–04.
70. Id. at 202.
71. Id.
72. Id. at 203 n. 25 (emphasis added).
73. Id. at 210 n. 32.
74. Id. at 209–10.
75. In the Matter of the Impartial Due Process Hearing on the Petition of Amy Rowley v. Hendrick Hudson Central School District, dated November 30, 1982, available in district court archives.
76. Rowley, supra note 3, at 49.
77. Affidavit by Michael Chatoff, filed April 29, 1983, available in district court archives.
78. Interview with Barry Felder, October 4, 2011.
79. Rowley, supra note 3, at 50.
80. Rowley, supra note 3, at 50.
81. Order, Rowley v. Board of Education, No. 80–7098 (2nd Cir. October 13, 1983), available in district court archives.
82. Letter from Michael A. Chatoff to Judge Broderick, available in district court archives.
83. Rowley v. Board of Education, No. 84–7160 (2nd Cir. April 9, 1984).
84. 34 C.F.R. § 300.34(a); (c)(4).
85. 34 C.F.R. § 300.101(b).
86. See Affirmation filed by Michael A. Chatoff in Rowley v. Board of Education, No. 79 Civil 2139 (VLB), dated December 7, 1982, available in district court archives.

CHAPTER 4

1. These facts are found in the hearing officer opinion, In Re: Michael P., BSEA # 2867 (Deborah D. Blumer January 31, 1980). This opinion is found in the Joint Appendix for School Committee of the Town of Burlington v. Department of Education, No. 84–433 (filed Jan. 18, 1985).

2. *Id.* at 4a.

3. *Id.* at 15a.

4. *Id.* at 13a–14a.

5. This matter is discussed in Town of Burlington v. Department of Education, 655 F.2d 428, 430 (1ˢᵗ Cir. 1981).

6. Town of Burlington v. The Department of Education of the Commonwealth of Massachusetts, No. 80–359-Z (D. Mass. Nov. 19, 1980).

7. Town of Burlington v. The Department of Education of the Commonwealth of Massachusetts, No. 80–1527 (1ˢᵗ Cir. Jan. 28, 1981).

8. Town of Burlington v. The Department of Education of the Commonwealth of Masschusetts, No. 80–359-Z (D. Mass. Feb. 12, 1981).

9. Town of Burlington v. Department of Education, 655 F.2d 428, 431 (1ˢᵗ Cir. 1981).

10. *Id.* at 433.

11. Interview with David Rosenberg (September 2011).

12. 458 U.S. 176 (1982).

13. Town of Burlington v. Department of Education, No, 80–359-Z 9D. Mass. Aug. 13, 1982), at 65a (emphasis added).

14. *Id.* at 66a.

15. *Id.* at 62a.

16. *Id.* at 66a.

17. *Id.*

18. *Id.* at 68a.

19. Michael's father worked as a security guard at the courthouse; I do not know if Michael's mother had paid employment.

20. Doe v. Anrig, 561 F. Supp. 121 (D. Mass. 1983).

21. *Id.* at 130.

22. Town of Burlington v. Department of Education, No. 80–359-Z (D. Mass. May 9, 1983).

23. Town of Burlington v. Department of Education, 736 F.2d 773 (1ˢᵗ Cir. 1984).

24. *Id.* at 788.

25. *Id.*

26. *Id.*

27. *Id.* at 792.

28. *Id.* at 793.

29. *Id.* at 796 (quoting provision).

30. *Id.* at 799.

31. *Id.*

32. *Id.* at 801.

33. *Id.* at 794.

34. *Id.* at 801.

35. School Committee of the Town of Burlington v. Department of Education, 471 U.S. 358 (1985).

36. *Id.* at 370.

CHAPTER 5

1. Public Law 95–49 (June 17, 1977).
2. H.R. Rep. 98–410, at 4.
3. H.R. Rep. 98–410, at 18.
4. *Id.* at 18.
5. See Public Law 98–199, at sec. 7.
6. H.R. Rep. 98–410, at 21–22.
7. *Id.* at 18.
8. Public Law 98–199, at sec. 17(a)(1).
9. *Id.* at 19.
10. 458 U.S. 175 (1982).
11. Public Law 99–372.
12. Public Law 99–457.
13. Smith v. Robinson, 468 U.S. 992, 1021 (1984).
14. *Id.* at 995.
15. *Id.*
16. *Id.* at 997, n. 3.
17. *Id.* at 997, n. 4 (1975 amendments became effective on October 1, 1977, and were effective while Tommy's case went through the state administrative process).
18. *See generally* Alyeska Pipeline Serv. Co. v. Wilderness Soc., 421 U.S. 240, 247 (1975).
19. 29 U.S.C. § 794.
20. *Id.* at 1031.
21. *Id.*
22. Public Law 99–372, section 2.
23. See 42 U.S.C. § 12102(2) (defining "major life activities").
24. See 20 U.S.C. § 1401(3) (defining "child with a disability").
25. H.R. Rep. 99–860, at 4.
26. *Id.* at 5.
27. Public Law 99–457, section 672(1).
28. Public Law 99–457, section 672(2).
29. H. Rep. 99–860, at 2410.
30. H.R. Rep. 99–860, at 2421.
31. H.R. Rep. 101–544, at 4.
32. *Id.* at 4.
33. *Id.* at 5.
34. *Id.* at 14.
35. *Id.* at 14–17.
36. *See generally* Beth Harry & Janette Klingner, Why Are So Many Minority Students in Special Education? (2006).
37. Public Law No. 102–119.
38. S. Rep. 102–84, at 6.
39. *Id.* at 9. The House Report contained similar language. See House Report 102–198.
40. Public Law No. 102–119, at sec. 15(7).
41. Lyke Thompson et al., *Pathways to Empowerment: Effects of Family-Centered Delivery of Early Intervention Services*, 64 Exceptional Children 99, 106 (1997).
42. *Id.* at 106.

43. Don Bailey et al., National Early Intervention Longitudinal Study—Families' First Experiences with Early Intervention: NEILS data report no. 2 (January 2003).

44. *Id.* at 16.

45. *Id.* at 14.

46. *Id.* at 17.

47. *Id.* at 18.

48. *Id.* at 29.

49. *Id.*

50. *Id.* at 30.

51. *Id.* at 31.

52. *Id.* at 32.

53. Paula Sue Lalinde, The Effects of Family Race/Ethnicity and Socioeconomic Status on Quality of Services and Family Outcomes for Families Participating in Part C Early Intervention Programs (2008), available at http://scholarlyrepository.miami.edu/oa_dissertations/65.

54. *Id.* at 46.

55. *Id.* at 49.

56. Public Law No. 103–382.

57. See U.S. House, Conference Report 103–761, at 386.

58. Public Law No. 105–17, 111 Stat. 37 (June 4, 1991)

59. 458 U.S. 176 (1982).

60. 111 Stat. at 39, codified at 20 U.S.C. § 1400(c)(4).

61. *Id.* at 39, codified at 20 U.S.C. § 1400(c)(5) (emphasis added).

62. See H.R. Rep. 105–95 (May 13, 1997); S. Rep. 105–17 (May 9, 1997).

63. 111 Stat. at 40, codified at 20 U.S.C. § 1400(c)(7)(A).

64. 20 U.S.C. § 1400(c)(8).

65. U.S. Senate, Hearings of the Committee on Labor and Human Resources 16 (January 29, 1997).

66. *Id.* at 81, codified at 20 U.S.C. § 1414.

67. *Id.* at 82, codified at 20 U.S.C. § 1414(d)(2)(C).

68. *Id.* at 82, codified at 20 U.S.C. § 1414(d)(3)(A)(i).

69. *Id.* at 82, codified at 20 U.S.C. § 1414(d)(5).

70. H. Rep. 105–95, at 99.

71. U.S. Senate, Hearing of the Committee on Labor and Human Resources, United States Senate 14 (January 29, 1997). (His last name is misspelled as "Hehr" in the transcript of the hearings.)

72. U.S. House, *Hearings on H.R. 5, The IDEA Improvement Act of 1997*, Subcommittee on Early Childhood, Youth and Families of the Committee on Education and the Workforce 41 (February 4 & 6, 1997).

73. *Id.* at 49.

74. *Id.* at 41.

75. 111 Stat. at 102, codified at 20 U.S.C. § 1418(c).

76. Thomas Hehir, *IDEA and Disproportionality: Federal Enforcement, Effective Advocacy, and Strategies for Change* in Racial Inequity in Special Education 219 (Daniel J. Losen & Gary Orfield eds. 2002).

77. *Id.* at 231.

78. *Id.*

79. 111 Stat. at 84, codified at 20 U.S.C. § 1414(d)(1)(A).

80. *Id.* at 83, codified at 20 U.S.C. § 1414(d)(1)(A).

81. *Id.*

82. *Id.* at 84, codified at 20 U.S.C. § 1414(d)(1)(B).

83. H. Rep. 105–95, at 108.

84. 111 Stat. at 41, codified at 20 US.C. § 1400(c)(8)(E)&(F).

85. U.S. House, *Hearings on H.R. 5, The IDEA Improvement Act of 1997*, Subcommittee on Early Childhood, Youth and Families of the Committee on Education and the Workforce 51 (February 4 & 6, 1997).

86. *Id.* at 63.

87. *Id.* at 60.

88. *Id.* at 62.

89. 20 U.S.C. § 1411(1)(1)(A)(1994).

90. 111 Stat. 120.

91. 20 U.S.C. § 1415(i)(3)(D)(ii).

92. Section 612(a)(24).

93. 2004 U.S.C.C.A.N. S43, 2004 WL 3670895 (Leg. Hist.), at 2.

94. Section 614(b)(6).

95. Section 615(b)(7); (c)(2).

96. Section 615(k)(1)(E).

97. H.R. Conf. Rep. 108–779, at 190.

98. Section 615(k)(3).

99. Data from U.S. Department of Education, Office of Special Education Programs, Data Analysis System (DANS). For 2007–8, in-school suspension and out-of-school suspensions were reported separately. I combined them to make data comparable over time.

100. See Michelle Alexander, The New Jim Crow: Mass Incarceration in the Age of Colorblindness (2010).

101. U.S. Senate, Subcommittee on the Handicapped of the Committee on Labor and Public Welfare 672–74 (May 14, 1973).

CHAPTER 6

1. 20 U.S.C. § 1400(c)(5).

2. The facts are taken from the hearing officer decisions. These decisions are contained in the Joint Appendix filed in the U.S. Supreme Court. See Schaffer v. Weast, No. 04–698 (filed April 29, 2005).

3. Hearing Officer Decision, *supra* note 2, at App. 77 (November 27, 2000).

4. *Id.* at App. 78.

5. *Id.* at App. 91.

6. *Id.* at App. 80.

7. *Id.* at App. 82 & 91.

8. *Id.* at App. 84.

9. *Id.* at App. 137.

10. *Id.* at App. 121 n. 1.

11. *Id.* at App. 147.

12. *Id.* at App. 144.

13. *Id.* at App. 145.

14. *Id.* at App. 147.
15. *Id.*
16. *Id.* at App. 153.
17. *Id.*
18. *Id.* at App. 155.
19. *Id.* at App. 150.
20. *Id.*
21. *Id.* at App. 156–157.
22. *Id.* at App. 154.
23. *Id.* at App. 156.
24. Brian S. v. Vance, 86 F. Supp.2d 538, 544 (D. Md. 2000).
25. *Id.* at 544.
26. *Id.* at 544 n.8.
27. *Id.*
28. Hearing Officer Decision, *supra* note 2, at App. 91.
29. *Id.* at 91.
30. *Id.*
31. *Id.* at 104.
32. *Id.* at 108.
33. *Id.* at 109.
34. Weast v. Schaffer, 240 F. Supp.2d 396, 406 (D. Md. 2002).
35. *Id.* at 408.
36. *Id.* at 409.
37. *Id.*
38. Weast v. Schaffer, 377 F.3d 449, 456 (4th Cir. 2004).
39. *Id.* at 458–59.
40. Schaffer v. Weast, 546 U.S. 49 (2005).
41. *Id.* at 62-63 (Stevens, J. concurring).
42. Schaffer v. Weast, 546 U.S. 49, 53 (2005).
43. *Id.* at 60–61.
44. Schaffer v. Weast, Civil Action No. PJM 99–15 (D. Md. Sept. 17, 2007).
45. Weast v. Schaffer, 377 F.3d 449, 474 (4th Cir. 2004).
46. Schaffer v. Weast, Civil Action No. PJM 99–15 (D. Md. Sept. 17, 2007), at 69.
47. *Id.* at 72.
48. Schaffer v. Weast, 554 F.3d 470 (4th Cir. 2009).
49. *Id.* at 474.

CHAPTER 7

1. Arlington Central School District Board of Education v. Murphy, 548 U.S. 291 (2006).
2. See Application of the Board of Education of the Arlington Central School District for review of a determination of a hearing officer relating to the provision of educational services to a child with a disability, No. 99–65 (Dec. 14, 1999).
3. *Id.* at 3.
4. *Id.* at 6.
5. In the Matter of T.M. & P.M. on Behalf of their Child, J.M., against Arlington Central School District (Feb. 26, 1999) (Leonard W. Krouner, Hearing Officer).

6. *Id.* at A-15.
7. *Id.*
8. *Id.*
9. *Id.* at A-9.
10. *Id.* at A-10.
11. See Schaffer v. Weast, 546 U.S. 49 (2005).
12. McKinney's Education Law § 4404 (1)(c). See 2007 Sess. Law News of N.Y. Ch. 583 (A. 5396–A) (McKinney's).
13. In the Matter of T.M. & P.M. on Behalf of their Child, J.M., against Arlington Central School District (Feb. 26, 1999) (Leonard W. Krouner, Hearing Officer), at A-17.
14. In the Matter of T.M. and P.M. on Behalf of their Child, J.M., against Arlington Central School District (July 7, 1999) (Leonard W. Krouner, Hearing Officer), at 12.
15. *Id.* at 19.
16. In the Matter of T.M. & P.M. on Behalf of their Child, J.M., against Arlington Central School District (Feb. 26, 1999) (Leonard W. Krouner, Hearing Officer), at 15.
17. *Id.* at 16.
18. *Id.* at 17.
19. *Id.*
20. Murphy v. Arlington Central School District Board of Education, 86 F. Supp.2d 354, 356 (S.D. N.Y. 2000).
21. *Id.* at 361.
22. *Id.* at 365.
23. *Id.* at 366.
24. *Id.* at 367.
25. *Id.* at 367 n.9.
26. Murphy v. Arlington Central School District Board of Education, 297 F.3d 195 (2nd Cir. 2002).
27. *Id.*
28. Winkelman v. Parma City School District, 550 U.S. 516 (2007).
29. Murphy v. Arlington Central School District Board of Education, No. 99 Civ. 9294 (CSH) (S.D. N.Y. Feb. 19, 2003), available at 2003 WL 367872.
30. *Id.* at *1 n. 1.
31. 20 U.S.C. § 1415(i)(D)(ii).
32. 20 U.S.C. § 1415(h)(1).
33. 165 F. Supp. 2d 570 (S.D. N.Y. 2001).
34. 34 F. Supp.2d 795 (N.D. N.Y. 1998).
35. See http://www.marilynsuearons.com/index.html.
36. See Murphy v. Arlington Central School District, No. 99 Civ. 9294 (CSH) (S.D. N.Y. 2003), available at 2003 WL 21694398; Murphy v. Arlington Central School District Board of Education, 402 F.3d 332 (2nd Cir. 2005).
37. Murphy, 402 F.3d at 336–337.
38. *Id.* at 338.
39. Arlington Central School District Board of Education v. Murphy, 548 U.S. 291 (2006).
40. *Id.* at 307 (Ginsburg, J., concurring).
41. See, e.g., H.R. 4188: IDEA Fairness Restoration Act, 110th Congress (2007–2008); H.R. 2740: IDEA Fairness Restoration Act, 111th Congress (2009–2010) (referred to committee).

CHAPTER 8

1. 20 U.S.C. § 1415(b)(3).
2. Some of these facts were taken from an Internet interview with Sandee Winkelman. http://www.blogtalkradio.com/specialed/2010/11/04/interview-with-sandee-
   winkelman. See also Parents O/B/O Child v. Parma City School District Board of
   Education, No. 1328–2003 (Feb. 19, 2004) (Joy M. Freda, Impartial Hearing Officer).
   The hearing officer opinion says that Jacob was one of five children, but his mother
   indicated in the interview that he was one of four children.
3. See http://www.achievementcenters.org/.
4. See http://monarchcenterforautism.com/.
5. http://www.news-herald.com/articles/2010/07/28/obituaries/nh2820512.txt.
6. SE–1328–2003.
7. See Parents O/B/O Child v. Parma City School District Board of Education, No.
   1328–2003 (Feb. 19, 2004) (Joy M. Freda, Impartial Hearing Officer); Student v.
   Parma City School District, No. 1328–2003 (June 2, 1004) (Theresa L. Hagen, State
   Level Review Officer Decision).
8. Winkelman v. Parma City School District, 411 F. Supp.2d 722 (N.D. Ohio 2005).
9. In the Matter of Student v. Parma School District, No. 1901–2006 (June 28, 2007)
   (Harry H. Taich, Impartial Hearing Officer), at 8.
10. Id. at 9.
11. In re Student v. Parma City School District, No. 1845–2005 (March 30, 2007) (T.
    Anthony Mazzola, Impartial Hearing Officer), at 60.
12. In the Matter of Student v. Parma School District, No. 1901–2006 (June 28, 2007)
    (Harry H. Taich, Impartial Hearing Officer), at 16.
13. Student v. Parma City School District, No. 1727–2005 (Sept. 2005) (Tobie Braverman,
    Impartial Hearing Officer).
14. Winkelman v. Parma City School District, 150 Fed. Appx. 406 (6th Cir. 2005).
15. In re Student v. Parma City School District, No. 1845–2005 (March 30, 2007) (T.
    Anthony Mazzola, Impartial Hearing Officer).
16. Parents O/B/O Student v. Parma City School District, No. 1845–2005 (Sept. 2007)
    (Robert L. Mues, State Level Review Officer).
17. In the Matter of Student v. Parma School District, No. 1901–2006 (June 28, 2007)
    (Harry H. Taich, Impartial Hearing Officer).
18. In the Matter of Student and Parents of Student v. Parma City School District, No.
    1901–2006 (Oct. 1, 2007) (Monica R. Bohlen).
19. Winkelman v. Parma City School District, 550 U.S. 516 (2007).
20. Winkelman v. Parma City School District, 294 Fed. Appx. 997 (6th Cir. 2008).
21. Parents O/B/O Student v. Parma City School District, No. 1995–2007 (March 7,
    2008) (Ronald E. Alexander, Impartial Hearing Officer), at 151.
22. Id.
23. Id. at 155–56.
24. Parents O/B/O/ Student, No. 1995–2007 (August 2008) (Robert L. Mues, State Level
    Review Officer).
25. See Board of Education v. Rowley, 458 U.S. 176 (1982). This case is discussed exten-
    sively in chapter 3.
26. 325 F.3d 724 (6th Cir. 2003).

27. Parent O/B/O Student v. Northwest Local School District, No. 1208–2002 (May 2003) (Robert L. Mues, State Level Review Officer).

28. Although hearing officer decisions are not supposed to disclose the name of the child, this opinion included the child's first name. See *id.* at 8.

29. Elida Local School District v. Erickson, 252 F. Supp.2d 476 (N.D. Ohio 2003).

30. Stancourt v. Worthington City Schools, 841 N.E.2d 812 (Ohio Ct. App. 2005), reconsidered 2005 WL 3481544 (Ohio Ct. App. 2005), appeal denied, 900 N.E.2d 624 (Ohio 2009), cert. denied, 130 S. Ct. 74 (2009).

31. Parent O/B/O Student v. Northwest Local School District, No. 1197–2002 (April 2, 2003) (Linda R. Warner, Impartial Hearing Officer).

CHAPTER 9

1. Child v. Broward County School Board, Case No. 10–3160E (Nov. 3, 2010) (Stuart M. Lerner, Hearing Officer).

2. *Id.* at 37.

3. *Id.* at 13.

4. These facts are taken from Child v. Collier County School Board, Case No. 06–0274E (Sept. 15, 2009) (Daniel Manry, Hearing Officer). *See also* Katherine Albers, *Collier School District settles suit concerning autistic student wanting service dog in class*, Naplesnews.com (April 21, 2010); Katherine Lewis, Boy with disabilities, parents file federal suit against school, National-College.com (December 1, 2006).

5. *Id.* at 11.

6. *Id.* at 18.

7. *Id.* at 28.

8. Child v. Duval County School Board, No. 08–2546E (Feb. 3, 2009) (Suzanne F. Hood, Hearing Officer).

9. 34 C.F.R. § 300.513.

10. Child v. Broward County School Board, No. 09–0568E (Sept. 9, 2009) (Robert E. Meale, Hearing Officer).

11. See Child v. Broward County School Board, Nos. 06–5243E & 07–1054E (Jan. 11, 2011) (Errol H. Powell, Hearing Officer).

CHAPTER 10

1. See N.J.S.A.18A:46–1.1 (enacted in 2008). See also Lascari v. Board of Education, 116 N.J. 30 (1989) (allocating burden of proof on school district).

2. See L.R. O/B/O E.R. v. Middletown Township Board of Education, EDS10263–09 (Oct. 15, 2009) (Joseph F. Martone, ALJ).

3. S.H. and M.H. O/B/O Minor Child, L.H. v. Caldwell–West Caldwell Board of Education, No. EDS5369–08 (June 17, 2008) (Jeffrey A. Gerson, Hearing Officer).

4. S.D. and C.D. O/B/O M.D. v. Moorestown Board of Education, No. EDS8971–08 (Dec. 11, 2009) (Donald J. Stein, Hearing Officer).

5. S.B. and J.B. O/B/O M.B. v. Bridgeton Board of Education, No. EDS14043–09 (Jan. 28, 2010) (W. Todd Miller, Hearing Officer).

6. See L.R. O/B/O E.R. v. Middletown Township Board of Education, EDS10263–09 (Oct. 15, 2009) (Joseph F. Martone, ALJ).

7. R.S. and D.S. O/B/O E.S., No. EDS14008–09 (July 19, 2010) (Elia A. Pelios, Hearing Officer).

8. See Crowe v. DeGoia, 90 N.J. 126, 132–34 (1982).

9. C.R. O/B/O P.B. v. Winslow Township Board of Education, No. EDS894–11 (Feb. 3, 2011) (Donald J. Stein, Hearing Officer).

10. See http://www.drnj.org/aboutdrnj.htm (website for Disability Rights New Jersey).

11. K.S. O/B/O K.S. v. Hackensack Board of Education, No. EDS12621–10 (Dec. 1, 2010) (Evelyn J. Marose, Hearing Officer).

CHAPTER 11

1. See Tracy Gershwin Mueller & Francisco Carranza, *An Examination of Special Education Due Process Hearings*, 22 J. Disability Policy Studies 131, 132 (2011).

2. Parent OBO Student v. Los Angeles Unified School District, No. 2011010405 (May 9, 2011) (Judith L. Pasewark, ALJ).

3. *Id.* at 3.

4. Board of Education of the Hendrick Hudson Central School District v. Rowley, 458 U.S. 176 (1982).

5. ALJ Opinion, *supra* note 2, at 7.

6. *Id.* at 8.

7. *Id.* at 6.

8. *Id.*

9. *Id.* at 8.

10. *Id.*

11. See chapter 8 (Joseph Winkelman).

12. See chapter 10.

13. In the matter of Coachella Valley Unified School District v. Parents O/B/O Student, No. 2010060472 (Dec. 27, 2010) (Robert F. Helfand, ALJ).

14. *Id.* at 21.

15. Parent O/B/O Student v. Desert Sands Unified School District, No. 2010100854 (April 8, 2011) (June R. Lehrman, ALJ).

16. Parent O/B/O Student v. East Whittier City School District, No. 2010050196 (Oct. 1, 2010) (Adrienne L. Krikorian, ALJ).

17. 34 C.F.R. § 300.304(c)(4).

18. Parent O/B/O Student v. Capistrano Unified School District, No. 2010050368 (Aug. 16, 2010) (Robert F. Helfand, ALJ).

19. Parents O/B/O Student v. Los Angeles Unified School District, No. 2010050661 (Nov. 2, 2010) (Glynda B. Gomez, ALJ).

20. Parents O/B/O Student v. Los Angeles Unified School District, No. 2010041011 (Aug. 12, 2010) (Clifford H. Woosley, ALJ).

21. Los Angeles Unified School District v. Parents O/B/O Student, No. 2011010957 (May 24, 2011) (Rebecca Freie, ALJ).

22. Schaffer v. Weast, 546 U.S. 49, 61 (2005).

23. OAH Case No. 2010100865 (Feb. 3, 2011) (Eileen M. Cohn, ALJ).

24. *Id.* at 2.

25. *Id.* at 6.

26. 34 C.F.R. § 300.301(c).

27. *Id.* at 11.

28. 34 C.F.R. § 300.306(a).

29. *Id.* at 15.

30. *Id.*

31. *Id.*

32. *Id.* at 16.

33. *Id.* at 14.

34. 34 C.F.R. § 300.306(a)(2).

35. 34 C.F.R. § 300.304(c)(iii).

36. Phillip L. Ackerman, Review of the Test of Visual Perceptual Skills, 3rd Edition in Mental Measurements Yearbook with Tests in Print, available at http://web.ebsco-host.com/ehost/detail?sid=28e2f981-10b1-4501-959e-85b88d0d1e8b%40sessionmgr1 04&vid=1&hid=126&bdata=JnNpdGU9ZWhvc3QtbGl2ZQ%3d%3d#db=mmt&AN= TIP18173428.

37. *Id.* at 4.

38. *Id.* at 24.

39. 34 C.F.R. § 300.304(c)(1)(v).

40. ALJ opinion, *supra* note 23, at 6.

41. *Id.* at 19.

42. 34 C.F.R. § 300.304(c)(4).

43. ALJ opinion, *supra* note 23, at 12.

44. *Id.*

45. *Id.* at 19.

46. K.S.N. v. Los Angeles Unified School District, No. CV 11–3270 CBM (MANx) (March 20, 2012) (Judge Consuelo v. Marshall).

47. See generally Gregory K. v. Longview School Dist., 811 F.2d 1307 (9th Cir. 1987).

48. *Id.* at 7.

49. *Id.* at 8.

50. *Id.* at 9.

51. *Id.*

52. *Id.* at 11.

53. *Id.* at 9.

54. *Id.* at 10.

55. See W.H. v. Clovis Unified School District, No. CV F 08–0374 LJO DLB (E.D. Cal. June 8, 2009), available at 2009 WL 1605356. This case is outside the scope of the 101 cases that I read for this study but is an excellent example of the kinds of errors I found in other ALJ opinions during the time period of my study that have not been subjected to appellate review.

56. *Id.* at *3.

57. *Id.* at *3.

58. *Id.* at *25.

59. See Schaffer v. Weast, 546 U.S. 49, 61 (2005) (discussed in chapter 6).

60. In the Matter of Student v. Clovis Unified School District, OAH Case No. N 2007060634 at 6 (December 17, 2007) (Debra R. Huston, ALJ).

61. *Id.* at 7.

62. *Id.* at 9.

63. *Id.* at 9.

64. *Id.* at 11.

65. *Id.* at 11–12.
66. *Id.* at 12 n. 8.
67. *Id.* at 13.
68. District Court Opinion, *supra* note 55, at *2.
69. *Id.* at *16.
70. ALJ Opinion, *supra* note 60, at 8–9.
71. *Id.* at 9.
72. *Id.* at 10.
73. District Court Opinion, *supra* note 55, at *18.
74. *Id.* at *16.
75. ALJ Opinion, *supra* note 60, at 25.
76. *Id.* at 16.
77. District Court Opinion, *supra* note 55, at *17.
78. ALJ Opinion, *supra* note 60, at 25.
79. District Court Opinion, *supra* note 55, at *16.
80. *Id.* at *18.
81. ALJ Opinion, *supra* note 60, at 16.
82. District Court Opinion, *supra* note 55, at *17.
83. ALJ Opinion, *supra* note 60, at 26 n. 13.
84. District Court Opinion, *supra* note 55, at *18.

CHAPTER 12

1. Hobson v. Hansen, 269 F. Supp. 401 (D.D.C. 1967).
2. *Id.* at 448.
3. *Id.* at 512 ("those who are being consigned to the lower tracks are the poor and the Negroes").
4. Mills v. Board of Education, 348 F. Supp. 866 (D.D.C. 1972).
5. See Pennsylvania Association for Retarded Children v. Pennsylvania, 334 F. Supp. 1257 (E.D. Pa. 1971).
6. See Blackman v. District of Columbia, 185 F.R.D. 4 (D.D.C. 1999).
7. *Id.* at *6.
8. Blackman v. District of Columbia, 633 F.3d 1088, 1096 (D.D.C. 2011).
9. See Parents O/B/O Student v. District of Columbia Public Schools, No. 31124 (Frances Raskin, Hearing Officer) (March 7, 2011). The decision does not provide the name of the child, so I have called her Amanda.
10. *Id.* at 10.
11. *Id.* at 12.
12. See http://datacenter.kidscount.org/data/bystate/Rankings.aspx?order=a&loct=3&dtm=11143&state=DC&tf=809&ind=4774&ch=3%2c894&by=a.
13. Parents O/B/O Student v. Charter School, No. 111001 (Wanda I. Resto Torres, Hearing Officer) (October 23, 2010).
14. Parents O/B/O Student v. District of Columbia Public School, No. 111011 (Ramona M. Justice, Hearing Officer) (November 5, 2010).
15. Parents O/B/O Student, No. 111014 (Coles R. Ruff, Hearing Officer) (November 12, 2010).
16. Justin Blum, *Lawyers Capitalize on D.C. School Gaps; Special Ed Clients Sent to Affiliated Firms*, Wash. Post, Feb. 18, 2002, at A01.

17. Justin Blum, *D.C. Strikes Deal with Special-Ed Schools; Fees for Private Programs Are Cut in Exchange for Enrollment Guarantees*, Wash. Post. April 9, 2003, at A01.

18. See informal admonishment from the District of Columbia Bar Counsel to James E. Brown (Oct. 31, 2002). See also http://www.dcbar.org/for_lawyers/ethics/discipline/discipline02.cfm?barNumber=%25%2C%2B)%2B%2B%3C%40%20%0A (list of all discipline actions taken against James E. Brown).

CHAPTER 13

1. Education for All Handicapped Children of 1975, Pub. L. No. 94–142, 89 Stat. 773 (codified as amended at 20 U.S.C. §§ 1400–1482 (2000)).

2. 121 Cong. Rec. 25,531 (daily ed. July 29, 1975) (statement of Rep. Bill Lehman).

3. *See id.* (discussing an agreement requiring the Commissioner of Education to "spell out" what is to be considered a specific learning disability as well as the process of determining if a child meets the definition).

4. *Compare* Education for All Handicapped Children Act of 1975, Pub. L. No. 94–142. 89 Stat. 773 (codified as amended at 20 U.S.C. § 1411 (2005)) ("[T]he term 'children with specific learning disabilities' means those children who have a disorder in one or more of the basic psychological processes involved in understanding or in using language, spoken or written, which disorder may manifest itself in imperfect ability to listen, think, speak, read, write, spell, or do mathematical calculations. Such disorders include such conditions as perceptual handicaps, brain injury, minimal brain dysfunction, dyslexia, and developmental aphasia. Such term does not include children who have learning problems which are primarily the result of visual, hearing, or motor handicaps, of mental retardation, of emotional disturbance, or environmental, cultural, or economic disadvantage"), *with* 20 U.S.C. § 140126 (2000) (current definition) ("(A) [I]n general. The term 'specific learning disability' means a disorder in 1 or more of the basic psychological processes involved in understanding or in using language, spoken or written, which disorder may manifest itself in the imperfect ability to listen, think, speak, read, write, spell, or do mathematical calculations. (B) Disorders included. Such term includes such conditions as perceptual disabilities, brain injury, minimal brain dysfunction, dyslexia, and developmental aphasia. (C) Disorders not included. Such term does not include a learning problem that is primarily the result of visual, hearing, or motor disabilities, of mental retardation, of emotional disturbance, or of environmental, cultural, or economic disadvantage").

5. *See* 20 U.S.C. § 1401 (2000 & Supp. V) ("(3) [C]hild with a disability (a) In general [t]he term 'child with a disability' means a child—(i) with mental retardation, hearing impairments (including deafness), speech or language impairments, visual impairments (including blindness), serious emotional disturbance (hereinafter referred to as 'emotional disturbance'), orthopedic impairments, autism, traumatic brain injury, other health impairments, or specific learning disabilities; and (ii) who, by reason thereof, needs special education and related services").

6. *See* Education of the Handicapped Act Amendments of 1990, Pub. L. No. 101–476, 104 Stat. 1103 (codified as amended at 20 U.S.C. § 1400 et seq. (2000)) (amending the EAHCA by renaming it the Individuals with Disabilities Education Act (IDEA) to align its terminology with that of the Americans with Disabilities Act).

7. *See generally* 20 U.S.C. § 1400(d) (2000) (explaining the purpose of the IDEA).

8. *See* 20 U.S.C. § 1401(3) (2000) ("[T]he term 'child with a disability' means a child—(i) with mental retardation, hearing impairments (including deafness), speech or language impairments, visual impairments (including blindness), serious emotional disturbance (referred to in this title as 'emotional disturbance'), orthopedic impairments, autism, traumatic brain injury, other health impairments, or specific learning disabilities; and (ii) who, by reason thereof, needs special education and related services").

9. *Id.*

10. The term "specific learning disabilities" is the technical term used in the special education statutes, but the term "learning disabilities" is also often found in special education law literature. This chapter uses both terms interchangeably.

11. *See* U.S. Dep't of Educ., Office of Special Educ. Programs, Data Analysis Sys. (DANS), OMB # 1820–0043: *Children with Disabilities Receiving Special Education Under Part B of the Individuals with Disabilities Education Act, Table 1-3. Students ages 6 through 21 served under IDEA, Part B, by disability category and state: Fall 2008* (data updated as of Aug. 3, 2009), *available at* https://www.ideadata.org/arc_toc10.asp#partbCC (last visited Sept. 30, 2010) (reporting that, out of the 5,889,849 children receiving special education services, the largest group, 2,525,898 children (42.8 percent), were classified as having "specific learning disabilities," while the next most common category was speech or language impairments with 1,121,961 children).

12. *See* Individuals with Disabilities Education Improvement Act of 2004, Pub. L. No. 108–446, 118 Stat. 2647 (codified as amended at 20 U.S.C. §1401 (2005)) (defining what a child with a disability means and the guidelines of what constitutes a disability).

13. *See* 20 U.S.C. § 1414(b)(6)(B) (2006) ("[I]n determining whether a child has a specific learning disability, a local educational agency may use a process that determines if the child responds to scientific, research-based intervention as part of the evaluation procedures described in paragraphs (2) and (3)"); *see* 20 U.S.C. § 7801(37) (2006) (defining "scientifically based research"); 34 C.F.R. § 300.309(a)(2)(i) (2006) ("[T]he child does not make sufficient progress to meet age or State-approved grade-level standards in one or more of the areas identified in paragraph (a)(1) of this section when using a process based on the child's response to scientific, research-based intervention . . . ").

14. *See* 34 C.F.R. § 300.309(a)(2)(ii) (2006) ("[T]he child exhibits a pattern of strengths and weaknesses in performance, achievement, or both, relative to age, State-approved grade-level standards, or intellectual development, that is determined by the group to be relevant to the identification of a specific learning disability, using appropriate assessments, consistent with §§ 300.304 and 300.305 . . . ").

15. *See* 20 U.S.C. § 1414(b)(6)(A) (2006) ("[N]otwithstanding section 1406(b) of this title, when determining whether a child has a specific learning disability as defined in section 1401, a local educational agency shall not be required to take into consideration whether a child has a severe discrepancy between achievement and intellectual ability in oral expression, listening comprehension, written expression, basic reading skill, reading comprehension, mathematical calculation, or mathematical reasoning").

16. *See* U.S. Dep't of Educ., Office of Special Educ. Programs, *supra* note 11 (noting the discrepancy in the reporting that, in Kentucky, out of the 87,977 children diagnosed with a disability, 13,587 of those children were classified as having a specific learning disability which accounts for approximately 15.4 percent of the disabled children, whereas, in Iowa, out of the 61,418 children diagnosed with a disability, 37,038 of those children were classified as having a specific learning disability accounting for approximately 60.2 percent of the disabled children).

17. *See* No Child Left Behind Act of 2001, Pub. L. No. 107–110, 115 Stat. 1425 (2002) (codified as amended at 20 U.S.C. § 6311 (2006)), (requiring every child to be proficient in reading and math by 2014).

18. *See, e.g.*, Conn. State Dep't of Educ., *2010 Guidelines for Identifying Children with Learning Disabilities*, 1 at 5 (2010) [hereinafter *Connecticut Guidelines*] *available at* http://www.sde.ct.gov/sde/lib/sde/PDF/DEPS/Special/2010_Learning_Disability_ Guidelines_Acc.pdf (recognizing the interconnected relationship between No Child Left Behind and the 2004 amendments to IDEA).

19. *Compare* Am. Psychiatric Ass'n, Diagnostic and Statistical Manual of Mental Disorders 46 (4th ed. 2000)) *with Proposed Draft Revisions to DSM Disorders and Criteria*, AM. Psychiatric Ass'n DSM-5 Dev., http://www.dsm5.org/proposedrevision/pages/ proposedrevision.aspx?rid=429 (last visited Aug. 17, 2012).

20. *See infra* text accompanying notes 62–64.

21. Samuel Alexander Kirk, Educating Exceptional Children (1962).

22. *Id.* at 263.

23. *See* 20 U.S.C. § 1401(30)(A) (2011) (referring to the definition of a specific learning disorder in IDEA as a "disorder in one or more of the basic psychological processes"); 20 U.S.C. § 1401(30)(C) (2010) (referring to the exclusionary clause in IDEA—the term "does not include a learning problem that is primarily the result of visual, hearing, or motor disabilities, of mental retardation, of emotional disturbance, or of environmental, cultural, or economic disadvantage").

24. Barbara Bateman, *An Educational View of a Diagnostic Approach to Learning Disorders*, in 1 Learning Disorders 219, 220 (J. Hellmuth ed. 1965).

25. *Id.*

26. *See id.* (maintaining that a learning disability need not be associated with physical disorders).

27. Kirk, *supra* note 22, at 263.

28. *See, e.g.*, Am. Psychiatric Ass'n, Diagnostic and Statistical Manual of Mental Disorders, 44 (3rd ed. rev. 1987) (using the discrepancy model to define "specific learning disabilities"); Corrine E. Kass & Helmer R. Myklebust, *Learning Disabilities: An Educational Definition*, 2 J. Learning Disabilities 377, 378–79 (1969) (discussing the U.S. government–sponsored organizations' endorsement of the use of the discrepancy model to diagnose learning disabilities).

29. Samuel A. Kirk, Special Education for Handicapped Children, First Annual Report of the National Advisory Committee on Handicapped Children (NACHC), 34 (1968).

30. Kenneth A. Kavale & Steven R. Forness, *What Definitions of Learning Disability Say and Don't Say: A Critical Analysis*, 33 J. Learning Disabilities 239, 242 (2000).

31. NACHC, *supra* note 30, at 34.

32. Kenneth A. Kavale et al., *A Time to Define: Making the Specific Learning Disability Definition Prescribe Specific Learning Disability*, 32 Learning Disability Q. 39, 41 (2009) (citing Smith & Polloway, 1979) (citation omitted).

33. Education for All Handicapped Children Act of 1975, Pub. L. No. 94–142, 89 Stat. 773 (codified as amended at 20 U.S.C. § 1411(i)(4)(A) (2005)).

34. 121 Cong. Rec. 25,531 (daily ed. July 29, 1975) (statement of Rep. Albert H. Quie).

35. 121 Cong. Rec. 25,531.

36. 121 Cong. Rec. 25,531 (statement of Rep. Bill Lehman).

37. *See* U.S. Dep't of Educ., Office of Special Educ. Programs, *supra* note 11.

38. *See* Kass, *supra* note 29, at 378–79 (discussing the importance of the discrepancy model and the practical application).

39. *Id.* at 379.

40. *Id.*

41. Am. Psychiatric Ass'n, Diagnostic and Statistical Manual of Mental Disorders 44 (3rd ed. rev. 1980).

42. *Id.* at 92.

43. *Id.* at 94.

44. American Psychiatric Association, Diagnostic and Statistical Manual of Mental Disorders, 44 (3rd ed. rev. 1987).

45. The National Joint Committee on Learning Disabilities (NJCLD) was founded in 1975. For further information, *see* http://www.ldonline.org/about/partners/njcld (last viewed October 6, 2010).

46. National Joint Committee on Learning Disabilities, Learning Disabilities: Issues on Definition, *in* Collective Perspectives on Issues Affecting Learning Disabilities 61–66 (1994).

47. *See What Is a Learning Disability?* LDonline, http://www.ldonline.org/ldbasics/whatisld (last visited Oct. 6, 2010).

48. *See* American Psychiatric Association, Diagnostic and Statistical Manual of Mental Disorders: Fourth Edition (1994).

49. *Id.* at 46.

50. *Connecticut Guidelines, supra* note 18, at 2.

51. 20 U.S.C. § 1414(b)(6) (2006).

52. 20 U.S.C. § 1401(30) (2006).

53. *Id.*

54. *Connecticut Guidelines, supra* note 18, at 2.

55. 70 Fed. Reg. 35802 (June 21, 2005).

56. *Id.*

57. *See* http://www.ldanatl.org/news/osep-012111-rtimemo.pdf

58. No Child Left Behind Act is another name for the Elementary and Secondary Education Act of 1975, as amended by Public Law 107–110 (requiring every child to be proficient in reading and math by 2014). As the state of North Dakota noted in its specific learning disabilities guidelines, "Guidelines for developing an intervention that may be considered to be 'scientific, research based' can be found in the No Child Left Behind (NCLB) Act, which uses scientifically based research as one of its educational cornerstones. The term itself defined at 20 U.S.C.A. § 7801(37), and repeated in the 2006 IDEA regulations at 34 C.F.R. § 300.35 to mean research that involves the application of rigorous, systematic, and objective procedures to obtain reliable and valid

knowledge relevant to education activities and programs." North Dakota Department of Public Instruction, *Guidelines, Identification and Evaluation of Students with Specific Learning Disabilities* 4 (May 2007). N.D. Dep't of Public Instruction, *Guidelines, Identification and Evaluation of Students with Specific Learning Disabilities*, U.S. Dep't of Educ. (May 2007), available at www.dpi.state.nd.us/speced/guide/SLDGuide07.pdf.

59. *See, e.g., Connecticut Guidelines, supra* note 18, at 5 (recognizing the relationship between No Child Left Behind and the 2004 amendments to IDEA).

60. *See* 34 C.F.R. § 300.35 (2007) ("Scientifically based research has the meaning given the term in section 9101(37) of the ESEA")

61. *See* Neuropsychological Perspectives on Learning Disabilities in the Era of RTI: Recommendations for Diagnosis and Intervention (Elaine Fletcher-Janzen & Cecil R. Reynolds, eds.) (2008) (hereinafter Neuropsychological Perspectives).

62. *See* 20 U.S.C. § 1401(30)(A) (2006).

63. *See infra* Part II.

64. *An 08 Specific Learning Disorder*, Am. Psychiatric Ass'n DSM-5 Dev. (http://www.dsm5.org/proposedrevision/pages/proposedrevision.aspx?rid=429 (last visited August 17, 2012).

65. *Id.*

66. *See supra* text accompanying note 52.

67. Linda Caterino et al., *A Survey of School Psychologists' Perceptions of the Reauthorization of IDEA 2004*, 62 Sch. Psychologist 45, 46 (2008).

68. Cecil R. Reynolds & Sally E. Shaywitz, Response to Intervention: Ready or Not? Or, From Wait-to-Fail to Watch-Them-Fail, 24 Sch. Psychologist 24 (2009).

69. *Id.* at 4.

70. *Id.* at 9.

71. *Id.*

72. See http://www.ncld.org/images/stories/OnCapitolHill/PolicyRelatedPublications/stateofld/2011_state_of_ld_final.pdf (table of students with learning disabilities by age group).

73. Cal. Code Regs. tit. 5, § 3030(j)(4)(A) (2011), *available at* http://www3.scoe.net/speced/laws_search/searchDetailsLaws.cfm?id=744&keywords=3030 (last visited Sept. 21, 2010).

74. Mo. State Plan for Special Education: Regulations Implementing Part B of the Individuals with Disabilities Education Act (IDEA), *available at* http://dese.mo.gov/divspeced/stateplan/documents/Regulation_III_2010.pdf (last visited Sept. 17, 2010).

75. Miss. State Policies Regarding Children with Disabilities Under the Individuals with Disabilities Education Act Amendments of 2004, State Board Policy 7210 (effective July 20, 2009), at 303, *available at* http://www.mde.k12.ms.us/special_education/policies.html (last visited Oct. 28, 2010). ("NOTE: Severe discrepancy is defined as 1.5 standard deviations below the mean of the standardized test measuring intellectual ability.")

76. S.D. Admin. R. 24:05:25:12(8) (2010).

77. Tenn. St. Dep't of Educ., *Special Education Manual*, at 61 (2008) *available at* http://www.state.tn.us/education/speced/doc/80608SEMManualfinal.pdf (last visited Sept. 20, 2010) (hereinafter *Tenn. Education Manual*).

78. Special Education Guide: Vermont State Board of Education, § 2362.2.4 Additional Procedures for Identifying Children with Specific Learning Disabilities, *available at*

http://education.vermont.gov/new/pdfdoc/pgm_sped/laws/educ_sped_guide.pdf (last visited Sept. 20, 2010).

79. Wyo. Admin. Code EDUC. GEN. Ch. 7 § 4(d)(x)(E)(I)(2) (2011).

80. New Mexico T.E.A.M., *Technical Evaluation and Assessment Manual*, New Mexico Public Education Department (Apr. 2007), *available at* http://apps.leg.wa.gov/WAC/default.aspx?cite=392-172A-03065 (last visited Sept. 20, 2010).

81. *WAC 392–172A–03065: Use of Discrepancy Tables for Determining Severe Discrepancy*, Washington State Legislature, available at http://apps.leg.wa.gov/WAC/default.aspx?cite=392-172A-03065 (last visited Sept. 21, 2010).

82. Wis. Admin. Code PI § 11.36(6)(c)(2.)(b.) (2011); Minn. R. 3525.1341 subp. 2(C) (2010).

83. 16 N.C. Admin. Code rule no. 2E.1503 (2011).

84. Ala. Admin. Code r. 290–8–9.03(10)(c)(6)(d)(2)(i) (2007 & Supp. 2011).

85. Fla. Admin. Code Ann. r. 6A–6.03011(4) (2011).

86. Mont. Admin. R. 10.16.3019B (2011).

87. Utah St. Bd. of Educ., *Special Education Rules* II(j)(10)(c)(4)(h), *available at* http://www.schools.utah.gov/sars/Laws,-State-Rules-and-Policies/Rules-and-Regulations.aspx (last visited June 25, 2011).

88. Ala. Admin. Code r. 290–8–9.03(10)(c)(6)(d)(2)(i) (2007 & Supp. 2011).

89. 5 CCR §3030(j), *available at* http://www3.scoe.net/speced/laws_search/searchDetail-sLaws.cfm?id=744&keywords=3030 (last visited Sept. 21, 2010).

90. See *Missouri State Plan for Special Education: Regulations Implementing Part B of the Individuals with Disabilities Education Act* (June 11, 2011 1:53 PM), *available at* http://dese.mo.gov/divspeced/stateplan/documents/Regulation_III_2010.pdf (last visited June 24, 2011).

91. Miss. Dep't of Educ., *State Policies Regarding Children with Disabilities under the Individuals with Disabilities Education Act Amendments of 2004* (2009), *available at* http://www.mde.k12.ms.ud/SPECIAL _EDUCATION/policies.html (last visited June 25, 2011). ("NOTE: Severe discrepancy is defined as 1.5 standard deviations below the mean of the standardized test measuring intellectual ability.")

92. S.D. Admin. R. 24:05:25:12 (2007).

93. *Tenn. Education Manual, supra* note 74, at 61.

94. Vt. State Bd. of Educ., *Special Education Guide* § 2362.2.4, *available at* http://education.vermont.gov/new/pdfdoc/pgm_sped/laws/educ_sped_guide.pdf (last visited on Sept. 20, 2010).

95. Wyo. Admin. Code EDUC. GEN. Ch. 7 § 4(d)(x)(E)(I)(2011).

96. *See Connecticut Guidelines, supra* note 18 at 3.

97. Ill. State Bd. of Educ. Special Educ. and Support Serv., *Illinois Special Education Eligibility and Entitlement Procedures and Criteria within a Response to Intervention (RtI) Framework: A Guidance Document*, at 9 (January 2010), *available at* http://www.isbe.state.il.us/SPEC-ED/pdfs/sped_rti_framework.pdf (last visited Oct. 28, 2010).

98. *Id.* at 16.

99. Christina A. Samuels, *The 'response to intervention' framework in Iowa is helping teachers better understand and address students' learning needs*, Education Week (Sept. 10, 2008), *available at* http://www.edweek.org/tsb/articles/2008/09/10/01rti.h02.html (last visited Oct. 7, 2010) (hereinafter Samuels).

100. *Id.*

101. *Id.*

102. *Id.*

103. Ga. Comp. R. & Regs. 160–4–7–.05(3)(i) (2010).

104. *See* United States Department of Education Data, *supra* note 11. Kentucky's definition of learning disability can be found at 707 K.A.R. 1:002(59) (2011) ("'Specific
learning disability' or 'LD' means a disorder that adversely affects the ability to
acquire, comprehend, or apply reading, mathematical, writing, reasoning, listening, or speaking skills to the extent that specially designed instruction is required to
benefit from education. The specific learning disability (LD) may include dyslexia,
dyscalculia, dysgraphia, developmental aphasia, and perceptual/motor disabilities.
The term does not include deficits that are the result of other primary determinant
or disabling factors such as vision, hearing, motor impairment, mental disability,
emotional-behavioral disability, environmental or economic disadvantages, cultural
factors, limited English proficiency, or lack of relevant research-based instruction in
the deficit area"). That definition is a generic one that makes no mention of how to
diagnose a learning disability, so it is impossible to know from the definition itself
why Kentucky has such a low rate of learning disability classification.

105. *See* United States Department of Education Data, *supra* note 11. Nationally, the
distributions are: Mental retardation: 475,713 (8.0 percent); Hearing impairments:
70,682 (1.2 percent); Speech or language impairments: 1,121,496 (19.0 percent);
Visual impairments: 25,790 (0.4 percent); Emotional disturbance: 417,872 (7.1
percent); Orthopedic impairments: 62,332 (1.0 percent); Other health impairments:
648,112 (11.0 percent); Specific learning disabilities: 2,522,735 (42.8 percent); Deaf-
blindness: 1,735 (0.0 percent); Multiple disabilities: 123,924 (2.1 percent); Autism:
292,638 (4.9 percent); Traumatic brain injury: 24,857 (0.4 percent); Developmental
delay: 96,853 (1.6 percent). Kentucky's numbers for mental retardation are quite high
as compared with the national average, suggesting that it is classifying as mentally
retarded (or "intellectually impaired") children whom our states would classify as
learning disabled.

106. These data were compiled from Digest of Education Statistics, National Center for
Education Statistics and United States Department of Education data *available at*
IDEADATE.org/PartBChildCount.asp (last visited Oct. 1, 2010).

107. Reynolds & Shaywitz, *supra* note 68, at 7–8.

108. *Id.* at 7–8.

109. 28 C.F.R. § 36.309(b)(v) (2011).

110. *See e.g.*, M. Kay Runyon, *The Effect of Extra Time on Reading Comprehension Scores
for University Students With and Without Learning Disabilities*, 24 J. Learning Disabilities 104 (1991).

111. *Id.* at 107.

112. *See e.g.*, Jennifer Hartwig Lindstrom, *The Role of Extended Time on the SAT for Students with Learning Disabilities and/or Attention-Deficit/Hyperactivity Disorder*, 22
Learning Disabilities Res. & Prac. 85, 86 (2007) (concluding that SAT results can be
interpreted in the same way when students with disabilities have an extended-time
administration as compared to the standard-time administration); Nicole Ofiesh et
al., *Using Speeded Cognitive, Reading, and Academic Measures to Determine the Need
for Extended Test Time Among University Students with Learning Disabilities*, 23 J.

of Psychoeducational Assessment 35, 37 (2005) (acknowledging the widespread use of extra time on exams and suggesting which tests are appropriate for determining allocation of extra time).

113. LSAC, *Guidelines for Documentation of Cognitive Impairments* at 2, *available at* http://lsac.org/JD/pdfs/GuidelinesCognitive.pdf (last visited June 26, 2011).

114. *Id.* at 4.

115. *See* College Board, *Learning Disabilities, available at* http://professionals.collegeboard.com/testing/ssd/application/disabilities/learning (last visited June 26, 2011).

116. *Id.*

117. *See* The ACT, *ACT Policy for Documentation to Support Requests for Test Accommodations on the ACT (No Writing) or ACT Plus Writing, available at* http://www.act.org/aap/disab/policy.html (last visited June 26, 2011) (hereinafter *ACT*).

118. *See* Ruth Colker, *Extra Time as an Accommodation*, 69 U. Pitt. L. Rev. 413, 416 (2008).

119. *See* Andrea E. Thornton, Lynda M. Reese, Peter J. Pashley & Susan P. Dalessandrot, Predictive Validity of Accommodated LSAT Scores: Law School Admission Council Technical Report 01–01 (May 2002), *available at* http://www.lsac.org/LsacResources/Research/TR/TR-01-01.pdf (last visited June 25, 2011).

120. *See* Law School Admissions Council, *available at* http://lsac.org/JD/LSAT/accommodated-testing.asp (last visited June 25, 2011) (hereinafter LSAC).

121. 121 Cong. Rec. 25531 (July 29, 1975) (statement of Rep. Bill Lehman).

CHAPTER 14

1. These data were generated from the following website: https://www.ideadata.org/DACAnalyticTool/Values_2.asp?STUDY=Part%20B%20Child. I thank Katherine Hall for helping me generate these data.

2. See U.S. Census Bureau, Sex by Age Universe: Total Population 2010 Census Summary File 1; Sex by Age (Black or African American Alone) Universe: People Who Are Black or African American Alone 2010 Census Summary File 1, available at http://www.census.gov/population/www/socdemo/age/c2kguide.html. See also Data Across States, http://datacenter.kidscount.org/data/acrossstates/Rankings.aspx?ind=103 (The Annie E. Casey Foundation) (2009 data). African-Americans were 12.6 percent of the overall population in 2010. See http://quickfacts.census.gov/qfd/states/00000.html.

3. See http://www.autism-society.org/about-autism/symptoms/.

4. See U.S. Census Bureau, Sex by Age (White Alone, Not Hispanic or Latino) Universe: People Who Are White Alone, not Hispanic or Latino 2010 Census Summary File 1, available at http://www.census.gov/population/www/socdemo/age/c2kguide.html.

5. 269 F. Supp. 401 (D.D.C. 1967).

6. *Id.* at 512.

7. See http://www2.ed.gov/about/offices/list/ocr/docs/impact.html.

8. The federal government reported in 2010 that 9.8 percent of children under age eighteen were uninsured despite various federal programs that target children. See http://money.cnn.com/2011/09/13/news/economy/census_bureau_health_insurance/index.htm.

9. Beth Harry & Janette Klingner, Why Are So Many Minority Students in Special Education? Understanding Race & Disability in Schools (2006).

10. U.S. House, Hearings before the Select Subcommittee on Education of the Committee on Education and Labor 342 (March 6, 1974) (emphasis added).

11. 34 C.F.R. § 300.8(10)(ii).

12. Beth Harry & Janette Klingner, Why Are So Many Minority Students in Special Education? Understanding Race & Disability in Schools (2006).

13. See TOPPS, INC, Targeting Our People's Priorities With Service, http://www.toppsinc.org/Default_V3.aspx.

14. *See generally* Norman Garmezy, *Resiliency and Vulnerability to Adverse Developmental Outcomes Associated with Poverty,* 34 Am. Beh. Scientist 416 (1991).

Index

About the Author

Ruth Colker is a nationally recognized scholar and activist in the fields of disability discrimination and special education who is frequently cited by the media and the courts for her expertise in these areas. This book reflects her experience as the parent of a child who has benefited from special education; as a researcher who has delved into the history, social science literature, and law underlying the field of special education; and as an attorney who frequently assists families with children who are disabled.